Warrior

Warrior

A Spiritual Odyssey

William "Rev. Bill" McDonald Jr.

Bill and his wife, Carol, 1970

Warrior: A Spiritual Odyssey
© 2015 by William "Rev. Bill" McDonald Jr.
All rights reserved.

Editor: Marie Beswick-Arthur
ISBN 13: 9781515126645
ISBN 10: 1515126641
Library of Congress Control Number: 2015911632
CreateSpace Independent Publishing Platform
North Charleston, South Carolina

1 Spirituality 2 Self Help 3 New Age 4 Metaphysical 5 Military History 6 Short Story 7 Memoir

First Edition

Dedicated To:
Paramahansa Yogananda
Polestar of my life

FOREWORD

Just as the Inuit have hundreds of descriptions for snow, and the Sami speak a thousand words for reindeer, 'warrior' would need an extra column in the dictionary to fully capture the essence of Bill McDonald.

Nonetheless, I will attempt to expand the definition of warrior here, even though my words about his valor may not measure up to the boundless expanse of his life and spirit.

Endlessly astonishing, inspiring, and humble, his unpretentious manner and immense inner strength will be whispered about for decades.

Recipient of the Distinguished Flying Cross, Bronze Star, Purple Heart, 14 air medals, and many of other awards, this fearless hero took on a whole platoon of Viet Cong with an M-60 and kept firing until the barrel melted.

Years later, he returned to Viet Nam with 'The Peace Patrol' and was welcomed with respect by his former enemies.

When told by surgeons they would have to remove his nose, ears, and lips (because of cancer) Bill was afraid for about 90 minutes before saying, "bring it on!"

A true Renaissance man, his mystical experiences are as intoxicating as his stories of facing life's challenges. His Faith is extraordinary—not the conviction of charismatic, educated ministers, but the kind of man who has grabbed a cobra by the neck and looked it in the eyes.

An award winning poet, inspiring minister, talented artist, uplifting motivational speaker, advocate for veteran's rights and PTSD treatment; knowledgeable about yoga, spirituality, and mystical powers, Bill can do anything—and does everything well—even basketball.

And he is an extraordinary story teller.

May you enjoy and be inspired by his tales of the inexplicable, and find inner strength for facing your own difficulties in life.

Bill McDonald is a true spiritual warrior, and I'm proud to call him my friend.

~*Shadoe Stevens*

The creative energy of luminary Shadoe Stevens is injected here with the same vitality as in his own fulfilled life: www.shadoe.com

INTRODUCTION

"For those who believe, no words are necessary.
For those who do not believe, no words are possible."
— Saint Ignatius of Loyola

This book is a road map of the spiritual journey that my life took before, during, and after my 'tour of duty' in Vietnam. It is about peace, though it contains a number of stories related to war.

Each story can be an independent read, but as a collective the words form my sacred pilgrimage that made me who I am today.

There are no specific categories—you might giggle, shed a tear, or tremble. Sometimes you might do that all in the same story. My hope is that a good number of them will leave you inspired and fill you with wonderment. The memories I've recorded are to provide a better understanding of how my spirit was altered in some way by each event.

And because it was never my intention to create a fully detailed account of my life, there are stories between the lines; of the emotional and spiritual footprints.

The time period is from my humble birth through 2004, though updates occur when they add new understanding to what had transpired.

May you be inspired to begin, or to continue, your own spiritual awakening. My heartfelt blessings to you as you reconcile, reignite, or further enlighten your own sacred soul

~William 'Rev. Bill' McDonald Jr.

William "Rev. Bill" McDonald Jr.

"Tell me a fact and I'll learn.
Tell me a truth and I'll believe.
But tell me a story and it will live in my heart forever."
Native American Proverb

PART ONE
1946–1965: MY CHILDHOOD

Me, eight years old

THE BEGINNING

Everyone's life has a beginning; a place in time and space where the stars line up to guide your spirit into the human womb of your chosen mother. On March 16, 1946 the midnight sky over San Francisco twinkled a unique constellation.

My mother arrived at the hospital in labor. The nurses did not agree with her prediction that she was about to give birth. They told her there was lots of time and decided to give her an enema as a pre-delivery procedure. They provided a metal bedpan.

Many are born with a symbolic silver spoon in their mouth; my arrival symbolized the opposite. My first earthly moments were spent with my head stuck in a load of crap. It has kept me humble.

Dysfunctional Family "R" Us. My mother married early and, at 19 years of age, she already had a son, my older brother Gary (1939). She divorced and soon after became pregnant with my older sister Melody (1943). Melody's father went to war.

My dad came along when my mother truly needed financial help. He married her and took care of my brother and sister before my arrival. He purchased a wonderful home for us on Lake Street in San Francisco in which my grandmother—a partner in the purchase—lived on the third floor. When the war came to an end Melody's father returned and reconnected with my mother. She obtained a quickie divorce in Reno faster than I could say 'stepfather.'

Dad moved out. My stepfather moved in.

I know almost nothing about my real dad's life other than he was born and raised in San Francisco. A promising All-American baseball player in high school, he signed a professional baseball contract before going to war, but was wounded (World War II) and never played professionally. Sadly, he never made contact after the divorce; nor did his parents or siblings, even though they lived in San Francisco. Six decades later there exists a space in my heart for that family experience.

My mother married my stepfather as soon as the divorce papers were filed. A hateful alcoholic, he created and ruled a household built on fear and intimidation, subjecting our family to tremendous emotional abuse. Violence was his solution and solace.

I lived in fear and grew up with a false premise that he hated me. It dawned on me in adulthood that because he hated himself, he hated everyone. *Nothing personal, kid.*

My stepfather suffered what we now call Post-Traumatic Stress Disorder. Perhaps some of his behaviors would have existed without the impact of the war—drinking, smoking, swearing, anger—but I imagine them amplified by battle experience.

He demonstrated no love for his stepsons. My position fell in the middle of his two biological children: Melody (1943) and Marsha (1948). The following years produced brothers: Roger (1949) and Bruce (1950). And so there I was, third out of six children born to my mother, and not a silver spoon in sight.

Despite her lack of foresight in my stepfather, my mother was considered by many to be a gifted psychic. She had an ability to read people and know things about them. She read cards for a small following. Her own mother had the gift of premonition as did several generations of my mother's Italian family.

Author's note: In 2012 and 2013 I had a couple of operations to get rid of cancer that had gone deep into my head. It developed from an old bump on my skull which had been caused by metal forceps that held me in place and delayed my arrival while awaiting that of the doctor. Six decades and I was still dealing with the birthing process.

Me with my siblings in 1948

Melody with her doll, and Gary holding Marsha's hands

OUR HOUSE ON LAKE STREET

During the late forties we lived in a large house—three stories if you counted the garage as the bottom floor—on Lake Street in San Francisco. My father purchased the house in a partnership with my grandmother who took up residence in the upstairs flat. After my parents divorced, my stepfather took over the house.

It was in the house on Lake Street that our family encountered many mysterious and frightening happenings. The same house that held tragedy and sorrow when my baby brothers died—one in the house, and one in the hospital after being rushed from the house in a state of respiratory failure.

My oldest brother, Gary, told me many years later how *he* had almost died in the same room from being unable to breathe. He said it felt as if someone had physically tried to choke him to death, though no one else was in the room with him.

I remember the day one of my brothers' bodies was carried from our home. The house was eerily quiet. No evidence of crying, no tears from my mother— at least none that any of us saw—but there was a pervasive cloud of sadness.

In retrospect, I'm sure it affected her greatly. I believe depression took hold because she repressed her emotions; handled the burden of her two dead children by herself. She never confided in anyone or had any kind of counseling; people didn't do 'go to therapists' back then.

Most people who know our family are not aware my two baby brothers existed. Bruce and Roger Engelking: infanthoods interrupted; each lived for less than a year.

My stepfather didn't make it any easier. His two sons had died. He'd wanted sons. His relationship with my mother netted two daughters. My brother and I became mirrors of boys lost. My stepfather's moods added to the dysfunction—non-verbal blame, as if it were somehow my mother's fault.

My mother molded her hurt into anger and struck the weakest target in the house, my innocent brother Gary. Moments after the body had been removed, standing in the room where her baby had died, she stared into the crib—crocheted blankets in that ever familiar scrunch that babies often create—as if it were an abyss. A second infant death in two years. When my 11-year-old brother approached to provide her comfort, she turned and looked directly into his eyes. "It should have been you that died," she screamed.

The anguish from a misplaced moment of rage remained with my brother, Gary. The wound never healed. Even in his 70s, as I write this, it continues to throb. A child wanting to help his mother; I don't think she ever realized how much damage she did that day to a living, breathing son. When Gary shared this story with me, I wanted to weep for him, for her, for my brothers. I wanted to sob his pain away.

The Lake Street House was a place of great mystery, but much greater fear. Downright scary at times. No one understood the goings on; the hows or whys. Worse, no one could stop the happenings. The house was either haunted or visited by some unknown beings each and every night. It all seemed to begin shortly after my stepfather moved in.

We knew someone had died at the house before we moved in. The room where the death occurred was always physically cold—of the 'almost see your breath' variety. It was the same room in which my younger brothers slept, and where my older brother, Gary, had nearly suffocated by some unknown source of trouble. Time spent in that room gave one a veil of depression: gloom and doom. This was also the room where my normally meek and passive mother went into a fit of anger against my brother. We all avoided it.

Each night footsteps moved down the hallway, and doors opened and closed. The visitors were ever-present, walking past our bedroom door, pausing, and then moving down the hallway. It almost drove my stepfather insane. My mother remained composed. I do not know or understand why that was so, but she kept telling all of us that it was just our nightly visitors and not to worry.

My stepfather was a World War II veteran who had seen a lot of combat. Today, he would be diagnosed as having a severe case of Post-Traumatic Stress Disorder (PTSD). He arrived in our lives and in our home complete with a lot of issues—namely anger, and a large handgun. He took that gun to bed with him every night. Under the circumstances, that may have been a sane and rational reaction for him.

When he heard the 'visitor' he'd jump up out of the bed with his fully loaded pistol and dash into the hallway to catch the intruder. Night after night he readied for combat. All of us children stayed in our rooms, avoiding the ghost and preventing ourselves from becoming targets of a frightened, lethally-armed man. After several months my stepfather stopped patrolling. Why he never found anyone, and why he gave up, I do not know.

We never saw anything ourselves or, better stated, we never remembered seeing anything. I do know that there was someone or something coming and going each night. I'm unsure if our rooms were trespassed. I remember only pieces of events. I can remember being very tired each morning. I often wonder if more was happening to us than we can remember.

The most astonishing part was how my parents could have slept through the nights with someone or something wandering around the house while their children lay helplessly alone in their beds. If it were my children, I could not have slept.

We may have been visited again in later years, even after leaving that house. I remember dreams of places and beings, but nothing more. Anything that might have happened is a lost or, perhaps, a repressed memory.

Of course, none of this was normal. Any functioning family would have questioned the events with greater curiosity and authority. Perhaps, being motivated by some well-deserved fears, others would have the good sense to move out of the house. But not our family; we accommodated the abnormal and terrifying, accepted it as a part of our routine.

I do remember my stepfather telling me that he once saw someone, or what appeared to be the backside and legs of someone, going through a window. Not an open window, mind you.

And of note, my grandmother never had any problems upstairs. The paranormal only involved the first and second floors—the part we occupied.

Of my family group, I'm the only one who wanted to dig below the surface. Though I was only four years old at the time, perhaps too young to realize what I was seeing and hearing, my brother, Gary, knew much more, but cannot remember the details.

What I know for certain is that at the time, I knew it was happening but knew that there was nothing we could do to stop the visits. Something happened to me, but I am not sure what. Maybe this whole experience was a nightmare we all somehow lived through and shared. But what kind of nightmare? In another realm? In whose truth?

My Mother and Father (on right side of photo) around 1945

STRANGE VISITORS

"There are no aliens, only Ascended Masters"
——Yogiraj SatGurunath Siddhanath

My parents sold our house in San Francisco and headed north to Oregon. My stepfather used the money made from the sale of the house to finance the move. We stayed at a cheap motel for a time, but began to run out of money while my stepfather was out looking for work—as a lumberjack—and a place for us to live.

During this time my parents drove by an abandoned government-housing complex in North Bend. 18 units of three-bedroom triplex apartments—previously used to house military dependents—stood in a field of uncut grass and dirt. The buildings were boarded up and decorated with large 'Warning! No trespassing—Government Property Keep Out' signs. Not a welcome sign for miles.

My mother came up with a bold idea: move in and claim squatters' rights. She informed the local media that she was breaking into one of the units and moving her entire family in that afternoon. She went on to say that her husband had earned the right as a veteran, and explained that we would have to be removed by force if 'they' wanted us out of there.

Her word-for-word ended up in print. Our family made the front page: a photo of us in one of the units unpacking our belongings. After radio newscaster Walter Winchell broadcast our story nationally, a crush of people showed up ready to move into the rest of the apartments.

The entire complex filled less than a day after the story aired. By the time the city council figured out what had happened my mother was a citywide and national hero. Nobody wanted to give the order to the police department to remove a poor veteran's family. She'd won the battle and found a place to live. We spent several days cleaning, fixed some small things, and got the lights and water turned on. A real home. No rent. Just as well; my parents didn't have much money.

Behind closed doors life began to get ghostly weird. We found ourselves in almost the same kind of frightening situation we'd moved from. But this time it was a whole new level of scary.

If I'd never had the experiences I've had, and someone told me the following story, I'd find it difficult to comprehend. 'Oh, you were dreaming,' might be the standard reply. But around 1951 I know this happened, and my siblings were witnesses.

I recall going to bed. I lay there fighting sleep while my brother was in deep slumber in the other bed. I felt uneasy, as if someone were watching me in the darkened room. I pulled up the blankets to warm up; the room temperature had dropped. I saw something move across the room.

I became scared and called out for my parents. I kept yelling, waking everyone—except my brother—in the process. My stepfather burst in, angry that I'd woken him. He turned on the lights, pronounced a 'nothing here', turned out the lights, and told me not to call out again. Left me in darkness.

My stepfather's footsteps fell silent and I heard him close his bedroom door. Several more anxious moments passed before my eyes adjusted.

I knew 'they' had returned because I saw 'them'. Several childlike figures wearing what appeared to be matching uniforms or jumpsuits. They stood nearby and stared with huge owl-like eyes. I got the impression they were not children. I thought their lips moved like they were talking, but I didn't hear or understand anything.

Terrified, I began yelling again. Gary remained in an almost comatose sleep. Everyone in the house should have heard me, even our neighbors. I screamed at the top of my lungs, but I later learned only my two sisters in the other room heard me and were too afraid to come help me. I have never understood how my brother could have slept right through all the noise, or why the beings left him alone in his bed, or why my parents didn't hear or didn't react to my screams of terror.

The beings looked human-like, but not exactly. I could see light through them. I knew that I was seeing 'beings' (for lack of a better term) and that they wanted to do something to me. I felt that they wanted to take me away from my home. I could not hide from them, nor could I make them go away.

The creatures, about five of them, were in my closet and around my bed. I saw them while I was wide-awake; this was no dream. I tried to hide from them under my covers, but it was as if there was an x-ray machine at work, because I could actually see light and their images through the blankets.

They carried a tool that reminded me of a fishing pole. They reached out to touch me with it. Two of them sat on the top shelf of my closet and used the pole to shoot what appeared to be bubbles onto me.

Each bubble had a hook or sharp object in it. I felt they were doing something to me. Overcome with fear and horror, I could not scream anymore. I froze to my bed in sheer terror, unable and unwilling to move. Then I found courage and, in a moment of extreme bravery coupled with manic fear, I jumped off my bed and bolted out of my bedroom and into my sisters' room. My two sisters were awake and wide-eyed with fear.

Later Melody and Marsha explained they saw a light glowing behind me, then witnessed these same creatures coming into their room. We all saw the beings standing directly in the bedroom's doorway, blocking our escape. Our next memory is of standing behind the sofa in the front room.

Just as the dawn's early light came shining through the windows, the 'beings' walked toward us. They smiled like a mother might to soothe a crying child; sympathetically. They raised their hands as if gesturing a goodbye. As they stood next to the sofa and stared at us, they transfixed me with their oval-shaped eyes. As frightened as I was, I found it difficult not to stare back into those lidless eyes. I had the feeling that they did not want to harm us, but I still felt angry with them for scaring me. They continued to move across the floor to us. Then, as the light from the windows hit them, they all disappeared, fading away into nothing.

My sisters and I stood silent for a long time, afraid to return to our bedrooms. We never shared it with our parents or with anyone else at the time. We all saw what happened that night, but we did not speak about it again for five decades.

It was around the time of the 'strange visits' that I began to get frequent, terrible nosebleeds. Many a morning there'd be blood on my pillow. I do not remember hitting it or doing any damage to it, so I decided weather changes brought them on. No one ever figured out why my nose bled as often as it did.

Over time, I realized that my paranormal psychic skill levels increased greatly around the times I experienced nosebleeds.

I began to sense that 'others' visited me during the night. I often woke up and felt the presence of 'others' near me, but would fall back to sleep. I never remembered anything except the feeling that someone had been there and that I had not been in my bed all night long. There was a sense I'd traveled during the night. Strange dreams about journeys and places occurred, but they were un-relatable to the real world that I woke to. I accepted this as normal at the time and did not question it until years later.

Author's note:When my sisters and I shared this experience Melody was eight years old, and Marsha was three years old. None of us ever talked about it again until 50 years later. It seems odd to me now that it took so long to discuss it, and that my sisters still would prefer not to.

FIREWALKER

There were no kindergarten classes at the local schools in North Bend, Oregon. Preschool was not an option either, so I spent my time hanging around the housing project in which we lived.

Though it was a common practice for some of the residents to burn their household garbage on the open ground between the rows of buildings, none stayed around to guard the fires or to ensure that they didn't get out of control. Most of the kids in the project enjoyed throwing sticks and leaves into the burning mess, pretending it was a campfire. We gathered around them playing camping or cowboys and Indians.

One afternoon found me playing near a pile of burning trash; nearer and nearer. At some point I decided to walk through the flames. It wasn't a 'hot coals' walk of spiritual significance. I was five; I'd decided I would and could walk through fire. Basically I chose to take a stroll through a pile of burning garbage.

Undaunted by lashing red fingers of fire which leapt at me, I began walking. Suddenly one of my pants' legs caught on fire. Within seconds fire engulfed me, flames shooting out from every piece of clothing. I flew out of the fire screaming and crying. My speed fed the fire: the faster I ran the more the flames flared. I became a red fireball screeching and moving through the housing project.

Luckily for me, my yelling reached the ears of an older woman. She ran out of her apartment so fast that she couldn't have had time to think about her actions. She raced to me then tackled me as if she were a football player. I went down and she threw dirt on my blazing body and rolled me on the ground.

Then she picked me up and looked into my eyes. She was visibly shaken and seemed more afraid of what had happened than I was. She may have been burned—perhaps her hands were scorched during the process of saving me; she'd used them to pat down the flames. She must have stripped off some of my clothing, or it came off during the patting down and dirt roll. Tears flowed down her checks as she looked at me. So much love came from her eyes. I have never forgotten that motherly look of worry.

She lifted me and carried me as gently as possible, but I felt as if I were still on fire. I screamed out in agony. My leg was seriously burned; other parts of my body were blistered.

I would have been totally disfigured for life or even dead if she had not taken such swift action. I do not remember ever seeing her before this incident. She was there when I needed her. I never saw her after. I know not who she was, but I know she loved me deeply.

I was passed from the arms of my rescuer to those of an emotionless mother, who removed the remnants of clothing and cleaned me up. She did the best she could without taking me to see any doctors. I remained in great pain. My right leg in particular looked like cooked meat. I eventually recovered from the burns without any medical attention or medication. I still have a large circular scar on the inside of my right leg.

We were very poor back then, so I assumed that my mother couldn't afford to pay for a doctor. At some point in my adulthood the message became clear that I simply hadn't been important enough to her.

Someone watched over me that day. I will always remember the woman with the loving eyes as my first true and faithful guardian angel.

ONE YEAR

Part One – Ward of The County Hospital

My schooling never got off on the right foot. I began first grade a couple of weeks after the school year had started.

My family had moved back to San Francisco from Oregon to grandmother's three-bedroom house. She was unhappy with the situation, and we'd even brought our dog into her house, but it was to be our home until we could find another.

With my grandmother in one bedroom, my parents in another, my two sisters received the third. My brother, Gary, and I had none. We were assigned the front room in which I had a rollaway bed.

And so I was the new kid, two weeks late with no friends. To make matters worse, I'd never attended any preschool or kindergarten classes, so this 'two weeks late first day' was my very first in any school. The deficit was more than social; I was behind in my schoolwork. I did not know my numbers or letters; couldn't sight read a word. From my first moments I decided I didn't want to look stupid, so I became the class clown and joked around to cover what I didn't know.

Survival describes the ordeal of second grade. I started on time, but a few weeks into the school year my family moved to a new house in Sunnyvale which required I attend a new school. Once again I began class not knowing anyone and, just like before, several weeks of school had passed. It got worse. My mother had decided I should use my stepfather's last name, Engelking. When the teacher asked me to write my name, I didn't know how to spell it correctly. Not know how to spell your name in grade two? Overwhelmed and zero confidence on the 'first day three weeks late.'

Grade two afternoon snack time consisted of graham crackers and milk. Students brought in milk money each Monday and the teacher then shopped for the food. Every afternoon the other students drank their milk and munched their crackers, and I watched them enjoy their snacks. I did not have money, and the teacher asked me why. I explained something about not getting hungry.

Sadly, sensitivity was lacking. I felt like an outcast.

Third grade was so much better. An on time start, no move, and I knew some of the kids from the year before. The problem was I became ill. I developed a high fever and my face swelled up like a balloon. I peed blood for weeks, and lost a tremendous amount of weight. My skin paled—I looked like a POW.

I attended school with a high fever, totally out of it, in pain and dizzy almost all the time. Eventually my teacher noticed and sent me to the school nurse. The fact was that I was slowly dying, and no one in my family noticed. I was sent home and my mother received the message to take me to a doctor and not to send me back until I was well. But she did not seek medical attention for me. It was not until about a week later, when my aunt came for a visit, that anyone did anything about my health. She took one look at me and demanded my mother call a doctor. This didn't happen immediately. Up until that moment I'd been just lying in bed every day, getting weaker and thinner. A little closer to death.

Finally someone did call a doctor. He ordered my parents to take me to the San Jose County Hospital, which they did that evening. When the doctors saw me in the admitting room they sprung to action, calling for a series of tests and x-rays. They told my mother and stepfather that I was already so far gone that there was a good possibility I would soon die.

My frail, eight-year-old body was strapped to a hospital gurney. Staff wheeled me away from my family; no goodbyes. I still remember looking up at the ceiling from the gurney, the bright lights hurting my eyes, as a nurse pushed me through the halls. A prisoner immobilized on the stretcher, I was confused, sick, and scared.

I was taken to an isolation ward in a separate facility outside the main hospital building. I wondered why I had to be kept alone. Was this a treatment or punishment? No one explained.

A door opened to a room that held a metal table with a lot of long needles on it. The longest ones I had ever seen. The nurse informed me that staff would be sticking the needles into my back and into my lungs to draw out fluid. That I was terrified is an understatement. Stripped down to my underwear, I was directed to sit backwards on a cold metal chair. They began their job of suctioning fluid from around my lungs. It hurt like hell, but they kept stabbing me over and over again. It seemed to go on forever. When they were finished, they left me sitting there alone until a nurse returned to put me in bed.

No one hugged me. No one empathized with a 'sorry, kid' or 'them's the breaks'. In fact, the nurse didn't say a word.

I cried myself to sleep. It would be the first night of a very long year as a ward of the San Jose County Hospital.

Part Two – The Playground In My Mind

I had only my imagination as a playground. No one provided me with any forms of entertainment such as reading material, toys, television, coloring books, or radio. Isolated most of the time—rarely any child patients to talk to—most conversations were with adults, namely medical staff. Days became long stretches of daydreams, though over time I realized that those daydreams also contained visions—I believe the concentrated time alone allowed a journey within and thus a focused time with my intuition; a visit with psychic powers that lay within that perhaps most people do not get due to the hurried pace of life.

Someone wheeled me in one of those old wooden wheelchairs over to the main building for x-rays and blood tests every day. Almost all the conversations were based on what medical information they needed to know and telling me what they wanted me to do. But I had a hurt inside that they didn't comprehend. I ached for attention and friendship. To them I was a patient, not a person; part of their job. They were paid to be with me for medical purposes.

The first few weeks the extraction of fluid was a regular occurrence; perhaps seven times. Then one day the nurse rolled me up to the main building and pushed me up onto a wooden platform. When I looked around, I saw rows of doctors seated in a small theater-like room. No one had prepared me for what was about to happen.

The nurse undressed me to my underwear in front of all those strangers. The medical community was to see a demonstration of my treatments. Had someone asked, I would have told him that I did not want to be displayed like some animal in an experiment in front of a crowd. But no one did ask.

I took my mind away from all that was happening to me so I would not have to endure all these people watching me suffer. I refused to cry out when it hurt because I did not want them to be a part of my pain.

The procedure took much longer than usual since they stopped intermittently to lecture about the process. They even had some members of the audience of doctors come up and try sticking me with needles. One after another practiced injecting me; long needles through my back and into my lungs. Not all of them hit the right place or did it correctly, and when that happened, the doctor in charge instructed them to do it again.

I endured every moment. The adults ran the show; an eight-year-old was unimportant. They spoke as if I were not even a person or not even there. Anger pulsed through my body, but I didn't express it because I knew that complaining would be futile. I practiced what I had learned well from dealing with my stepdad—I suppressed my rage.

A medical sideshow: I considered it an emotional rape.

When it was over there were no acknowledgments. I was left sitting on stage in my underwear while the discussion wrapped up. Finally, someone rolled me offstage and back to my ward where I lay alone in my bed and wept silently.

Neglect. Mistreatment. Disregard. Abandonment. Yes, emotional rape.

Part Three – Dreams of A Future

The staff woke me dutifully every day at six in the morning when the shift changed. The long, dull hours stretched endlessly before me. I had no clock, so I never knew what time it was. I didn't know the date or even the day of the week. I spent my time going within my mind to keep myself entertained. I had vivid dreams—visions really—about people, events, and places that many years later I would recognize in my real life. Many of these dreams became reality some five, ten, twenty and even forty years later. To this day, things unfolding from these long-ago imaginings that I had as a child.

I had entered the hospital at eight years old and stayed for one year—until I was almost six months past my ninth birthday. Thanksgiving was meaningless; nothing happened, and nothing happened in the presence of no visitors.

At Christmas someone dressed as Santa came into my room to say 'hello'. He brought some candy which the nurses promptly took away after he left. No gift to unwrap.

My own family took a page from Santa's guidebook and dropped in but brought no gift. The staff did not celebrate with patients; the only Christmas decorations were at the nurses' station. I heard seasonal tunes playing down the hall, along with occasional laughter from one of the staff. There existed not a single strand of tinsel in my own world. I did my best to think of the real reason for the celebration—Christ and his birth.

Even at the young age of eight I felt things inside me about love and God. I knew that there must be a purpose to all that had happened to me. I refused to think of myself as a victim. I knew this experience would make me a different and perhaps better person. The time I spent in the playground in my mind altered my life forever. Though I had the regular kind of dreams—the fall asleep and see a movie kind—many of my 'dreams' were visions within a meditative state I'd created through my desire to escape.

I could not physically leave the hospital, but I had the freedom to think and imagine. Free inside my mind, I searched for the deeper parts of myself. I prayed and talked to God all day long. He became my confidante, I thought he was perhaps the only real friend that I would ever be able to count on and trust. In many ways I was blessed that all this had happened to me because it gave me a new perspective on my life.

I developed a hunger to change. I might have been physically in the hospital, but I was never mentally or spiritually a captive of that place. I took my mind on magical trips into new worlds and on great adventures. I created stories and did anything I wanted to in my own mind. I found that the harsh world that held my body as a prisoner did not exist for me in my inner world. I learned a lot by staying silent and lying still on my bed. I quieted my thoughts and emotions. I became one with peace.

Part Four – Outpatient

Because I was never informed of anything, and could not put together the snippets of information I overheard, I did not understand my full diagnosis until later.

I had several things wrong with me due to what started off as just a bad case of the mumps which went untreated. Both lungs became infected and I developed pneumonia, which caused fluids to surround my lungs, a condition called pleurisy. In this weakened condition I developed Bright's disease, now known as Glomerulonephritis—a kidney disease. This resulted in my dangerously low blood pressure (I peed blood) and intense chest and back pain. The dizziness made it so I couldn't even stand up straight.

There was no fanfare when I left the hospital. I was no longer a captive, but I had a parole of sorts. My kidney disease was not cured. Every week for one year after discharge, and then every other week for about five years, I returned to the hospital for treatment. Eventually I returned once a month—I was a high school student by then.

My mother did not drive a car. Getting some twenty-five miles to the hospital took lots of walking and unreliable public transportation. No citywide bus service existed in Sunnyvale in the 1950s. My mother and I had to walk across the town into the downtown area—four miles one way.

On appointment day we'd get up before sunrise and trek across town to the only bus stop. From there we caught a bus that took us to the center of San Jose where we transferred to another bus to get to the hospital. It was a physical workout and logistical nightmare, especially when it was cold and/or raining.

The hospital expected us at eight in the morning so that we could wait with others in order to get X-rays and blood work. This took up most of the morning. When the tests were done we'd walk to the closest restaurant and have lunch then return to the hospital and wait with more than a hundred others to see the doctor and hear the results of the tests. It always seemed to me that people were called in random order so everyone had to be there and not outside. With no television and few, if any, magazines to read, it was a tiresome time.

It always seemed my name was one of the last ones called. I never saw the same doctor, but the treatment was identical: the doctor would ignore me while reading things over then ask several questions, the kind that made me wonder if they had been informed why I was there. There was no feeling of anyone being invested in my health or me as a person. Medications would be renewed for an additional week. Gavel down, next case.

We'd walk to the bus stop and reverse everything we'd done that morning. By the time we arrived home I'd be exhausted; a zombie at school the next day. The entire ordeal created huge problems for my classroom work. I missed about a week of school every month that year, after losing a whole year when I was in hospital.

Looking back I realize the doctors I saw were new ones. I've decided my experience resembles going to court with a public defender that is reading your case files for the first time while standing in front of the judge.

This process of enduring these medical appointments taught me patience and tolerance. I became a daydreamer and spent my waiting time by exploring my own inner resources. I survived and, in some ways, became stronger for having endured it all; it was another of those gifts that, at the time, did not resemble presents in any form.

Author's note: This was the longest year of my life. Restricted to total bed rest, most of my time was spent alone. Virtually no other children, nothing for entertainment— except my imagination. Family visited Sunday afternoons for less than fifteen minutes. Sorry, kid.

Of interest: In 2010 I had an unexpected reunion with one of the few boys who spent time in the hospital ward (he'd been a patient for a couple of months). When a pest control man checked my garage attic for termites he stepped onto the sheetrock surface, creating quite a bit of damage. As a result, the company sent out one of their old supervisors to repair it.

The supervisor and I got to talking and San Jose came up. We compared notes and realized we'd both been in the children's clinic during the same period. We remembered each other, embraced, and exchanged stories.

Sixty years removed from the events, we'd randomly found each other. The odd thing about this is that I never talk about being in the hospital to strangers, let alone people I know, but I felt that he was the right person to talk to about it—there'd been a connection as soon as I saw him.

ANGELS AND DOGS

"If trouble hearing Angels song with thine ears, try listening with thy heart."
—— MERIEL STELLIGER

My tenth year, 1956, marked a new beginning. My one year of captivity at the San Jose County Hospital was to be placed in the past. I was overjoyed to be alive and home.

Even though I was a child, I felt a strong urge and need to draw closer in my personal relationship with God. I looked for ways to make myself better, not just physically, but spiritually

One of my first decisions was to take a vow never again to eat meat. My thinking was that if the Catholics did not eat meat on Fridays, I could go without it altogether. My mother was supportive of my decision, but she did suggest that I eat some fish and fowl since otherwise there wouldn't be much for me to eat.

Shortly after making this personal decision I shared a very beautiful experience with my mother. The moment still stands out brightly in my heart and mind. We were resting on the sofa in the living room when I heard what sounded like the singing of a church choir. Never before had I heard singing as glorious as this. The multitude of gentle, feminine-like voices seemed to come from all around and inside me.

A flash of thought led me to believe someone had left a radio or record player on.

My mother heard the chorus too. I could tell from the look on her face. We got up and searched the entire house, but we could not locate the source. No matter where I went, the music followed me. Outside, it seemed to be coming from the sky itself. A pleasurable, blissful chill came over my entire body, and a joyful shiver raced up my spine. It was like being loved and being in love.

It followed my mother, too. No matter where we went, the music remained the same volume as if it were a part of us. The voices were everywhere, singing, praising, and loving. We finally stood side by side, mother and son, listening. Peaceful waves of energy washed over us. I felt as if I were being hugged by a divine being. I embraced the feeling of love that blossomed within me. We absorbed all that awesome peace. Finally, after a blissfully long time, the voices gently faded.

I felt lightheaded and joyous for several days following that event; my mother seemed that way too. Later, when she suggested that we'd perhaps been blessed to hear the angels themselves singing, I fully accepted that as a fact. Her suggestion felt more than theory. It felt right. It felt true.

Not long after this shared experience, a passing car hit one of our dogs. He could barely move when I found him lying there in the street. I carried him inside the house to the sofa where I knelt down on my knees and prayed through my tears. I prayed with all my heart and soul for God to heal my dog. Resolved in my faith, I tensed my entire body then gently laid my hands on the dog and wished with all my strength for God to transfer my faith and life energy to him.

Power, like electricity, shot from my fingertips into my dog's body. To my astonishment, he suddenly jumped off the sofa. He paraded around the house as if nothing had happened. He was healed. I believed that God healed my dog because I had trusted and believed in Him. My faith in God had healed my dog.

More strange and wondrous experiences began to unfold after that healing. I found that I was often aware of events in the future, not just my own but in the futures of people I didn't even know.

At the time, I did not realize what was unfolding or why these things were happening to me. I was just a small, trusting child graced somehow with the wonder and holiness of God's angels. I had heard them sing and they touched my heart and soul forever.

MIND GAMES

"Fairy tales do not tell children the dragons exist. Children already know
that dragons exist. Fairy tales tell children the dragons can be killed."
— G.K. CHESTERTON

My younger sister Marsha and I had a phenomenal mental connection. We could actually read each other's thoughts; not something that we could do with others with the same rate of success.

We played a couple of different mental games with each other.

The first one required a deck of cards. We'd shuffle and then my sister would retrieve the first card on the pile and send me a mental image of it. The object of the game was to guess the value of the card AND the suit. For example, if she focused on a 'four of spades' then I would have to say 'four of spades' to get it right. Guessing a 'four of clubs' would be a wrong.

The idea was for each to go through the entire 52 cards to see who could get the most correct with only one guess.

When my sister sent me mental images of the cards it was almost like a television turned on inside my brain. I could sense the color and feel the card value. We got so good at this game that I often got 25-30 correct cards out of 52; sometimes closer to 40.

Images I sent to her produced a lower score, but still respectable, and beyond a random guessing range. She'd identify 15-20. She'd get many more by the value but not the suit.

We could never get all of them, even though we tried.

We played another 'mind game' where we would each have to think of common sayings (Mary had a little lamb, or Merry Christmas) or lyrics from a song, a book title, or name of a television show. We'd see how few 'guesses' we'd have to make without clues. We hit a good percentage on the first guess based on what we were feeling inside our mind, and got the rest after a few guesses.

At the time I never thought much about the impact of these games, nor did Marsha. It seemed normal and felt natural. Later, after having read about this kind of communication, I realize our results were better than random guesses. My sister's ability to send and receive was at its super peak when she was a young child. The years have taken their toll on most of that ability. She was more open to the positive energies of life and had a much stronger belief system when younger.

I used to play another game called "Pushing The Clouds". I'd lie on the ground outside at our home in Oregon looking up at the sky. I'd try to push away or dissolve a selected cloud. I was a five year-old successful cloud pusher.

I never felt the story worthy of sharing when I wrote my first book *A Spiritual Warrior's Journey,* but someone pointed out to me that the games we played might demonstrate the potential energy generated by the innocence of children who truly believe.

The faith and trust of children should never be underestimated. When teachers, parents and other adults welcome children to the 'real world' and erase silly notions of fairies, and angels, invisible friends, and impossible things like dissolving clouds, they dissolve a concept that likely has merit for all ages.

A NEIGHBOR'S LOVE

"Insight is better than eyesight when it comes to seeing an angel."
— EILEEN ELIAS FREEMAN

When I was eleven years old I used to go to a friend's house every day after school. His place was about six blocks from my family's home, but I'm pretty sure my mother didn't know where it was; she never asked for an address, a family name, or a phone number.

I used to hang there for as long as I could. My friend and I watched television and played with his toys until it was time for his dinner. I sat in front of their TV set while they ate. I didn't want to go home.

Sadly, after one visit, I paused in front of their closed garage door and heard my friend's mother lecturing him about my being there all the time. She asked her son if I had a home to go to, which she knew I did because she made some unkind remarks about my family and me. Her remarks hurt me deeply because I'd thought I was welcome. Heck, I didn't cause any trouble, and all I wanted to do was stay there and enjoy their family.

I ran home feeling rejected and hurt by that mother's unkind words. I vowed never to visit them again, which I never did. Looking back, I understand I over-stayed my welcome. I was a lonely little kid looking for love, some friendship, and a refuge from my own dysfunctional family. Besides, they had a TV set and we didn't.

Later, a new family moved into our neighborhood four houses down from us. They were the nicest people, and I was still that lonely little kid looking for love and refuge. The young mother may have sensed my needs because she gave it to me. She let me talk to her and actually listened. I told her what I thought about life and other important stuff. She let me play with her children's toys, and one time when she saw that I was attached to an old cowboy outfit and a couple of beat-up toy guns, she asked me if I would mind taking them home with me since her children didn't need them anymore.

I was overjoyed.

Sometimes she baked cookies for me and poured a tall glass of milk to go with them. When she did this, it was the most enjoyable experience of the day for me. I really loved this woman and her whole family. Her children were much older than I was, but she let me come over to play and just hang around even when her own children were not there.

She lived a wholesome lifestyle and projected an image of stability. She made me feel good about being me. I did not worry about saying or doing anything wrong around her. I had the feeling that she would always like me no matter what I did. I visited her often and she treated me as if I were a part of her family. I certainly felt welcomed and loved there.

My experience with the concept of unconditional love was short, but sweet. When she told me that her family was moving I was devastated. I stopped going to their house. The funny thing is that I have absolutely no memory of the day she and her family moved. I'm totally blank. After she was gone it was as if she had never been there. My mind wrote off the whole history of that relationship and the associated memories.

She was one of the most positive people in my young life, yet I find it odd that I so easily wrote off the whole experience of that relationship after she moved away. I learned early in life how to shut off my emotions in an attempt to protect myself. I guess I did not want to feel abandoned once again, so I did not mourn her moving. It was much the same with the responses I had in Vietnam to death, battles, and relationships. The mind is an incredible combination of magical wonder and powerful science: perhaps they are the same thing.

LESSONS FROM A DRUNK

Part One—Life 101

When my stepfather got drunk he sometimes exploded with rage. He aimed his anger at the entire world. Though he did not always erupt into violence, the anxiety he created in me and others occupied us full time. We didn't want to find ourselves anywhere near him after he'd been drinking, which was most of his waking hours when he wasn't at work.

He carried with him a large Bowie knife, hidden under the back of his shirt. The knife was at least a foot long and lived in a leather sheath that he tucked into his belt. He had few problems moving around with it and when it did get in the way he'd pull it out and put it on the bar next to his drink. He also packed a loaded .357 Magnum in a concealed holster under his jacket. He wore the gun all the time except when he was at work—then it was in his car. He was Dirty Harry's alter ego; prepared for war—any place, any time, any 'body'.

One time, after he had disappeared for several weeks, he returned to explain that he'd been under investigation for shooting someone in the head with a shotgun. He'd told the cops it was an unfortunate accident resulting from cleaning the gun. He had witnesses testify that was what happened. The truth, he told us, was that he'd been paid by the witnesses to do it—murder for hire. I believed him wholeheartedly.

When I was about twelve years old, my stepfather was involved in a knife fight in a bar in Palo Alto. He cut and sliced his victim to the point of the man needing hospitalization, then claimed self-defense and beat another rap.

One of the worst memories is when he used a leather bullwhip on our family dog, a large German Shepherd. The dog barked in great fear and pain, but my stepfather continued to strike. The dog's flesh tore and there was blood everywhere.

I couldn't stand for it. I went into my parent's bedroom where the assault was taking place and I demanded he stop.

He turned and looked at me with rage in his eyes then told me to stay away or he would take the whip to me next.

I placed myself in front of the dog and watched my stepfather raise his arm and peel back the whip. I waited for the lashing, but he hesitated and dropped his arm. He cursed me and walked away.

The dog was bleeding badly. I wanted to cry for my dog, but couldn't; my anger blocked my tears. I held it all in, not daring to show my anger outwardly, knowing that it might lead to more violent consequences.

The dog whimpered, as any injured animal would. As I stood quietly, thinking how insane my stepfather was, he returned to the room and told me that if I told my mother what had happened he would kill me. *Beyond insane, yes.*

I did not want to take the chance. I figured my mother could see what had taken place by all the blood on the bedroom floor and on the walls, and by the huge, raw bloody marks on the dog.

His cruelty knew no bounds. One summer he decided our dogs were too much trouble. Over the course of a couple of months, he took a dog out to a friend's property, and insisted I come along as a witness to each execution. Both times he walked the dog away from the view of the road and then performed his insane deed. Each one looked so trustingly at him as he aimed his pistol directly at its head.

It was over quickly. But more than a half century later the pain is locked inside me. Their eyes still haunt me. I could not cry then. I held it all inside. However, anytime now that I watch a movie or television show where an animal is killed I cry more than a few tears. And since that fateful summer, I have never owned another dog.

More than one night I was awakened from a sound sleep by the *thwack* of a large knife hitting the wall just above my head. He was drunk and coming to talk to me about his life; his sad childhood. I learned to be a great listener at a very young age in order to survive. I listened to all his stories about beating, robbing, and even killing people. I never knew which to believe, but I did not doubt the possibility that he would and could have killed as many people as he claimed.

On another occasion he pulled his pistol out and put it right to my forehead.

He then pulled back the hammer with his thumb. I could see the actual bullets in each cylinder, just inches from my face. It was fully loaded and cocked, ready to fire. I remember looking at each of them and wondering what it would feel like if he really did pull the trigger and those bullets penetrated my forehead.

He talked to me for what seemed like an hour but was probably a few minutes. It could have been a lifetime. I listened attentively, without comments. I stood there not moving, breathing slowly and shallowly. I was tranquil and at peace. He reached up with his left hand and gently put down the gun's hammer to its resting position on the cylinder. He pulled the gun away from my forehead and put it on top of a shelf in the hall closet as if nothing had ever happened between us.

I remained in place, not wanting to make any sudden or wrong moves, concerned what the crazy man might do next, but he just walked away.

I felt no emotion at all. I returned to my room and played some records as if it were just a normal day. No fear, no tears, and no anger.

Confrontation would have been dangerous at best, so I chose not to judge him openly or confront him with the obvious nature of his insanity. I left him alone both physically and emotionally, avoiding confrontation. I stayed as invisible as possible and when I wasn't, I listened. That was the secret weapon that protected me from the craziness around me.

His own friends—that he had any is strange—were afraid of him. No one gave him lip. Most people just wanted to keep to themselves, staying quiet and cool-headed around him, so as not to set him off.

Part Two—Gone Fishin'. Not.

My stepfather always promised to do things with me when he was drunk or when he went through a melancholy guilt. He talked a good talk and I always wanted to believe him. It was the guilt that stemmed from another broken promise after the only uncle I knew, Uncle Johnny, gave me his personal shortwave radio. It was a transoceanic radio that could pick up stations from around the world. I was thrilled to get it even though it didn't work. It needed some minor work.

My stepfather promised to get the radio fixed and packed it into his car shortly after my uncle gave it to me. Months went by. Every time I asked about it he told me to be patient. He said he had some guy working on it, but the part he needed had not arrived. A full year or more expired when, after I asked again, he told me to stop bugging him. He went on to say it wasn't a great radio and that he'd given it to a friend at a bar.

The next thing I knew he promised to take me fishing—perhaps to make up for what he'd done. It would be my first fishing trip ever. On the Saturday we were to go fishing, I rose before sunrise and grabbed the beat-up old fishing pole and a metal box containing a handful of hooks and lures that my brother, Gary, had given me. I sat at the kitchen table waiting for my stepfather to get up and have his breakfast.

When he came into the kitchen and saw me sitting there, pole leaning against the wall, he told me he had to do a small job first thing that morning. He asked me to wait and he'd be right back for me. The morning dragged on and bled into the afternoon. I waited.

At six o'clock he returned; said he'd forgotten about me, but that we'd still go fishing. We got into the car and he said he needed to stop at a bar first to see a guy who would tell him where there was a good fishing spot. He returned to the car about an hour later and said the guy didn't know any good places. He then said he'd remembered one. We drove to Stanford University (where he worked at that time) and pulled in near a fenced area behind the university. Large 'No Trespassing' and 'No Fishing' signs were posted in plain view.

My stepfather told me that there was a small lake just a short walk from the fence. I didn't feel good about going over the barbed wire. I went anyway, concerned the whole time that we'd be busted and someone would take my fishing pole. When we reached the water he stood and looked at it and declared there were no fish in the lake so we would be going home.

I never even got my fishing line wet.

I did not show any anger at the time and told him it was okay. I knew I had been messed about again, but I decided to let it pass. My mother never said anything nor did anyone else. The fishing pole sat unused in my bedroom closet until years later when I finally gave it away. I have never had the desire to go fishing again.

Part Three—Swimming Class

I was about 11 years of age and I had not learned to swim yet.

My stepfather thought my lack of knowledge about how to swim could be taught by him in the 'old school' way. Sink or swim. He took me to a place called Stevens Creek Dam.

He parked his car alongside the road and we walked down to the edge of the lake. We stood on a dirt mound that formed a bit of a precipice about four feet above the water. The water's depth was unknown to me and to him, but I guess he assumed it was deep enough to motivate me to swim.

He began the lesson by attaching a rough rope around my waist. The idea, he told me, was that if I went under he'd be pulling me up and toward the edge so not to worry He emphasized this was a proven way to teach people to swim and that I needed to trust him. Then he took me by the waist and tossed me into the air.

Downward I fell and then entered the cold and deep water below.

My body plunged below the surface. I moved my legs and arms as fast as I could but I continued to descend. I felt tension on the rope, but his pulling it only dragged me toward the edge and not above the surface. I struggled and fought. As with terrifying experiences, it seemed forever. When I surfaced I wanted to get back on land. I kept swallowing water and coughing while begging him to get me back to the dirty shore.

That day I vowed I'd never allow him to do that to me again. I knew I could be a great swimmer, and I was going to learn despite the ordeal he'd put me through with drowning lessons.

That summer I persuaded my parents to pay for community swim lessons at the local pool. The first lesson at the first class was about opening one's eyes underwater. Within an hour we were holding our breath and actually swimming underwater in a shallow pool.

I returned after one lesson for public swimming. Confident I could swim underwater and open my eyes to see, I went straight to the separate pool meant for diving. I lined up for the low diving board and when it was my turn I walked out and without hesitation, no rope around my middle or stepfather high above, I jumped into twelve feet of pure bliss. I held my breath and calmly swam underwater all the way to the poolside ladder. Though it was only about twenty-five feet from where I'd landed, I felt as if I'd just completed an English Channel crossing.

There was not an ounce of fear within me. I knew within a short time I'd be a good swimmer on the surface as well.

I spent the whole afternoon fearlessly jumping in and swimming to the ladder. By the end of the day I'd decided to go to the high diving board, ten feet above the water. Ten feet looks a lot higher from the top than the bottom; when I looked down I wanted to change my mind, but I had friends watching. I took a running jump and managed to go head first into the water below me. I knew that after what my crazy stepfather had done to me (related to water) nothing would scare me again. Indirectly he'd helped: his 'water-boarding' torture technique made me want to become a good swimmer if for no other reason than to protect myself from him ever doing that to me again.

The following year I became a great competitive swimmer and was on the city's swim team. The races were by age groups. I was the fastest in the breaststroke for my group on the team even beating out older kids as well. However, my inexperience regarding swim meets and competition caused me to make a mistake in my first public race—a race against the top team in the area.

I was way out in the lead without knowing I was out front, and when I looked to each side of me and got ready to touch the wall I saw no one and assumed I was in last place. I stopped to look around and was disqualified for stopping and standing up—just a foot short of the wall.

I felt really bad. I hadn't known I was out front. I hadn't intended to make the team look foolish.

The swim coach yelled at me like a Marine Corp's drill instructor and put me down in front of others. He belittled me and called me stupid.

William "Rev. Bill" McDonald Jr.

This was the exact kind of behavior (from an adult) that I received at home. The same kind of stuff I was trying to get away from by joining a club. I picked up my towel, walked out of the pool area, and never came back to the team again.

Author's note: Later on in my life I swam a few long distant open water races, surfed in California and Hawaii, was a professional lifeguard, helped with the US Army Ranger School Water Survival Testing at Fort Benning, Georgia, and taught SCUBA Diving for a living for four years in California.

MYSTERIOUS FIREBALL

In the late 1950s one could still see stars in the night sky over the Santa Clara Valley.

Silicon Valley and Google had yet to be developed. An Apple was a popular fruit to give teachers; the first picture in an ABC book.

One Saturday night, circa 1958, a good friend and I decided to camp in his backyard. We wanted a big fire and planned on using the scrap wood his father had piled. We set up our tent out behind his house then built a deep pit for our all-night blaze which we planned would keep us warm. We had bags of popped corn and some soft drinks. It was the kind of thing that two kids in junior high called fun—and I'd never done much official camping so I welcomed a backyard adventure.

The entire cosmos was filled with massive displays of shooting stars which entertained us in spectacular style more than any 4th of July fireworks' display. We lay on our backs next to our blazing fire and took in the heavens.

Around midnight something caught our attention. It became larger. A huge glowing fireball traveled slowly across the sky then suddenly took a sharp turn and came directly overhead; its speed and direction changed.

It came over us slowly then fell into the farmer's open field behind my friend's house. Although we were certain it had fallen into the adjacent field there were no sounds One would have thought something that big and fiery hitting the ground would have woken people with vibration, sound, and brightness. But not one porch light came on nor did one dog bark.

We looked at each other and being curious young kids we hopped up onto the backyard fence. We tried to see where the fireball had crashed, but could see no crater, no rise of dust or dirt in the air.

The next thing we both knew was that we were sitting by our fire pit—which had burned out; reduced to a pile of ashes—at sunrise. We looked at each other. I got up and said I had to go home.

We never talked about that night. We never asked what might have happened or how come we did not remember more. There remained several unasked questions: the lost time between a little after midnight and sunrise on Sunday morning; what landed or crashed in the field, and why did no one else know about it or see it. The bigger question is just as strange: what happened to us? Why didn't we question what happened at the time?

Author's note: Many decades later I came across a copy of J.Z. Knight's autobiography, A State of Mind: My Story of Ramtha Begins. *She wrote something similar about what happened to her and some friends in Texas when she was in high school. I mention this because when I read her mystical life story I noticed that we had peculiar life experiences in common. Coincidentally, we share the same birthdate and year (March 16th 1946).We very briefly corresponded with each other and I brought this subject up with her.*

JFK DREAMS

When I was a senior in high school I had frequent dreams about President Kennedy getting shot. Not only shot, but killed. I saw images of people watching television and crying. I sensed from my dreams that the President was going to be killed soon. I felt overwhelmed by certainty. Though I didn't announce any solid information—I didn't have any—I did share the dream content with a few close friends at school.

On November 22, 1963, I felt anxious. I knew something was going to happen that day. I wasn't totally sure if what would happen was related to my repeated dreams, but the uneasiness I'd experienced for several weeks reached a climax. I was watchful that morning; vigilant because of the premonition.

The announcement came over the school intercom as I sat at my desk in my government class. The words came out slowly then blanketed the room in silence. As the announcement came to an end some kids began to cry softly.

Later that morning we heard a live radio broadcast from the United Nations. The announcer said the delegates were standing for a minute of silent prayer in honor of the fallen President. I immediately arose! Others joined me, including the teacher.

The principal's voice came over the intercom again and announced that we were all dismissed. We hung around the halls, talking quietly and trying to figure out what had happened.

I met up with my girlfriend Carol, and we walked to my house to watch the televised coverage. All the stations had film of the event and follow-up stories. I remained glued to the television for the next three days. It was as if I was watching video footage from my previous dreams—surreal. The black and white images on the television screen reflected what I'd already seen—a replay of events I'd witnessed in my dreams.

In addition to receiving and digesting the knowledge of the assassination in real time through the media, I'd foreseen the event—even though I hadn't known the details. The tragedy took on a mirror effect inside me; real time shock reflecting previous time visions.

I felt I'd lost a friend and, like many, I was angry at the world for taking away a hero. When I returned to school it was difficult to get excited about football and basketball games, or school dances. None of it seemed important.

Life went on, but it took a while to get moving, and was never the same.

Carol and me at the High School Prom 1963

ENGELKING

When I was in second grade, my stepfather decided he wanted my brother and I to use his last name. It came as a surprise to me first day of school that I'd been registered with his surname rather than McDonald—I knew how to spell McDonald. Not only did it cause me embarrassment when I was shamed by the teacher for not knowing how to spell my name, but the moniker troubled me—much like my stepfather himself—throughout my school years and into adulthood when I'd returned to *McDonald*, but was also known as *Engelking*.

From Social Security card to draft card the name popped up as a required answer on the AKA questions.

One of the strangest repercussions from using Engelking as my last name happened in my senior year in high school. Some people in the school thought it was a Jewish name. How naïve I was back then. I didn't realize intolerance and anti-Semitism lived in our sleepy town. One morning on arriving at school the principal stood waiting. I was escorted into the cafeteria area and told to sit and wait. I assumed that I was in some kind of trouble.

The school lunch lady put her arm around me and said it was okay that I was a Jew. No need to be ashamed about it, she'd relayed. When I informed her I wasn't Jewish she patted my shoulder and offered a look of pity mixed with compassion. The principal returned and explained that he had the janitorial staff cleaning the graffiti that was painted on lockers and walls around the school. I still had no clue as to what he was talking about.

Then it was explained to me that someone had painted Anti-Jewish slogans with me as the target; rather the last name, Engelking, had been the target.

Frankly it didn't bother me if people wanted to think I was a Jew, but all hurtful words and actions upset me. I never got to see the graffiti or understand what would make them decide the name was Jewish.

The event was a wake-up call. I'd always figured everyone had an open heart and mind as I believed I did. Small-minded people with deep prejudices apparently survive in what I had thought to be more a liberal and advanced community. It made me aware of the insensitivity to different races and cultures, and opened my awareness to religious intolerance.

THE MIDNIGHT THREE

I decided to organize a folk singing group in my last couple of years in high school. Many of my friends were talented, but my two best friends, Bill Martin and Bob Amick, were a cut above the rest. They could play various instruments and sing like professionals. In addition, they had great stage skills and a sense of humor; the perfect combination for entertaining.

We began singing at the occasional spot around the Bay Area, but every Friday night after our high school's football game we'd perform in a pancake house in Palo Alto. We'd bring our instruments in and occupy a large booth then politely ask permission to sing our folk music.

Permission was granted: 'sing away as long as no one complains'. After a few weeks, free food began arriving at our table; tip money too in appreciation of the music. People expected us to be there and looked forward to our singing. We were always there until after midnight and thus our group name was born. I decided to call our folk singing trio "The Midnight Three". We started getting small gigs around the Bay Area. Of course, we were the cheapest entertainment anyone could afford to hire, so we did a lot of schools and local events. All we really needed was enough money for gas and food—and anything extra was great.

The San Francisco Bay Area had many adult venues for folk singers and their audiences. The Purple Onion and The Hungry Eye featured The Kingston Trio, and Peter, Paul, and Mary. College campuses headlined a group that began at San Jose State College: The Smothers Brothers. And in the smaller world of high school our little group sang their hearts out.

Naturally, we stole lots of our singing material from the big groups and added our own touches of humor for stage presence. My two partners stood over six-two, each over 200 pounds. I was 139 wet and reached a questionable five-six when stretched. Stage value dictated I be in the middle, a rose between two thorns, not. But I centered myself and played my Congo and bongo drums as if I was on tour.

Aside from the visual effect, my being in the middle allowed me to hear my friends' excellent voices; an essential logistic so I could stay in tune. Sometimes I almost sounded like I could sing well. They used to batter me around in jest. I would play the fool on stage; all in good fun. Fortunately, my presence was needed and valued—I managed the group and lined up the jobs.

We used to get together with other friends for late night gatherings on the weekend at someone's home and there would be over a dozen people playing music and singing with us. Good times, good fun. The parents loved us too. In hindsight I guess they could see we were not getting into trouble.

They say all good things must eventually come to an end. Though I know not who *they* are, and hope it's not true of all things, our group disbanded after my high school graduation. Bob Amick had two years left of high school then went on to serve in the US Navy in Vietnam. Bill Martin was in the Merchant Marines (MSTS) for a very short period then attended college and eventually served in the Peace Corp. I was drafted and joined the Army.

Our group's name, however, still had life after we parted. A southern folk singing group took it over before changing both their music genre and later the name of the group—they won a Grammy!

On a sad note for me personally, my good friend Bob died unexpectedly from a heart attack in 2010. I did have a vision of him at the time of his death. I knew he had left the world.

CUTTING SCHOOL TIES

Always the school jokester and clown—I'd used it in first grade to cover up what I didn't know. It stuck and in 1964 my classmates voted me The Class Clown. Making others laugh or smile was pure joy for me. I'm sure asking me to carry out one last deed seemed natural—The Class Clown does the Final Folly.

We stayed up all night celebrating our graduation, then in the morning we headed to the school gym to attend an assembly of more than 2000 people headed by our principal, Mr. Adrian Stanga. A somber and formal guy, I sensed Mr. S liked me because I often saw him laughing at something I said or did.

Before the assembly began a fellow partner in crime, Ken Wing, approached me with an idea. He stated he did not wish to do 'it' alone but would assist if I agreed to be the fall guy. He showed me a large pair of scissors he'd concealed inside his suit jacket pocket. He'd decided I should walk up to the principal during the delivery of the 'sad to see you go' part of his farewell speech and literally cut the tie. I saw the genius of the concept immediately.

Not one concern entered my mind; I already had my diploma in my hand. But for this final address from Mr. Sanga it was over. Ken and I sat in the front row with our 425 classmates. Only our closet buddies knew the plan. It would surprise almost everyone in the building.

When the principal reached the saddest part of his talk—everyone riveted on his words, some students looking like they were ready to cry—it was the perfect moment and we seized it in order to write eternal jokester history. We stood then walked directly at him. His expression became one of concern. And then we were in his face. I grabbed his tied tie with one hand and reached out with the other. Ken placed the scissors in my hand with the efficiency an OR nurse would pass a scalpel to a surgeon.

I cut it right at the neck.

As I held up the severed tie in my hand in victory stance, the entire audience of students and teachers laughed hysterically. They shouted and applauded. Mr. Stanga remained speechless while I briefly danced around. I walked out of the gym and kept walking the three blocks home. I could hear the laughter when I reached my house.

I'd totally destroyed the serious talk and sentimental gathering. In what was becoming a predictable post exit for me, I never went back until after the Vietnam War.

It is kind of a sad irony that no student could do this in today's politically correct society. Possessing a sharp object, scissors, at a public gathering—weapon. Grabbing a principal by his tie—physical interference. Using a blade near his neck—emotional trauma. Destroying personal property—mischief. Planning prior to the event—premeditation. Assault punishable by law.

In today's fearful world we would have been tackled and handcuffed, or shot by high school security guards before we reached the speaker.

The cutting ties-farewell story remained alive and became a school legend. Students talked about it decades later. At my high school's twenty-fifth reunion I was asked to give a serious talk, which I thought was odd, but I accepted. I began my speech as planned at dinner, keeping it more serious than I normally did. Then I noticed some movement. An old man came at me. He wore a huge smile.

He moved fast, and before I could say Mr. Stanga he had grabbed my tie, produced a pair of scissors, and exercised revenge.

The blades cut through my tie like a hot knife through butter. He held it up by the tail and danced around the stage announcing he'd waited a quarter of a century for this. He left abruptly. I stood with my jaw dropped. Speechless.

It was the ultimate payback and I enjoyed every moment. When I saw Mr. Stanga at the fiftieth reunion I thought the conversation would be about the tie cutting or some of the funny things I did in high school, but I was totally surprised by what he did, and what he told me in front of several of the old teachers and a couple of my former classmates.

He put his arm across my shoulders and said he was honored to know me; that I was his personal hero. He went on to say that he'd been following my story all these years. He'd read about me and read my books. He shared that he was very proud of me and of whom I had become.

His sincerity touched my heart. I didn't know what to say other than a humble thank you. I'd never realized he saw this other side of me. He validated a huge part of my life.

HAWAIIAN ADVENTURE

My plan in high school was that after graduation (1964) I'd fly to the Hawaiian Islands and let life blissfully unfold. This ideal of finding my fortune and fame in Hawaii was born from naiveté. I was, however, practical enough to know I wouldn't grow wings to fly there. I purchased a one-way ticket on United States Overseas Airlines (USOA). The flight would leave from the Oakland Airport the day after graduation.

My parents knew about my plan and made a point of telling me that I was on my own when I left home. They provided no money and little emotional support. At that time I wasn't sure if I would ever return, but I did know I had forty dollars, one suitcase of clothing, and a lot of big dreams. As backup, my sister, Marsha, gave me the address of her boyfriend's grandfather. Even though the man wouldn't know me, she wanted me to have an emergency contact in Hawaii.

A group of my friends went to the airport as did my mother and stepfather. My mother made a point of telling me that, if I got into trouble, I was not to call her because she and my stepfather had no money and could not help. *You're on your own, kid.*

She finished her 'poverty' statement then marched directly to the flight insurance machine and purchased a ten thousand dollar policy on me.

When I witnessed this my heart ached. She was betting on my life with money. To her I was worth more dead than alive.

When I got on the plane, I almost cried. My fantasy had been marred by the hurtful events at the airport. Reality hit and I felt so alone in heading off to somewhere I'd never been. I did not know what I would find there.

The flight took more than eight hours on a four engine propeller plane. The aircraft resembled one from the black and white film era—in other words, it was old even by 1964 standards. When we landed the employees rolled out a ramp for passengers to deplane. But those were not the only workers we saw. FAA officials came out and put locks on the airplane's wheels. My flight was USOAs last official one. The airline was shut down; went out of business.

I caught a bus for Waikiki Beach on the island of Oahu. There, I met up with a guy about my age that I'd met on the airplane. I paid him ten bucks so I could sleep on the floor of his hotel room for a couple of nights.

The hotel was a block from the beach. I put on my shorts and went for a walk that first night along the ocean's edge. It was already late, but the water was the warmest I'd ever experienced. I waded and walked a few miles, drinking in all the sights and sounds of the beach and the people who were wandering around.

My money couldn't be wasted on luxuries like food so I began to fast. I knew that with only thirty dollars left I'd need a plan yesterday.

I decided to look up Marsha's boyfriend's grandfather. I hoped he might assist me with my job search or might know someplace I could flop on a sofa for a few days.

I walked out of the hotel and showed his address to a passerby. The person I asked instructed me to look up at the street sign. The grandfather lived on the same street as the hotel, less than a hundred feet away. My luck seemed to be working for me, as always.

I knocked on the apartment door. An older man who looked like a Buddha figure opened the door. I'd never met a real-live Kahuna priest before, but David "Daddy" Kaonohiokala Bray looked every bit like I thought a Hawaiian Kahuna should.

He looked through me as if he were searching my very soul. It was a penetrating gaze that focused on my eyes. I was a little uncomfortable with him looking at me that deeply. I felt spiritually naked. He followed my brief introduction, in which I told him my name and my circumstances, with a few moments of silence. I used the time to study. We stood eye to eye—both about five-seven. His dark skinned stomach hung over his belt—fat Buddha style. His sea salt-like hair flared wild and white. I later learned he was sixty-six years old when we met that summer of 1964.

Approved for an invitation inside, I stepped over the threshold and into the surrounds of what appeared to me a New Age native church. On one wall hung a sizable painting of the Hawaiian goddess Pele coming out of a volcano. Strange artifacts, seashells, and Hawaiian paraphernalia littered the room.

We sat and talked as if we knew each other. He offered to let me stay at his apartment for a few days and to assist me in finding employment.

Daddy Bray, as the locals called him, was a local god to the people on the islands. He'd written many books on the history and religion of the Hawaiian Islands and its people. Those first few days we talked for countless hours. I listened to him talk about his thoughts on life and God. I told him about some of my feelings and dreams. He was the first person who really seemed to understand me. I felt I had found a long lost piece of the puzzle to my inner self.

He seemed to know things about me that no one else ever had. He stated his desire to have me follow in his path. He went on to tell me that he had been waiting for me to come to him for many years. For some reason, he made a point to tell me that he felt I was gifted with much more spiritual energy and power than he had. I was unsure of why he was telling me all this, but my youthful ego was flattered. I really did not know or even care if he was right; it just sounded good to have someone believe in my abilities.

All kinds of people came to his apartment for prayers and blessings at all hours of the day and night. The movie *In Harm's Way* with John Wayne, Kirk Douglas, and other famous actors was being filmed in Honolulu. At night, some of the cast and crew came by to see and spend time with Daddy. (The film was released in 1965.)

I saw Daddy use his occult powers in ways that brought about healing, but he also had a dark side. He activated supernatural powers by chanting or praying. I sensed his ego, along with sensual living, corrupted some of his power.

It is hard to explain everything that happened over the several months of our association.

There was a lot of good in the man's soul. He showed me strange and wonderful ways to cure people of ailments through the use of herbs, chants, and potions made from frog hearts and ground coral. He could also cast spells for success, and even love. I learned a lot, but when he asked me to begin an apprenticeship with him, so he could pass on his powers and knowledge, I respectfully answered that I did not want that kind of power.

I was looking for my own personal enlightenment. I didn't want to become a cult leader and have followers. His dark side convinced me that what he was doing could become dangerous for my own ego. I knew I wouldn't feel comfortable promoting that kind of spiritual path for others. But there was also so much goodness and spiritual love in the man as well. I was torn between his mystical teachings and my own personal spiritual journey.

Daddy was kind enough to get me a couple of jobs on Oahu.

The first one was on the other side of the island in Kailua. I lived in a small cabin on the beach and worked at a nearby restaurant which was fine until I spilled a large pot of boiling rice on myself. When a significant amount of hot rice splashed on my stomach and chest I dropped the pot. It landed on my legs and tennis shoes. The sticky grains stuck to my clothing, shoes, and skin. It was like fiery pellets had been placed on my body, each searing the skin. I was severely scalded. Blisters formed all over my legs and feet. Since I couldn't afford a doctor, I suffered the pain from huge fluid-filled wounds. I was unable to wear anything except a swimsuit for several weeks; did not wear shoes for four months.

A long stretch of unemployment ensued.

My next job was school custodian. I received one dollar and twenty-five cents an hour and worked a full-time schedule. I put anything over survival costs toward an airline ticket to San Francisco.

When it was time to leave, Daddy Bray told me several things about what would happen to me in the future. These all proved correct. He also shared that we were long lost friends from a past life on these very islands where, at that time, we were both big Kahunas. I listened to him and at some level believed what he had to say, but I could not afford, either financially or spiritually, to stay any longer. It was time to close that chapter of my life and move on.

When I left the islands I got a big sendoff from Daddy and some Hawaiian girls. Several garlands of flowers, leis, were draped around my neck as I boarded the plane. I wore a suit and did not wear socks or shoes. With the leis around my neck, swaying across my chest I was quite a sight. It was rather interesting in that a few years later my look reminded others of how Paul McCartney appeared on the cover of the Abbey Road album—bare feet with a suit.

When we landed I chose to get off the plane last. When I emerged I saw a large crowd. My friends were sensitive to how I felt when I left for Hawaii so they took it upon themselves to be there to welcome me home. They cheered when I got off the airplane. This attracted other people who thought I might be a celebrity. Soon a small crowd of total strangers tried to get a closer look at me. I loved it all. I felt I'd been very successful on my first journey away from home. The thing was, I didn't want to go home again. I vowed that this was going to be a rest stop before another adventure.

Author's note: I left for the Hawaiian Islands within twenty-four hours of my last day in high school. I meet the man who is still considered the last pre-eminent Kahuna of the last century and a half, "Daddy" David K. Bray. He had by this time of his life written about thirty books on the Hawaiian history and culture. (Only one of his books is still in print, The Kahuna Religion of Hawaii, *which is coauthored by Douglas Low.) He also had an acting role in an old Hollywood movie with Louis Jourdan and Jeff Chandler in 1951, called* Bird of Paradise. *In the movie he plays a Kahuna.*

David K. Bray attempted to instill in me the fundamentals of Hawaiian mysticism. Although I was able to absorb and learn a lot I made a conscious choice to avoid this path with my life. Daddy Bray showed the dark side to his spiritual quest. He was not above using his psychic and mystical powers in negative and harmful ways.

Unfortunately, a short time after I left the islands, my mother formed a spiritual alliance with him and his cohorts, unbeknownst to me until her death more than twenty years later. She knew that I never would have approved; that is why she never told me.

"Daddy" Bray spent his lifetime exploring what was beyond the horizon of our material world. On November 11, 1968, his spirit sailed out from these shores for the last time to embrace that other reality that so few of us in our busy daily lives ever attempt to explore or understand.

ASLEEP AT THE WHEEL

In 1965, when I was nineteen years old, my dreams of traveling and seeing the world included flying from New York City to Europe, despite not having much—sometimes any—money. I devised a two parter and purchased the airline ticket attached to the second stage of the plan. This left the first part—getting to New York.

There was no turning back. A seat on the plane would be waiting for me, and so I set off on what must have looked to others as a foolishly conceived adventure; hitchhiking from San Francisco to New York City.

When I'd been thumbing almost nonstop for three days, only sleeping when I was in someone's vehicle, I became disheartened. An Indiana wind chilled me to the bone. The only thing that kept me from falling asleep was that I was standing on the roadside. There was no time to take a motel, nor could I afford accommodation. I needed to stay with my plan.

Around midnight, as I watched car after car pass me, my mind wandered to how my own family didn't seem to care where I was or what might happen to me—it was a theme my mind often covered. Sadness moved in and I thought some more. Perhaps I was traveling to escape my family, not just to see the world. The underlying message I took in that night was that no one loved me.

Eventually a car pulled over. The driver honked the horn and waved. I ran the distance between us in the darkness and jumped into his warm car. I looked forward to falling asleep, but when I got in the only occupant, a man in a business suit, asked me to drive. He said he was so tired he needed sleep.

It was either comply or keep hitchhiking, so I put my sleepiness aside and told myself I could manage. Within minutes of pulling onto the interstate the businessman was snoozing and I had the vehicle up to about seventy miles per hour.

It felt so good to be out of the harsh wind, but the warmth and my exhaustion caused me to drift between sleep and wakefulness. After a while I wasn't sure which was which. For some reason I had the impression that the speed had increased, but the next thing I knew the car had left the paved highway. It spun around, and around, and around. It continued spinning within a huge cloud of dust then came to a complete stop all on its own.

I did nothing but hang onto the steering wheel—not even touch the brakes. Fully awake, I surveyed my surroundings. The businessman was wide-eyed too. We stared out the windows. Spoke not a word. My heart pumped wildly.

Trees—only a few feet apart—surrounded the vehicle.

We got out of the car and took a look around. We saw the car had ripped through a dense forest. Not a straight line or track on which to travel. It would have been impossible for any car to have avoided colliding with the massive trunks. But this car had. Tracks and skid marks indicated we should have been wrapped around the trees. It was an amazing sight; neither of us could figure out why we were not dead or seriously injured.

As the man came to his senses, he returned to the driver's seat, none too pleased with me. Nevertheless, he didn't abandon me. It took several minutes of backing up and pulling forward—in order to avoid hitting anything—before we pulled back onto the highway.

When we were safely on firm pavement he looked at me and said, "You're one very lucky kid. We should have both been killed back there; somebody upstairs must really love you."

His words impacted me; traveled directly to the space created by my neglectful parents. I began to drift off into a peaceful sleep on the back seat of his car. Yes, I thought. 'Somebody' does.

THE CONTINENT

Part One: Europe on A Dollar A Day

The spring after I graduated, I hitchhiked across the United States (airline ticket already purchased as incentive to expedite the hitchhiking—San Francisco to New York City) and hopped on a flight to Europe.

Oh, the innocence of youth—19 years old in 1965—I had no idea where Luxembourg was in relation to the rest of Europe, let alone the world, but I deplaned and delighted. I was ready for anything and everything.

Strangely enough, the arriving felt like a homecoming—as if I would be welcomed, comforted, and loved here. I left the airport and walked out to the road. There appeared to be several directions I could take. I went with my feelings and walked east.

I ended up at the edge of Luxembourg City where I met a young traveler from England. He informed me about youth hostels. I followed him to the hostel and he told the clerk that I'd lost my membership card. Grateful to have run into this helpful chap, I ended up using my 'replacement' card all over Europe. Of course, in life there are never any accidental meetings.

I was wide-eyed and filled with excitement. The first night at the hostel I stayed with a group of German, Italian, and English students. We spent hours singing both American and German folk songs. The group was very open and friendly, and gave me their best advice on how to make my money last, where to go and what to see, and even what to do and what not to do. I gave thanks for all I'd received that first day.

Despite the overwhelming sense of joy and adventure, my thoughts wandered to family. It struck me as odd that they weren't concerned about my whereabouts—six thousand miles away. They had no way to contact me and didn't even know if I'd arrived safely in New York, let alone Europe. It was their way. I knew that. And I knew 'someone' was looking after me. I truly believed everything would turn out okay if I kept the faith and stayed within the boundaries of my moral code.

As quickly as the sad thoughts about family had surfaced, they disappeared. That first night I went to sleep feeling really free—I recorded it as the first time I'd ever felt that way. I had no place to be, no outstanding bills, and no one depending on me for support. Free as the wind.

Fed and rested, I began my day's adventures at an old castle on a cliff. The guided tour cost the equivalent of twenty-five cents. When we came to several passageways under the castle, I took my own path (metaphorically and physically) to explore a different route from the group. Additional passageways twisted and backtracked under the castle. Several hours of wandering produced more tunnels and dungeon like rooms. I never worried; rather I had a familiar sense of place. When I found the main passage, the last tour group was finishing up. I joined them and left the castle before the guards locked up.

I loved the city of Luxemburg. It looked exactly like the Europe I'd seen in movies and on postcards. I wandered around there for several more days exploring the streets and buildings and observing the people. Someone was always able to speak enough English so I had little trouble communicating my needs. When it felt right, I made the decision to move on. I walked out of the city and country of Luxembourg and headed south. I had no maps and very little sense of where I was, but in my heart I knew I would end up where I wanted to be.

Next stop: Paris. Paris to see the flowers that bloomed in April—the song *April In Paris* playing in my head.

Funny how the dark changes things. It was after midnight as I walked an isolated country road, southbound to France. I couldn't even see my feet. My surroundings began to stimulate my imagination. I had a feeling, which was more like a fear, that someone or something was watching me—aliens from a UFO preparing to take me away with them. My conscious mind knew it couldn't be real but my heart pounded regardless.

Normally the sounds of an owl brought comfort, but in my heightened state of paranoia I compared an owl's eyes to what I imagined those of an alien might look like. I couldn't shake the feeling of being watched. I kept walking down the center of the road; there was no way I was going to stop and unroll my sleeping bag in the open fields.

I lost track of time, but the next thing I knew a truck driver stopped. Though he did not speak any English, he let me crawl into the back of his truck and sleep while he drove to within a few miles of Paris.

It was raining hard and the dark skies shot out massive forks of lightning. The truck driver turned me out at about five in the morning. With nowhere to shelter, I began hiking up a hill. When I reached the top the panorama was awe inspiring: the skyline of Paris. A streak of lightning reached down and struck the Eiffel Tower. The experience was reminiscent of seeing a movie and being in it at the same time. I felt alive and fell in love with the city of lights that lay ahead. I knew that good things awaited me there.

When I arrived in the city I continued to walk. I traversed the city all day long, rain soaked. I did not care about the cold or wet; I was in Paris. I bought a large loaf of French bread—was it three feet long?—and managed to slide it into my pack. I wasn't fond of wine, but purchased a small bottle because I could trust the contents to be safe, and the bottle could hold water afterwards. I ate and drank as I explored the city and watched the people. The entire experience impressed me as holy and sacred, and I was very much at peace within.

Every street delivered new and exciting discoveries. Paris was everything I had expected and so much more. I was in love with this city and it loved me back.

A top-floor room in a rundown hotel next to the Seine River cost me five francs—about a dollar twenty-five. A thirteen flight climb led me to a six by eight, clean room—the size of a walk-in closet. The space was further reduced because of the slanted ceiling which came down to five feet at the window which I hoped would offer a view come first light—even though that view was only manageable from the bed. That I discovered the washrooms were four flights below was of no concern. I was in Paris!

William "Rev. Bill" McDonald Jr.

Sleep came instantly. I woke early and I looked out of my window expecting to see the city. Instead, I had a view of the roof and art studio next door. Even this made me joyous. I thanked God for my being there. I meditated, wrote poetry in my journal, got dressed, and left to go see more of the city, leaving my belongings in the room so as to explore unencumbered.

My plan to find old churches and museums proved easy. I sat for long periods of time in each church, feeling and absorbing all the energy of devotion and prayers that had been offered by so many over the centuries. It was as if each church was an old friend that I had come to visit. As peace entered my heart I said prayers of gratitude.

Though I wanted to stay in each church I visited, I hungered to see other sights. Next stop: Louvre.

The famous French museum of art was so large I had to return three more times and I still saw less than three-quarters of it. The painting I didn't see was the Mona Lisa—ironically it was on loan to New York City for the 1964–1965 World's Fair.

I'd heard a joke at a youth hostel about a young track star from Japan who did a sub-four-minute tour of the Louvre. I witnessed it for myself as tour busses whipped in and out of the area. It summed up the instant gratification, the been-there-seen-that of many travelers. I found it sad that people taking those kinds of trips had no time to sit and absorb the energy of such magnificent places.

The grand image of sacred architecture came next: that saintly church that sits beside the Seine River—Notre Dame. It was truly a sanctuary for God. Once inside, I looked for a stairway to the roof, and found one hidden from the public. When I reached the top I climbed out a window onto the roof then climbed another stairway to the highest point of the structure. The view was all that I had dreamed it would be. I sat on the roof, so as not to be seen from the ground, and meditated for some time. I felt the holy vibrations all around me. I spent the better part of the day there. Even as I write this, decades later, I can recreate it all.

As for basics, one cultural practice new to me was the use of a French restroom. When I needed to go, a helpful man told me that the funny looking structure on the corner of the street was a men's water closet (restroom). It consisted of a metal wall about six feet tall, but it had no structure from the ground up to about two feet. I had to walk inside this rounded metal fence and pee on a wall with water flowing down it.

In Paris the public toilets, called pissoirs, dated back to 1841 and were a Roman invention originally called vespasiennes, after a Roman Emperor who installed the first public system. By 1914 there were 4000 of them in the city. Fifty years later I found myself maneuvering into one of these pissoirs. I adopted a 'when in Rome' attitude. When I finally relaxed and stood at the wall the nearby traffic light turned red and a double decker bus filled with young college-age American students pulled up next to the wall. Cameras clicked as students shot photos of me standing at the 'peeing wall'. I waited until the light changed green before zipping up. I left while thinking that I may be featured in a few 'vacation' albums stateside.

I remained in Paris for several weeks. I never tired of watching the nightlife or the street artists creating chalk masterpieces during the day. I spent many enjoyable hours in outdoor cafés where I sipped French coffee, wrote poetry, and conversed with strangers. I thought of myself as a beatnik. I told myself that I was absorbing the whole emotional experience around me for future poetry and writings; which, as it turns out, I really was.

Part Two: Roman Holiday

1964, my nineteenth year, and I'd hitchhiked across the US to take a flight from New York to the 'continent'. I'd explored the historic splendor of Europe, from Luxemburg to France; immersed myself in its energy so that it had become a part of my own history. And now I was in Rome, once the seat of a powerful empire, now glorified for its contributions and vilified for its savagery. Rome, dripping with culture.

A new English friend and I took in all the sights and even explored the catacombs along the old Apian Way, where early Christians had hidden from persecution. The tunnels and caves were quiet reminders to me of how the love of God could not be destroyed by any man. I wandered through those tunnels and felt as if I was walking on holy ground. There were several early Popes and Saints entombed in some of the ones I explored.

We saw dozens of sites in several days, and stopped at the Spanish Steps; ran up and down all 137 of them. I took note that the church, Trinità dei Monti, at the top of the steps, was built about the time America was discovered.

I wanted to explore Vatican City and perhaps catch a glimpse of the Pope, if he were home. What did I know? I was young and not too smart in the ways of the world.

My friend and I set off to explore the Sistine Chapel where Michelangelo painted the ceiling. I wandered around, and my friend followed me, as I went to the room where the Cardinals elect the new popes. We saw the potbelly stove that they burned the ballots in. We trailed down the halls and explored the other rooms and buildings. And we strolled through the area where the Pope resided. Of course, there is no way that this should have happened; security guards were present, but no one took notice of two bold, young men traipsing through the Pope's residential compound.

We were having fun and feeling at home until a Swiss Guard finally asked us what we were doing there. We explained that we were lost. By this time we were ready to leave anyway, so we allowed him to escort us out of the area.

It bears additional mention. Looking back, I do not understand how anyone could have just walked around the Vatican as we did. We had entered a home and looked into a huge walk-in closet that appeared to contain the Pope's ceremonial robes. It was almost as if no one could see us.

Later, we decided to pick up some young women at the Rome airport with my new friend's old London taxicab that he'd purchased in England and was driving around Europe. This turned out to be a big mistake and not a very smart decision for us. It seems that taxi drivers the world over have an unwillingness to let young punk kids take business away from them.

We were parked at the airport when a group of Australian flight attendants called out to us for a ride. Apparently they thought it would be fun to ride in a real London cab, so they all jumped in and we took them to their hotel. When we got there we realized we were in trouble. There were a few taxis following us. Worse yet, with every street that we passed we picked up more cabs; a parade behind us.

We began to drive faster, but they were on our bumper and pushing us. We turned the corners as fast as we could and headed out of the city. However, they continued to follow us no matter how fast we went. The road narrowed and there were high cliffs going down to the ocean to our right. We knew we had to try to talk some sense into the taxi drivers before they forced us off the cliff. We pulled over. They stopped next to us, in front of us, beside us, and all around us, blocking the entire road with at least a dozen cabs.

They got out and quickly surrounded us, looking angry and mean. Some of them had knives in their hands and a couple had metal tools and car jacks. I knew it would take some fast-talking and some good old luck to get out of this mess.

We tried to explain in English that we were not charging money and that we were just passing through Rome. They told us never to come back, or they would kill us. They sounded serious about it.

Yet, my young English friend, after waiting just a couple of hours after the taxis cleared the highway, turned his London cab around and drove back into the city. I was a little concerned, but I trusted my luck and went along for the ride. We tried to be as invisible as possible with our old London cab, even though it had a large and easy-to-see TAXI sign bolted to the roof. We went to a party that evening where we met some young women. We took them on as fare-paying passengers, which paid for our gas and food. We left early the next morning, heading north on the Italian coastal roads to Pisa and as far away from Rome as we could.

WAITING FOR MY SHIP

I'd hitchhiked from San Francisco to New York City to fly on a previously purchased ticket to Europe. I'd discovered Luxemburg, hitchhiked to France, and fallen in love with Paris. The trip would soon be coming to an end for me, 19 in '65.

I'd spent the day hitchhiking; successful too. Everyone who'd given me a ride had fed me and provided something to drink. I ended up in a small village along the banks of the Seine a little hungry and knowing I needed a place to spend the night. Buying food and paying for a room were not options. A few coins jingled in my pocket which also held a ticket for my passage to America.

I had the greatest faith that my needs would be met. God had provided for me very well that day, and I felt confident that he'd take care of my dinner and accommodation.

I sat on the street curb and checked my watch, then decided I'd give God three minutes. Within two-and-a-half a striking woman, late twenties, came over and inquired why I was sitting on the curb. I told her I was waiting for dinner and a place to stay.

She told me to follow her into a building in which a community meeting was taking place. She sat me down in the back of the room and went to talk to the people running the meeting. It turned out that this woman was the local schoolteacher.

Conversation stopped and heads turned in my direction after which an older woman approached me, took me by the hand, and led me outside. The schoolteacher explained to me that the older woman was a sea captain's wife and would take me home with her. The teacher clarified that the sea captain's wife did not speak any English, but that some of her nine children did.

I was welcomed into the sea captain's home. The 'sea captain's wife' was a kind woman who treated me like one of her own sons. In addition, the entire village took an interest in my situation and in me. Each day, as I wandered around the streets of the village, someone would give me a copy of an American newspaper. Others would provide food, often pastries.

The schoolteacher who had originally helped me requested that I spend some time in her school in English lessons. I went a few times and conversed in English with students who were only slightly younger than me. It was a lot of fun for everyone, including me. I told them about surfing, American football, and dating in the good old USA, and they told me about sports, dating, and their favorite music in France.

I helped paint the sea captain's house, and did yard work there too. When I made a mistake and pulled flowers instead of weeds the sea captain's wife tried to make me feel okay about it and gave me a big motherly hug. The sense of family I experienced was deep and true.

Several villagers toured me around the countryside, one taking me to the famous beaches of the D-day invasions. It was while I was there, overlooking one of the beaches, that I had a strange vision—kind of like a flash and a dream; much like a memory that popped into my mind.

The content was the struggle and fear of a young American soldier who had been wounded and was drowning in the surf of that beach. I felt an instant sorrow and then relief. It was as if I had experienced it myself. I sensed all of what that young man had thought and feared as he rolled about, dying, in the surf that day. The loss he felt at having never seen France and having died without ever getting to fight in the war.

I realized, at some level within, that I was that same man coming back to where it had ended twenty-one years before. I wasn't sure if it was real or just my imagination at work, but it was such a strong vision that I believed it had to be a mirror in time, that it was me seeing and feeling that day.

When it was time to leave the village and I was close to my departure date (to return to the US), someone arranged for me to stay with a college professor and his wife. They told me that the man and his wife had waited more than two decades to repay an American for freeing their city and ejecting the Germans.

When I arrived at their home the professor recited his personal accounts of the invasion as he saw it from his residence. He'd seen the dead GIs floating in the waves and his heart went out to them. He made a point to show me everything that he could. He treated me as his token American so that he might pay his gratitude to this karmic debt.

I continued to 'remember within' the feelings of regret I believed the American GI at the beach had felt. He remained in my heart. He'd wanted to see Europe and to fight the war, but never got off the beach alive. I somehow knew that through me his desire had now been fulfilled, even if it took a second lifetime to do so.

BACK IN THE USA

I returned from Europe onboard a cruise ship that had been refitted and upgraded in Germany.

The passage was a cheap way to travel to New York. There were few passengers on board the vessel which was breaking in a new crew. Of the small group of American teenagers with which I shared a room, I made friends with a college student from San Jose State. Since he and I had no ride or money to get us back to California we decided we'd hitchhike together for safety and for the company.

We berthed in New York City and realized we'd need a place to sleep that first night. We decided to go to the college campus and call on one of the dorms and see if we could get some assistance. We chose one dorm at random then read the list of names at the mailboxes. We selected the one to call with the stick the pin (finger) on the list method.

We rang the room and presented ourselves to a group of college residents. We told them that we had just gotten off the boat from Europe and were going back to California and had no money. The idea was to get them to ask us to stay. I started telling stories about my trip and the next thing we were fed and had the use of their sofa.

The next day one of them took us to the freeway entrance so we could begin our hitchhiking journey back to the west coast. The first guy who picked us up had a loaded pistol sitting on his dashboard. He was wildly ranting about a guy who stole his girlfriend. When finally he asked where we were headed we told him 'the next exit'. And that is where he dropped us, even though he'd offered us a ride five hundred miles further west.

William "Rev. Bill" McDonald Jr.

The next ride came in short order, and when the driver told us his destination was Chicago, my friend became excited. Turned out he had relatives there; a good place to rest and eat before we hit the road again.

Chicago turned out to be a lucky break. All my new friend's Italian family were thrilled to see us, even though they didn't know who I was. It was even better when I explained my mother was a full blooded Italian. We spent three weeks as real family; shown the sites of Chicago, taken to a Cub's game, and fed delicious Italian food. Heaven.

They were upset when we announced we'd be leaving. They couldn't believe we planned to hitchhike across the country. It amazed them we'd done so in Europe, and from New York to get to Chicago. The night before we left they arranged a going away party. At least fifty people showed up at their small home to say goodbye to both of us. They went over the top and had taken a collection of sorts, asking everyone to chip in for two Greyhound tickets to San Francisco. When the party was over they presented us with the tickets. The only thing left was to receive huge Italian style hugs from everyone.

Their generosity did not end. The next morning we were driven to the bus station and when we got out of the car they handed us a large shopping bag. Inside that bag were a dozen or more sandwiches. We were truly grateful because we did not have any money at all.

Those sandwiches lasted until we got into the state of Nevada. At that time my friend of little faith complained about his hunger. I explained not to worry, that we would be taken care of by the universe.

I knew we would be fed; not a single doubt. When we pulled into Reno for a stopover I told him to go to the café and order something to eat. He reminded me we had no money. I instructed him to order something from the menu and I went to the restroom where I promptly found a twenty-dollar bill.

When I returned he'd still not ordered. I waved the twenty and announced breakfast was on me.

Once we arrived in the Bay Area we each found rides home.

The entire trip had changed me. It had solidified my belief that God provides for those who have faith and trust.

PART TWO
TOUR OF DUTY

March 1967, South Vietnam

"War is the greatest evil Satan has invented to corrupt our hearts and souls.
We should honor our soldiers, but we should never honor war."
Dean Hughes, Far From Home

THE DRAFT:
THE END OF MY CHILDHOOD

"Military men are just dumb, stupid animals to be used as pawns in foreign policy."
— SUPPOSED QUOTE FROM HENRY KISSINGER

When I arrived home from Europe, I discovered my family had sold their home and moved to a small apartment in which there was no room for me.

Almost immediately I wanted to take off again. It was time to look at the possibilities; time to make a life plan.

Over the next few weeks I took the physical examinations for the Army, Navy, Marines, and Air Force at the Oakland Induction Center. Though I wanted to get into the service (when many were trying their hardest not to join) rejection after rejection took place—classified 4F—based on my childhood medical history and my chest x-rays. The military believed that I could be looking to defraud the system by enlisting then requesting a pension for medical reasons.

My next stop was at the Military Sea Transportation Service (MSTS), previously called the Merchant Marine Service. It was known that the work paid well and ports of call included Saigon and the war zone. I obtained my overseas and Asian shots and took care of all the paperwork. As they were ready to ship me off to Vietnam they mentioned that I needed to be cleared by my draft board. I complied, feeling this would be a mere formality since the services considered me physically unfit to join.

William "Rev. Bill" McDonald Jr.

When I arrived at the draft board I was told I needed to have a complete pre-draft physical to establish my draft status and rating—and the medical would take place in Oakland where I'd just spent the past weeks failing those same tests.

I reported for my free bus ride to Oakland at four-thirty in the morning at the San Jose Draft Board offices where a fleet of five chartered buses delivered me and many others to the Oakland Induction Center.

We stood in long lines all day wearing nothing but our underwear, and were poked and prodded and given paperwork to hand to the next doctor. I was asked the same questions about my medical history and I supplied the same answers I had given them previously.

It seemed there was a consensus I was avoiding the draft. All my medical history was discounted and I was classified as 1-A; fully fit for military service. During the procedure I discovered that my draft board had listed me as a volunteer for the draft—this wasn't a set of qualifying tests but an induction physical. How those same doctors pronounced me unfit one week and fit the next seemed based on whim rather than science. Nothing had changed in my history; the only thing that had altered was their decision.

As I stood thinking about the situation, unsure as to what to do, a recruiter, who happened to be in the same building, approached me. He explained it would be to my advantage to join for an extra year, so I could receive decent career schooling. His idea of good training was helicopter maintenance because it would provide excellent training for a civilian job when I left the Army.

I followed his advice, signed up for the extra year, received the Oath, ate a meal at a cheap restaurant (on the Army's tab), and hauled myself onto another bus that headed for basic training at Fort Ord, California. I didn't even have a toothbrush or a change of underwear with me. *Welcome to the Army.*

Author's note: Basic training at Fort Ord, California took place November 8, 1965, to January 1966. After that I went to Fort Rucker, Alabama, for three months, to learn how to work on Huey helicopters. Then I was assigned to Fort Campbell, Kentucky, where I waited for my orders to Vietnam.

ORDERS FOR NAM

"Politics is war without blood, while war is politics with blood."
— MAO TSE-TUNG

Part One: Thirty-Day Leave

When I received my orders in Fort Campbell, Kentucky, I was granted a standard thirty-day leave. A fellow Californian and I decided to head home, and since we were both from the Bay Area, we split the gas and headed west in his old car.

So proud were we that we'd volunteered to serve our country that we put a sign on the car that read 'Vietnam Bound.' We looked forward to doing our part in what we both thought was going to be a quick little war in Asia to rid the world of the evils of communism.

When we reached his home of Hayward I caught a ride to Sunnyvale, a few miles down the road. I knew my parents had sold their home and moved to an apartment complex, but I went there anyway. I didn't have anyone I could bunk with—no matter how uncomfortable—so it had to do.

While on leave I discovered that one of my high school classmates, Mike Harrison, was home on leave and going to Vietnam on the same day I was to report. Not only that, Mike and another classmate of ours, Donna Dixon, were getting married before he left. They invited me to their wedding, which turned out to be a sad affair because we were shipping out—for a year—three days later. It wasn't only me who harbored concerns about what the next twelve months would bring; the guests also seemed to have some dark thoughts that Mike or I could be killed or injured.

I tried to find small pleasures in visiting friends and relatives before I left, but my attempts were futile. I experienced a series of judgmental and negative comments from almost everyone, even my own family, who questioned the war and why I was participating. There were no friendly exchanges of well wishes and hugs; more like there existed a series of self-righteous sermons from people that felt they had a duty to give me a lecture about the morals and ethics of this war.

I decided to spend my final time stateside in San Francisco doing what I enjoyed best—walking around Broadway and mingling with the crowds. At night I often sat in a coffee shop writing poetry on napkins or any scraps of paper I could find.

One foggy night, Karen—friend to me and best friend to Donna—accompanied me on one of my sojourns into China Town and then up to Telegraph Hill where there was a great view of the bay and all the lights of the city. We talked about Mike and Donna and how they would be separated from each other so early in their marriage. We also talked about the dangers of the war and the possibility of something actually happening to one of us while we were there.

We ended up driving to a fortuneteller's place where the seer read my palm. She foretold I'd return from Nam, get married to a woman with dark hair, and have two children—first a boy and then a girl. At that time Karen and I thought it was funny because we believed the seer assumed Karen was my girlfriend, which she was not.

The thing was, I had visited my ex-girlfriend, Carol, during that leave as well. She attended Cal (University of California) and lived on campus at Berkley. It was not the best visit. She had a whole new life and let me know I was not part of her future. Though I wanted to patch things up she felt we were through forever and told me she would not be writing me. She said if I wanted to write to her mother, however, she'd keep track of what was happening with me in that way. I was emotionally torn up inside about the outcome of our meeting as I said goodbye. *Not even one letter?*

Mike and I had to report to the Oakland Army Base on an October morning in 1966. We had orders for the same place so we decided to go together. I rode in the car with Mike and Donna, and Karen came along to give both of us her best wishes and prayers.

We pulled up in front of the gates while it was still dark outside and Donna took me aside and made me vow to look after Mike and bring him home safe and alive. I promised her I would take care of him as best I could. But I knew it was up to God, not me.

Mike and Donna embraced for a long time. I felt bad for them, but I was also a little envious that they had each other for loving support. Karen gave me a friendly hug then Mike and I dragged our duffle bags toward the lights of the entry gate. We looked back at Donna and Karen standing next to the car, waving goodbye. Donna's tears were visible in the little light there was. I noticed a tear or two in Mike's eyes too, so I stopped looking at him. We reported in and waited for our flight to Nam; no conversation, each with his own thoughts.

Author's note: True to the palm reading, I did come home. I did have two children, one boy and one girl. I also married my high school sweetheart, Carol, who has black hair. We wed in 1970 and are still married.

Part Two: Flight of the Damned

Herbert Hoover said, *"Older men declare war. But it is youth that must fight and die."*

Mike and I boarded a commercial airline out of Travis Air Force Base in northern California, which was just a short bus ride from the Oakland Army Base where we had in-processed.

I remember looking out of the bus windows at people whizzing by us on the freeway—people who were totally unaware or did not give a damn about a busload of virgin warriors.

At the airfield, we walked up the ramp and flight attendants greeted us. Back then the job title was 'stewardess' and, being the sixties, miniskirts were the current fashion. It was, for some of the young soldiers, their last image of an American woman.

Mike and I sat next to each other and exchanged some small talk for the first hour or two then fell into a reflective silence. What we would find when we got to Vietnam was all a big mystery as well as a great adventure into the unknown.

Shortly into our quiet time the plane developed engine trouble. It was directed to land at Honolulu International Airport. Though I thought this might be a pleasant interruption—seeing Hawaii again—I noticed military police (MPs) watching the airport exits. Perhaps they thought we might attempt an escape and run away. I was a little annoyed about being treated like a prisoner, but I couldn't do anything about it. The layover lasted about four hours during which we hung about and chatted.

When the repair had been made we took off, only to land at night on the island of Guam—same engine issues again. We deplaned into a muggy, hot setting and stood about in an old hangar with no air conditioning, no food. An old watercooler dispensed lukewarm, funny tasting liquid. We wore the same clothing we'd had on at the start of the trip; the air smelled a special kind of ripe.

After six hours of sitting on the floor we re-boarded, a hungry, sweaty bunch of soldiers. (The food onboard was stale from sitting too long.)

Then it happened again—more engine problems. We landed at Clark AFB in the Philippine Islands. The same fate awaited us—no special services, no food, no drinks. We were rounded up and put back on the plane. The crew had grown irritable, too; tired and smelly themselves. With the exception of peanuts, all the stale food was gone and there were no more drinks. The toilets weren't in great shape either.

We flew several more hours on the 'Voyage Of The Damned' flight. I looked bad and felt even worse. The flying time should have been about twenty-five hours, but with all the detours and stops we'd been en route the better part of two days. I held out great hope that Saigon was near.

And we were close, but my hopes of planting my feet on terra firma were shattered as the plane began its approach. The wheels locked for landing and I could see the ground, but sniper fire aimed at the plane caused the pilot to pull up. The nose of the aircraft abruptly rose and we turned away from the airfield.

A few hours later the airplane sat on the tarmac at Bangkok Airport. In order to save fuel the crew cut the engines. We remained inside the plane, under the tropical sun, for two hours as the temperature inside the aircraft climbed higher. I felt like a small child locked in a car with the windows up—a shopping mall parking lot summer day horror story. It became so unbearable that we all began to complain. In an attempt to settle a small, volatile army the door was opened and a ramp installed to allow access to the air-conditioned terminal.

We were so hungry, but neither the crew nor the U.S. Army provided a morsel. Several of the guys went to the restaurants inside the main terminal, waited in lines, were seated and ordered. Sadly an announcement in English informed us all to report back to the plane. I had very little money, so I had not ordered anything to eat, but—with the help of the airport police—the guys who did order got stuck paying for the meals they never received. I thought there might be a riot but cooler heads prevailed.

We lifted off once again, heading back for Vietnam. East because of the detour, instead of west, the direction we'd headed after leaving California.

It was around noon when we stepped off the plane. The humid climate made it difficult to breathe, and the combined smell of our three-day no-change of clothes created a fog that nearly knocked me over when I took that first whiff of hot, smelly Nam air. There has never been another moment like that in my life.

My feet sunk into the asphalt which was soft from the heat. I felt the intensity through the soles of my boots. We stood around under direct sunlight. Our late arrival had impacted the 'pick-up the soldiers' plan. We stood around waiting for someone to tell us what to do or where to go while the flight crew left us, and the ground crew dumped our duffels into a couple of huge piles on the tarmac. We had all day to locate our own bags.

Eventually we all ended up at the side of the airport and used our duffel bags as pillows It wasn't until the next morning that a bus came for us. Unlike the bus that took us to Travis, this one sported wire mesh and bars across the windows to keep hand grenades from being tossed inside.

Thus began the first day of my tour of duty in Nam.

WELCOME TO THE NAM

"We were eighteen and had begun to love life and the world; and we had to shoot it to pieces. The first bomb, the first explosion, burst in our hearts. We are cut off from activity, from striving, from progress. We believe in such things no longer, we believe in the war."
All Quiet On The Western Front, Ch. 5
— ERICH MARIA REMARQUE

My introduction to the 128th Assault Helicopter Company, the Tomahawks, was a rude one. I'd been shipped around Vietnam to several locations, including a week at Nha Trang along the South China Sea, before getting my final orders to report to the 128th AHC. I had no clean clothing, no money, and I needed a haircut. I didn't smell too good either.

When I reported to the company I was told to find a bunk in the maintenance hooch and report immediately for duty. (Hooch is slang for a simple dwelling either military or civilian.)

There were few introductions. Aside from telling me where the toolboxes were, everyone was too busy. My weeks of training at Fort Rucker, Alabama, were a blur. I wasn't sure what I was doing, and I became more concerned about 'not knowing my job' than the actual war going on around us.

I ended up working all night fixing Hueys.

We worked past sunrise then I staggered to the mess hall for breakfast where I discovered the 'company' had let the nationals who worked for us take the day off. Apparently it was Thanksgiving Day. A little anger pinched my insides; though I was new to the country I knew it wasn't 'their' holiday. I held the mentality it was 'our holiday'. As I went through the breakfast line someone signaled me to 'go see the mess sergeant.' It wasn't a happy meeting.

Exhausted from the ridiculous journey from the States to Vietnam, having been bounced around the country for almost three weeks, and working my entire first night, I desperately needed shower and sleep. Now a 'high-school-dropout-lifer-sergeant' ordered me to wash pots and pans—on Thanksgiving Day.

I went off in a rant in my mind: here I was, willing to do my tour of duty and had volunteered for Vietnam, this was not a holiday for a bunch of Vietnamese peasants who lived out in the countryside and had probably never heard of Thanksgiving Day. Why did they get the day off and I had to work?

I was lucky I was much too tired to mouth off and, being the new guy, it didn't seem right. Washing dishes in Vietnam, however, on Thanksgiving Day was not what I had envisioned John Wayne ever being asked to do for his country.

Far from home, no friends with whom to share a meal, exhausted from being up all night, desperately in need of the blessings of a long, warm shower, I finished the kitchen only to be told all the shower water was gone for the day. I dragged my hot, stinky body back to my hooch. *Thank YOU very much, Uncle Sam.*

It was late afternoon by the time I got 'home.' Everyone else was up and moving about, having showered and slept while I'd been on kitchen duty. Several of the guys were listening to their individual brand of music. The sounds came from several record players and radios competing with each other for volume. I glanced around at the guys and attempted to introduce myself to some of them then crashed on my bunk—my uniform soaking wet with sweat and dirty from the grease and oil. The temperature and the humidity were unbearably high but I didn't care, I needed sleep.

I moaned something about needing to rest, and some joker yelled, "Hey FNG, welcome to The Nam!"

Four hours later I was woken to begin another night shift of maintenance work.

Author's note: FNG is a term for Fucking New Guy. It was made popular by the military during the Vietnam War.

OUTRAGED AT MY
FELLOW SOLDIERS

"Those who understand see themselves in all, and all, in themselves."
— BHAGAVAD-GITA

Though I'd only been in the 128th a few weeks I felt I needed to take some time away from the maintenance platoon. Like so many others, I was waiting for a shot at getting an assignment as a crew chief to my own aircraft. I also wanted to get out of the base camp and see the country and meet the people. I ascribed to the sentiment of General Westmoreland who said we were not there only to win on the battlefields but to win the hearts and minds of the South Vietnamese people. This prompted me to volunteer for some local community work.

I went one day to the local community hospital to paint it and to do some repairs. The clinic was run by a group of Vietnamese Catholic nuns, and I spent an entire day enjoying my labor there. It felt good working with the locals—part of the winning hearts and minds strategy that the General had spoken of. Sadly, that belief would later be shattered by the futility of the conflict.

At the end of the day our company truck came by to take me back to base. I rode in the back with four short-timers; guys who had less than ninety days left in their tour. They carried M-14s (M-16s were not issued until I'd been in Vietnam a few months) and they used these weapons to 'have fun,' pointing their rifles at the peasants as we passed by. These locals would get huge eyes and freeze, afraid to move. My supposed colleagues thought it was a great game.

They began firing rounds at livestock, killing or wounding several water buffaloes, and a bunch of ducks and chickens. Their cruelty broke my heart.

I told them to stop, and one of them casually told me I'd feel the same after I'd been there as long as they had.

I wanted to punch him, but I knew I'd never survive the fight. I'd not even brought my weapon with me, not wanting to worry about it when I was painting. I also knew they were capable of lying about what happened. It was a risk—if I reported what I saw them doing I'd be marked, and it would be their word against mine. I was pissed off and decided to complain and face the consequences anyway. I figured if I did not say anything, who would?

It was a very rude awakening for me that afternoon. I could see that not everyone wanted to do good things for the people of Vietnam. That was confirmed when I complained about what I'd seen. No one wanted to listen. The other men told me to stop making trouble for myself and mind my own business. Someone told me that I was still too new to fully understand and judge these men.

Well, half a century later, I still don't understand. It was horrifying, and sadly not an isolated incident.

ANSWER TO A PRAYER

Author's note: To those not familiar with the use of the term Charlie, it was GI slang for the Viet Cong, from the phonetic alphabet for VC (Victor Charlie). Sometimes we called him a respectful Mr. Charlie.

In March 1967 Binh Duong Province saw a lot of action. In particular, a place known as Ho Bo Woods which contained large elements of the politico-military forces of the Viet Cong's Region 4 Headquarters.

This area was laced with tunnels and spider holes (camouflaged sniper holes the VC created and used). Our troops had discovered a large underground complex that included a three-story hospital and offices for the officers—all of it buried deep under the forest. There had been some heavy fighting in this area over the previous fifteen months and there was no end in sight. Basically, Charlie owned this piece of real estate. He made us pay dearly for every inch of ground we walked on or flew over.

This was one of those bad places where I could feel the fear creep up my spine, and I could taste it in my mouth anytime I entered the area. It was a very nasty place to do business, and I never looked forward to flying missions into or around it. It was not a location in which to fly alone.

We began one particular morning, before sunrise, and had a very difficult time locating anything below us in the darkness. When daylight broke over the forest, we had to contend with thick ground fog; below us, for as far as we could see, there appeared thick rolling cloud on the ground. Most of the time we couldn't even tell if we were flying over open areas or trees. The few Landing

Zones (LZs) inside Ho Bo Woods were small clearings where GIs had cut down the trees or blown them up with explosives; no bed of roses. They all had tree stumps and fallen logs, which forced choppers to hover a few feet from the ground and required troops to jump out. We also had to deliver the supplies this way—throwing them out of the aircraft.

We'd been flying support for some elements of the 25th Infantry Division and were alone; single-ship missions supplying fresh food and ammo for the ground troops. So distracted were we in looking for Charlie, we neglected to check the fuel consumption.

It became impossible to carry on with the mission; the pilots had become a little disoriented by the fog (which covered guiding references). We circled around to get our exact bearings, while the fog remained thick, and slowly rose to about one-hundred feet. The only good news was that no one could see us, so we were safe from any ground fire.

The fuel warning light came on with its accompanying audio alarm. Both pilots froze. We had enough fuel to fly out of the fog-shrouded forest but all the ground below was hostile and forbidding, and not just because the enemy might be there—we couldn't see where to land. All directions held a mystery. We were stuck in between certain death and fog.

With five to ten minutes of fuel remaining we anticipated our aircraft dropping.

If we plunged into trees the rotor blades would thrash them and twist the body of the helicopter and those (bodies) inside it. We knew what that looked like because we'd seen one of our company ships do it a week before. That image played over and over inside my head.

If we crash landed and survived we'd be at high risk of being captured or killed. It'd be a long time before a rescue, the fog would hide our aircraft and, when it lifted, no one would have any idea where we were since we didn't know ourselves. The pilots had been in radio contact with our other company helicopters, but none of them were close, assuming our guess about where we were was remotely accurate. Even after a mayday distress call, no one would have been able to respond instantly.

Our fuel should have run out, and we knew we were running on sheer luck. The fog was endless in all directions; there was no opening to be seen.

William "Rev. Bill" McDonald Jr.

My heart pounded like that of a long distance runner in a hard fought race which had moments ago been lost. I looked around, as I would normally do in this kind of situation, figuring out what I might need once we crashed. I grabbed my M-16 and some magazine clips.

(I wasn't carrying any food or water. We did, however, have lots of colored smoke grenades to use to signal a rescue, but in this fog no one would have able to see them.) I knew we were all mentally ready for the worst kind of crash; the certain destruction to come from the rotor blades destroying the aircraft.

I began a silent conversation with God, asking for His divine help to find us a landing spot before we crashed into the forest below.

And out just below where we'd already looked there appeared an opening which gave a view through to a grassy meadow. A fairy tale LZ. The pilots lined up with the Landing Zone just as the engine died. Less than 25 feet from the ground, the blades rotated with enough force that we did not drop hard. A text book landing.

I immediately jumped out of the ship with my weapon.

I saw movement beyond the trees lining the meadow. Though we'd made it to the ground, we were completely surrounded by soldiers. We readied ourselves for defense but knew we were outnumbered. Any resistance on our part would have been a death warrant, so we just held our position and waited.

The uniformed men began to show themselves. They were elements of the 25th Infantry. By some unbelievable luck we had dropped right on top of one of their temporary camps. Not only were we surrounded by our own troops, but they had a supply of JP-4 jet fuel.

Why did the LZ just open up in the middle of so many square miles of solid fog? Why had we not seen this opening before? Why hadn't our helicopter run out of fuel before we saw this opening?

Lucky or blessed? The result of a small, silent prayer? We did not crash, and no one was killed or injured—good enough for me. I did not need anyone to tell me that prayers worked—I believed. Still do to this day.

A HELLHOLE

In the beginning of 1967, when I was 20 years old, I was thrown into the middle of Operation Cedar Falls. I'd only been flying combat missions a couple of weeks. The 128th Assault Helicopter Company, of which I was a member, was actively engaged in supporting the operation. My position was crew chief/door gunner on a UH1-D model helicopter, better known as a Huey. Our company had been taking lots of fire from the ground, and there had been some damage to several of our unit's aircraft. But so far that week, none had been shot down.

We happened to be in an area next to the Parrot's Beak. This is the part of Nam where Cambodia sticks out into South Vietnam. This also is where many trails from North Vietnam used to empty into the south. We'd been conducting operations in and around a large mountain that overshadowed a flat area below.

The weather was hot and dry, and our rotors kicked up a ton of dust every time we landed or took off; lousy for the troops living in tents on the ground, but not much better for the helicopter crews. In spite of the cooling air from the rotors blowing on me most of the day, I sat in my own pool of muddy sweat, my head boiling under the flight helmet.

On this particular day we landed at a small base camp used to supply the forces in the area; no fences, bunkers, or watchtowers, just a few strands of barbed wire and a few guys sitting behind a couple layers of sandbags. Six flatbed trucks piled with ammo sat waiting to be unloaded. Several of the trucks had large artillery shells on them.

We'd dropped in that morning to refuel and, if possible, catch a meal. We were only about a hundred yards from the flatbeds when I heard and felt the blast. I looked up and saw a ball of fire form. There followed many more explosions.

The force of the blasts knocked us off our feet. The explosion and fire caused hundreds of rounds to heat up, which then fired randomly from the truck's bed. They were going in every conceivable direction. It was a death zone as fire exploded everywhere. What made it even worse were the hundreds of cans of machine gun rounds that heated up and fired off indiscriminately.

Some of the artillery rounds shot straight into the air and rained back down on the camp. The helicopter was not an option either, the sky a massive target. We decided to make a run for it and take cover. My door gunner and I ran for a nearby hole that had been dug into the ground about twenty-five yards from our aircraft. It seemed to take forever to cover the distance. Meanwhile machine gun rounds zipped past our heads and the ground shook from dozens of artillery explosions. Dirt flew into our faces and I felt the heat of the fire as we jumped into the hole.

Out of breath, we rolled to the bottom of the ditch and covered ourselves with our arms and hands, but it didn't feel right to me. I felt an urging to get out of there. An inner voice—a sense—that we should not be there. I told my gunner to get out and move as quickly as possible.

He wouldn't move and so I grabbed his uniform and pushed him up and out of the hole.

He fought me every inch of the way. Finally, we were exposed to the open rounds.

I pointed in the direction of another hole. We took off, half crawling, half running.

There is an unwritten rule of combat that you do not put all your men in the same hole—this prevents one round from taking everyone out of commission.

The two guys in the new hole reminded us of that when a flash of light followed by a thundering force of energy came at us from the other hole. An artillery round had directly come down into our abandoned hole.

Smoke and fire rose out of the enlarged hole that we'd evacuated moments before. The hole looked like an entrance to hell, with flames billowing out. Silence ensued within our group. We'd come extremely close to cashing in our chips and knew it. Seconds had spared us from death.

Puzzlement replaced my gunner's anger. He asked me how I knew we should leave the hole. I didn't know how to explain it. The feelings inside me were so overwhelming that I had no choice but to take action.

As soon as we could the crew assembled at the helicopter, which for some fortunate reason had not taken a hit. We flew up, alongside the smoke which curled into the skies around the camp. The ammo had destroyed the trucks and a big part of the camp, but we were safe.

We flew around the mountain and back to our airfield at Phu Loi. Inside the aircraft the crew remained shaken by the experience, but I felt something else— blessed by the unfolding of the events, I knew that 'Someone' had been looking after me—there was no other explanation.

A deep sense of peace enveloped me as we flew back to base camp; I was loved.

LIFE OR DEATH DECISION

In the spring of 1967, in an area about 35 miles northwest of Saigon, I had to make one of the biggest decisions of my life.

We'd been flying solo flights, mostly supply runs into small encampments of the 1st Infantry Division. The troops were there to slow down the movement of supplies that came directly from North Vietnam off the Ho Chi Minh Trail.

There had been some fighting, but not nearly as bloody as we had expected it to be—even though men were getting wounded and killed daily.

Our intelligence reports indicated we should look for large movements of supplies and troops.

We hadn't seen any signs, but we kept a watchful eye on everything that moved below us.

My helicopter commander, a major, had just arrived from a tour of several years in Germany. He was a West Point graduate and was a strictly-by-the-book style military leader. That was the way he had managed his duties in Germany. He was determined to continue those ways in the Nam. He appeared to me as a no nonsense guy with little sense of humor. When he gave an order, he expected full obedience by those he commanded. He made it clear he had no intentions of fostering friendships with lower ranking personnel. He was in charge and those of us who did not outrank him were there to support and obey. We knew he wouldn't be open to any questions or suggestions—we had to do as he said— there were never going to be any debates.

During his first couple of weeks in the Nam, the major was still trying to figure out how to find the Landing Zones (LZs) and how to read the maps of the area. He did not know the names of places we had to fly to, and he had no clue as to where these places were in relation to other places or to our base camp. Without a map in his hand, this guy wouldn't have had any clue to where we were. (The "old guys" who had been there for a while could follow roads and rivers and head toward landmarks such as Black Virgin Mountain.) Yet, he asked very few questions, if any.

On this particular morning, we flew higher in the sky (about 500 to 800 feet) than felt comfortable to me; our normal was treetop-level altitude. The major had an aversion to flying too close to the ground, but he had not yet realized the risks of flying at higher altitudes. Eventually he would learn—like all new pilots did—that flying at treetop level was actually much safer. We could sneak up on enemy troops well before they could see or hear us coming; the common proce-dure in Nam—fly low and fast. Keep your profile close to the ground.

From our lofty position in the sky, we could see much farther around the countryside and I think it may have been helpful for him in spotting landmarks for his navigation. We did have a greater view of all that was down below, but it also made us an easier target. We were not high enough to avoid small arms fire and not low enough to sneak up on anyone. We just kind of hung in the sky like a big, fat, slow moving target.

We were flying just a click (a kilometer or .62 of a mile) outside of a small hamlet when I spotted a group of about thirty people who appeared to be mov-ing down the road in a military formation. They carried what looked like some kind of weapon on their shoulders. There was a man in the front who seemed to be leading. All were dressed in the typical black pajamas that the VC (and most everyone living in Nam) wore. Since this was so close to the Ho Chi Minh Trail, it certainly appeared that it could be a squad of VC (Viet Cong).

The major immediately determined that they were VC troops—he had no doubts—and gave orders for me to fire my M-60 machine gun on the formation below. Now, an M-60 can fire 750 rounds of 7.62 mm ammo a minute—the group would have been shredded in a matter of seconds. I looked down at the formation and thought what he saw was correct, but then I froze. I couldn't pull the trigger on the machine gun. I couldn't squeeze off a single round.

Great apprehension filled my entire being. Something wasn't right.

I did nothing. The major yelled at me, informing me he'd given a direct order to fire and that disobeying was not optional. But I just sat there. Then I told the major I would not fire. I explained that I had doubts about what we saw.

The major was mad as hell. He reminded me disobeying a direct order in combat was a punishable offense and that he'd be bringing me up on charges. I knew those charges could mean two decades or more in a military prison at Leavenworth. Charges the major could bring against me were not to be taken lightly. The system within the military is much tougher than civilian court. The foundation of the military is discipline and rules. Directly disobeying an order in combat could land me in prison for a significant part of my adult life.

I told him I wanted him to make a pass over the group's formation so we could get a better identification. In the meantime, he'd had the aircraft circle so that the left door gunner was in line to fire his weapon on the group. To my surprise, that door gunner also refused the order. He showed exceptional courage by supporting my position. His action for non-action took my breath away.

This was a serious breach of military law. I was in awe that he had such courage and conviction. His future hung on my feelings. I hoped to God that I was right, for both of our futures.

The major debated with the copilot, a young warrant officer, about calling in an air strike or at least some artillery. It was suggested that we take the aircraft down for a closer look.

Finally the major caved. We dropped down from the higher than normal altitude and descended closer to the group of people on the ground. Our M-60 machine guns were in the ready position, aimed at the heart of the group, ready for all hell to break loose when we passed down the right side of them.

The first clue that they might not be the enemy was the fact that they stayed on the road the whole time we were above them. Not one took cover in the surrounding jungle. The second was that no one fired at us as we passed by.

Identification brought a mammoth sense of relief. What marched below us was a group of innocent children with their garden tools; their leader a priest dressed in black. Tears rolled down my cheeks as I processed it all and attempted to let go of the horror of what had almost happened. Chills ran down my spine and my hands shook.

I couldn't see the major's face, but I liked to imagine that it paled. He remained silent.

Why had I refused to fire? Why had the other gunner followed my lead? I have no answers. I went with my feelings, which at the time were so very clear and strong that I should not pull the trigger. I risked going to jail because I followed my intuition and not the orders. What if I had been wrong and the group had been VC? I had risked the helicopter getting shot down and the life of every crewmember based only on my feelings.

In Viet Nam I learned never to question my gut. Premonition or intuition seemed heightened in combat and dangerous situations.

After that day the major and I became better friends. He learned to trust those working for him and began to ask questions and rely on the advice of combat-experienced men around him. He turned out to be a good human being and a fine officer. He also proved many times over to be a brave and courageous pilot—someone with whom I felt confident flying. Someone for whom I'd risk my own life.

I think we both learned something that day that forever changed the way we looked at life and ourselves.

The mountain in the background is Nui Ba den, known
locally as "Black Virgin Mountain"

MY MOTHER'S DREAM LETTER

My mother made an impression on some of the guys I was stationed with in Nam because of a letter she wrote to me in the spring of 1967. As with all of my family, to varying degrees each member seems to have a gift for knowing things ahead of time.

In her letter, she went into great detail about two dreams she'd had about me in Vietnam. At first reading one might have dismissed them as the power of imagination, but there was such a parallel to what took place that it was more than coincidence or a lucky guess.

Dream #1:

My mother described—in vivid detail—seeing my helicopter fly at treetop level with me firing my machine gun into the jungle below. She even saw the canvas seat in my aircraft. She saw all the soldiers sitting nervously on the floor, and went on to describe what the men looked like and what they carried. Her dream contained detailed information about the Landing Zone (LZ) where we would land our Huey.

She pointed out trees on fire along the right side of the LZ and she saw tracers going from my aircraft to the tree line and tracers coming back toward the ship. Then she described how the men jumped out of the Huey as it touched down—not waiting for it to come to a full stop.

She saw a soldier carrying a machine gun jump out and run forward. A guy carrying more ammo for the gun followed him. Her detailed description of the surrounding jungle was as if she'd been an eyewitness.

When I put down her letter that contained the first dream I realized she'd described exactly what had happened the same day she'd written it. When she dreamed it during the night in California the events would have been taking place in Viet Nam—there is a fourteen hour time difference.

I showed the letter to some of the guys who had flown the mission with me, and they agreed that it was an accurate account of the whole experience. It was as if she had been there flying with us on the combat assault. I was not really amazed by my mother's dream—I guess I had seen her predict too many events—but a couple of the guys thought it was spooky.

Dream #2:

My mother stated that the events in her second dream had not yet taken place, but that she firmly believed would happen soon after I received the letter. She shared that she understood it was a strange dream, but she recounted it nonetheless. It began with her seeing two soldiers standing on a dirt street in a Vietnamese village. They appeared intoxicated as they staggered around yelling insults at each other from about 100 feet apart. She went on to say that it looked like a scene from the old TV show Gun Smoke—two gunfighters engaged in a shootout on the streets of Dodge City.

In her dream, the two soldiers faced off, each drawing weapons from waist holsters. She said they fired at each other but missed and so no one was hurt. She wrote that while she felt sure this would happen she had no idea of the significance or its relationship to me. She stated she did not understand, but was passing it along to me as she felt she should.

I read that part of the letter to some of my buddies and received a good round of laughs about my mom's prediction. So I told them, "If my mother says it will happen, then it will happen!"

So strong was my trust in my inner feelings and my mother's belief that it would take place that I challenged them to go with me to the village that afternoon and witness it for themselves. I think they went along to prove I was wrong and have a good laugh.

We caught a ride to the village in the back of a half-ton military truck and went to the local bar for a few beers. I decided to sit outdoors so I would not miss any of the action that would surely take place that afternoon. After several hours of drinking and waiting, the guys started kidding me about the letter. I stood firm and said that it would happen. We went inside to get a last beer before heading back to base.

It was then we heard a couple of gunshots. We ran outside while everyone else in town ran for cover. By the time we got outside, it was all over. Someone told us two drunken soldiers had shot at each other. No one had been hurt.

Sufficiently spooked, my friends stood there in a collective frozen state. They remained silent all the way back to base camp.

PANIC IN THE LZ

Working with any troops from the Army of the Republic of Vietnam (ARVN) always posed a risk. We could rarely count on their support when things got tough—never knew how they'd react to certain combat situations.

It was spring 1967, a perfect day weather-wise in Nam—warm sunshine, no rain, and a gentle breeze. It made flying a lot more comfortable for my door-gunner and me. Our positions were at the doors and faced whatever weather conditions were present. Though there was always a wind from the rotor and the forward airspeed of the aircraft—which helped in the heat—we became chilled and soaked when there were heavy rains.

We were doing some easy hash and trash (resupply) missions along the Cambodian border when we received a call asking us to pick up several wounded ARVN troops in a remote Landing Zone (LZ), not too far from where we were currently flying. The pilots changed course; the only thing we knew was that the site was under mortar attack and the wounded needed to be taken to a Mobile Army Surgical Hospital (MASH) unit. It was almost a routine dust off (medical evacuation), so we were not expecting much trouble since the LZ was secured by 300 ARVN troops. The estimated attack force was just one VC mortar team, which had been dropping rounds at random in the LZ.

Our plan was to fly in at treetop level, undetected until the last few hundred yards then drop down for loading—a matter of seconds before we'd lift out of there; certainly before the mortar team could zero in on us and place their rounds on our aircraft.

We pulled over the last few trees and descended to where they had popped yellow smoke. For some reason we hit the ground hard; perhaps the pilots were hurried. A couple of medics began to load wounded troops onboard, slowly. I had time to look across the LZ and could not believe what I saw. Almost half the ARVN troops had panicked. As they ran for our helicopter I felt the craft shrink—that was the effect of having so many people try to board. Before I could do anything, several dozen of them were attempting to get in. They pulled at the wounded to make more room for themselves. When I looked to the other side of the ship I saw my left door gunner trying to keep his own seat from being taken.

The ARVN soldiers had turned into a panicked herd of animals. They stepped on each other, including on their own wounded men. The pilots tried to pull up and get some lift but dozens of men were inside the ship and more clung to the skids.

They kept coming at us until we were completely engulfed with bodies of panicked, frightened men. It was an ugly sight; there seemed to be no way we could leave that LZ.

It was as if it were a large insect being devoured by an army of hungry ants.

Meanwhile, we'd been on the ground long enough for the mortar team to zero in on our position. Rounds dropped closer and closer. The enemy had enough time to 'walk' the rounds up to the LZ about ten yards at a time. The rounds came so close that we felt the impact of the explosions as they shook the helicopter. Time was critical. We had to get out of there or get out of the helicopter before a round hit it.

The pilots shouted through the intercom to shoot or do whatever it took to get them out of and off the aircraft. My gunner and I were not about to shoot any of them; but we began kicking and pushing them off as the ship struggled to rise off the ground.

There were so many of them, and they just kept hanging on. We could see the fear in their eyes. Some had even pissed in their pants. These ARVN troops were going to stay in that helicopter even if it meant that all of us crashed into a treetop or were hit by a mortar round.

When we managed to lift a couple of feet, the pilots turned the helicopter into a giant buzz saw by swinging the tail rotor around a few times to stop the advancement of other troops. Luckily we saw no one cut up or killed by the turning blades. The crew turned the aircraft in the opposite direction and chased away a few dozen men who were attempting to get on board. In the meantime my gunner and I had shoved and thrown off as many as we could. It was a fight for our lives in the back of the chopper.

They screamed, cried, and hit us. We hit back—two gunners against a mob of 50 or more. Rifle butts and fists battered my flight helmet. At one point I saw my gunner swing an ammo can at about a half dozen troops' heads in an attempt to fight them off. The pilots cried out for us to shoot but that was something that neither of us felt was an option—after all, these guys were on our side.

When we lifted to about nine feet, several men remained clinging to the skids. We stomped on their fingers and kicked at them until they fell to the ground. This effort allowed us to pull up a few more feet, but we began to feel the dirt from the mortar explosions that were now hitting under us. We headed across the LZ as rounds exploded behind us where we'd parked. That meant the troops were taking hits too. We couldn't think about them—we had to get enough forward airspeed to clear the tree line ahead.

With an overflow crowd onboard we needed the full length of the LZ to get enough translational lift to make it over the treetops at the end. We were lucky that we did not have a full tank of fuel because we couldn't have carried any more weight and made it out. We cleared the trees by a foot or two at the most—less than 24 inches.

The wounded were scattered on the ground. Their 'comrades' had pulled some of them from the aircraft; others hadn't made it that far. They'd been walked over and stomped on by their fellow soldiers. We had risked our lives to evacuate their wounded, but not one of them was on his way to the MASH unit.

I looked around at the young South Vietnamese soldiers and was disgusted by what I saw. They huddled together, and some of them were crying. It angered me to be there fighting 'their war.' Their behavior showed me that they did not have the enduring will to win a war.

My reasons for being there, to help the South Vietnamese stop the communist aggression, were totally shattered in one scary afternoon. I would never have the same zest and enthusiasm for the war effort again.

When we dropped off the South Vietnamese 'deserters,' we were asked to go back and get their wounded and killed. We declined the request. There was no way we would go back to that LZ ever again.

Author's note: I was never again able to endure crowds. Waiting in lines for movies or wading through crowds at sporting events still makes me uncomfortable. Too vivid are the memories of the panic in that LZ.

My Huey in action in an unknown LZ 1967

SPIRITUAL ARMOR

In April '67 our crew sat around on standby, waiting for action that would require more ground troops to be transported to locations—yet unknown—when our guys made enemy contact. The rest of my helicopter company had left on 'eagle flights'. Several would fly troops into areas suspected of having enemy concentrations and, if there were, a backup force would be dropped into the Landing Zone (LZ) to overwhelm opposing forces.

My helicopter gunship was the command and control (C & C) and therefore the ground commanders were a part of the ridership. We supported ARVN (Army of the Republic of Vietnam) Rangers out of the Phu Loi area; not a large force, perhaps 150 men plus a handful of American advisors. All morning the search had been on for suspected Viet Cong (VC) elements hiding along the Saigon River across from Chu Chi.

Late in the morning frantic voices on radio calls alerted us that our guys were under heavy fire. We responded immediately, the ARVN commanders onboard, and flew to the hot (under fire) LZ.

The radio chatter between the helicopters indicated all nine of our ships had taken hits and the gunships were escorting them back to the base camp at Phu Loi. All nine made it safely back, but it meant there were no more gunships on station to protect us—our single aircraft—when we landed, and no one there to rescue us if we got into trouble.

On arrival, our view from the sky above the LZ was that of a full on hostile engagement. The ARVN had stumbled upon an enemy force of around 500 who seriously outnumbered and outgunned the ARVN Rangers. A commander decided to get closer to the action and requested a drop off on the edge of the hot LZ.

Within 20 feet of the ground all hell broke loose. The sky filled with red and white tracers (red were NATO ammo and white were Chinese and Warsaw ammo). Each tracer round usually represented five rounds of shot ammo, every fifth round being a tracer.

Our own M-60 machine guns featured an ammo belt which came set up from supply with a tracer for every fifth round out of the ammo can. However, I'd made my own ammo belts for combat assaults, putting together solid tracers for the first 2,000–3,000 rounds, to make the enemy believe I had more firepower.

I hoped to get a psychological edge over the enemy by firing the belts and lighting the sky—in essence it'd appear more rounds fired than actually were.

I don't know if it really worked, but it made it easier to direct my aim and make quick adjustments; and it did make me feel more powerful.

As we got lower, closer, and slower, dozens of rounds from automatic weapons pelted our ship. I could hear the pings, but mostly I could feel the vibrations of bullets ripping holes in the metal walls. The sky was filled with tracers, yet I had orders not to return fire since there were friendly troops on the ground. I faced the wall of fire that assaulted me from every angle. Our small helicopter was being shredded by the impact of heavy firepower.

When we hit the ground, the ARVN commanders scurried off like rats leaving a sinking ship. One of them stopped, turned, and faced me. He pulled his automatic weapon up to his shoulder and sighted directly on me sitting behind my idle machine gun.

I checked for an enemy toward the rear of the helicopter just as the ARVN commander pulled off a short burst—my pilot later told me that the commander put in a new ammo magazine and aimed his weapon right at my chest. There were about 18 rounds in the clip; he fired them all in seconds.

I saw a stream of light enter my body and felt the impact in my chest— which would have struck my heart if I had not been wearing a new ceramic protective plate—then felt my body hit the wall of the transmission well. The impact sucked out my breath and the force of the hit severed the radio cord to my flight helmet.

I sat in total silence, fire and smoke escaping from what appeared to be a large hole in my chest protector. For a moment, I considered I might be dead.

Three days prior to the mission, I'd agreed to test a ceramic chest protector. If I'd been wearing a flak vest I'd not have survived. I stared at the two-day-old chest protector. The white smoke and red embers seeped out of a deep cavity over my heart. No blood, no pain in the area, only a sore neck from the whiplash from when my body flew backward.

The pilot managed to pull the ship about 12 feet above the ground and we were able to move a few hundred yards past all the fighting before involuntarily dropping hard to the ground and then sliding forward a bit.

I rushed to help the aircraft commander get out then raced to assist the copilot. When I looked back I saw the left door gunner and blood splattered everywhere. Red flowed across the nylon seat, onto the grey metal floor, and down the outside of the aircraft.

When I reached him I saw multiple holes in his neck, shoulders, back, and buttocks. He was alive but in a great pain.

The NVA troops could be at this site in minutes. I got him out of the helicopter, rendered some quick first aid then heaved him across my shoulders. My back felt badly sprained but I sprinted—adrenalin powering me about 100 yards to a safer location—away from the helicopter.

The two pilots joined me and we huddled at the edge of a clearing away from the downed Huey. Soon the familiar *whop, whop* of another Huey filled the sky and one of our B-models landed. I dragged and lifted my gunner to that gunship. I gently laid his body on the helicopter's metal floor and pushed his legs inside. My aircraft commander rushed past me and jumped onboard. As I began to climb in I was informed there was no room for my co-pilot and me.

We stood under the rising gunship in bewilderment.

500 enemy troops fought a short distance away—the length of a football field—the ARVN forces were present, and I'd been shot by one of their own commanders.

Rather the hunter than the hunted, I refused to wait for the enemy to find us. I returned to the Huey and pulled an M-60 machine gun from the mount and seized a few thousand rounds of ammo. I held my machine gun hip high, ready for battle. The co-pilot carried an Army issue pistol with a couple of ammo clips. Mutt and Jeff, two Americans against 500 fighters.

From the vantage point of old age I do not think this was a bright idea at all. But it is what we did.

A thick tree line edged the shore of the river. My plan was that none of the enemy should approach from that covered position. I walked toward it with my M-60 blazing from my hip. I became a giant mulcher rolling through the jungle. Birds and monkeys flew and jumped—everything in my path was blown away by massive firepower. I was John Wayne in a war movie—a surreal scene. The copilot remained behind me, covering the rear with his little handgun. Courage beyond courage.

We forged ahead, thousands of rounds fired, and then: silence. I pulled the trigger. Nothing. I looked at my weapon, its barrel was bent. I realized it was smoking and hot—melted from the heat generated by firepower.

We mutually agreed it was time for intelligent E & E (Escape and Evasion). We spent the rest of the day hidden, but close to the helicopter because that was where we knew that our rescue would eventually take place. At some point I discovered my hand had been injured—shrapnel—and I added that to our list of deficiencies. We killed a lot of time (no pun intended) before the popping of old rotor blades announced our rescue. We boarded before the skids settled on the ground.

Later, a Chinook helicopter hoisted our damaged Huey out of the crash site and carried it back to Phu Loi Airfield for repairs. When we examined it, we were baffled by what we found—or what we didn't find.

The logistics were such that the left door gunner and I were like silhouettes, our backs directly in line as we faced in opposite directions to fire our machine guns on the left and right sides. Between our mirror images existed a transmission and a wall. On his wall there were 17 exit holes. Yet, on my side there was nothing, not one single hole.

We went over it again. There were 17 holes in the transmission-housing-wall on the left side of the aircraft, behind where the gunner sat. The bullet fragments had exited here before entering the door gunner's body.

There should have been 17 entry holes on the right side of the ship where I sat. They had to have come in to have gone out.

When we took a straight line from where the bullets exited the only place they could have entered would have been through my body.

We all knew that the gunfire had come from the right side of the ship. We all saw the sky, aflame with tracer rounds heading toward where I had been positioned.

The evidence puzzled Army safety board investigators. No one could offer an explanation of what had taken place.

18 rounds were fired directly at me. One entered my chest protector and the other 17 exited the far side of the aircraft without ever hitting me. It was as if they went through me. I can offer nothing more to explain this, except to believe there must have been some kind of spiritual armor protecting me that morning near the Saigon River.

A direct result of my actions that day led to being awarded a Purple Heart, and further honored with The Distinguished Flying Cross.

Author's note: When the helicopter was brought back to Phu Loi, the Army sent top level investigators. They questioned me relentlessly about how the bullets could go around me to have exited the other side. Their skepticism and arrogance over my theory bothered me for almost half a century.

Then, in the fall of 2013 I received a call from a CIA contractor from Langley, Virginia. Somehow, the contractor had the files about the incident and were interested in talking to me.

I was surprised to learn that the CIA had given the contractor millions of dollars to research this phenomenon. I discovered the military had not discarded my theory, and that there existed a classified file. That was all he would share with me on the phone, but he asked me to provide the 'secret' to the protection I'd received because they were involved in developing the ultimate armor.

HEALING HANDS

Following a concentrated period of combat in Vietnam, called 'Operation Junction City,' my commanding officer (CO) strongly suggested I take a few days Rest and Relaxation (R&R). To his credit he'd recognized my physical and emotional health was weak. I'd lived through some nightmarish flight missions during the past weeks, including suffering an injury, being shot down three times, and almost being captured.

(Of that intense period of combat: I was recognized by being awarded the Distinguished Flying Cross and by being nominated for a Silver Star. I also earned a handful of Air Medals, and a Purple Heart for a very minor hand wound.)

My CO essentially ordered me to recharge. I didn't fight the idea. He knew I'd been interested in returning to the northern coastal city of Nha Trang. I'd pictured what it would be like to spend some lazy days on the beaches and swim in the South China Sea.

Early the next morning I caught a helicopter to the base in Nha Trang. I took very little with me; chose not to bring a weapon.

A young Vietnamese man transported me on his Pedi cab to a small, clean hotel—no more than half a dozen rooms for rent. It had a peaceful feel; just what I wanted. I didn't need to be near the Army. I wanted to be in the city with the people who lived there. I was also the only American for several miles, and probably the only GI dumb enough to stay overnight in the city without any kind of weapon.

Though the city was fairly safe, there were VC living there—VC that occasionally attacked the bases a few miles away. The hotel and the area was not a protected compound and there were no security personnel to stop anyone from capturing or killing me. It is strange, but those facts and related concerns come to me as I write this—at the time I felt invincible. Youth does that.

On check-in, I told the manager not to bother me with anything, and insisted 'NO GIRLS' since I was not interested in having a prostitute in my room.

All I wanted to do was rest.

The vista from my window provided a magnificent view of the large Buddha on the hillside at the edge of the city. I'd seen it when we'd flown in that afternoon—we'd actually flown circles around it, and discovered it was a temple—from the air we'd watched people walk under it and into a chapel-like area. The statue served as the roof over the place of worship.

The 'movie' in the other direction from the window in my room delivered the most wonderful rolling surf washing onto one of the world's finest beaches. White sand—as far as I could see—melted into the soft blue water of the South China Sea. Such contrast to the war torn part of the country where I'd been living and fighting.

I gave thanks for the room with the soul-refreshing view.

Then I focused on rest, but my mind was so overstimulated—exhaustion beyond exhaustion—that I could not shut down, could not relax. Even if I'd wanted to go out and explore the city, I couldn't. My physical energy was so low I could barely walk, and my mental energy too wrapped up in fighting the battles of the war that I thought I'd left behind.

I lay there half awake, daydreaming about home, when a gentle tap at the door interrupted my thoughts. When I opened the door there stood a stunning young woman who appeared to be part Asian and perhaps part French. She might have been in her twenties but had an ageless look to her—she could have been any age I imagined. Ethereal would be the closest description. Her skin was brilliant white—she seemed to glow. The light around her hung like a veil and radiated from within, not from the outside sunlight.

She spoke not a word and cast her eyes down, yet managed to connect with a demure expression. I made it clear I wasn't interested in whatever she had on offer. I didn't want to pay for anything, nor did I want her services. I told her to go away. I closed the door and returned to my bed, falling face down and burying my head in the pillow. I hoped for sleep.

Suddenly, the gentle pressure of two soft, feminine hands gently rubbed my back. I did not look up. I lay there, transfixed on the feeling of peace. I did not move nor did I say anything to her while she massaged all the tension, anger, and depression out of my body.

I drifted between wake and an altered state. I felt so loved, but not at all in any sexual way. It was more like a spiritual uplifting—the same kind of feeling when I used to fast for long periods of time—light-headed, other-worldly floating, an almost out-of-body experience. Yet, I was fully there. And so was she.

I rolled over to look at her eyes but I couldn't see what they looked like; the light from the window blurred my vision. I did see her kind, motherly smile as she rolled me back over to continue rubbing my back.

When all my pains and tension were gone, and I felt alive and well, I knew I needed to see this woman who had gifted healing energy. My mind and body were stimulated by natural desires, and I had decided that I wanted to spend some time with her—take her around the city, and to the beaches. I rolled over. There was no woman. The room was empty but for me.

I scanned the room, all possible recesses. The door remained closed. I jumped out of the bed and raced into the hallway. I looked both directions then ran downstairs to the street. She was not to be found.

When I asked the people outside the hotel which way she went, they told me that no one had left the hotel for hours, nor had anyone entered.

I returned to the manager and demanded to know whom she had sent to my room. The manager looked at me as if I were crazy. She vehemently stated no one had been sent to my room, and no one had come and gone all day. She inquired if I'd been drinking or taken drugs.

Of course, I had not used drugs or alcohol. I had tried to rest. Someone had come to my room. I'd been transformed, not just physically.

I wandered back to my empty room and stopped worrying about understanding the mysterious healing. I submitted to the love and peace within me. That surge of bliss allowed me to forget the battles of war. I slept as soon as my head touched the pillow—slumbered like a baby—never slept that well in my whole life before or since.

When I woke I felt connected to the world. I walked along the wet sand in the twilight. The warm water touched my bare feet as I looked up at the stars and felt attached to the divine—God's love filling me.

I have no answers about the visitor to my room, but I know it was not a dream. It was many years before I felt comfortable to share the story, and then only to a few friends.

Who was she? Who sent her? How did she disappear without a trace?

I will never know for sure, but that I was touched by an angel is certain. It matters not that anyone else believe—I will forever cherish the memory of my time in Nha Trang.

OUT, OUT, DAMNED SPOT!

The 1st Infantry became involved with 'Operation Billings' whereby troops were inserted into extremely hostile areas. The dense jungles held not only VC (Viet Cong) but also a large number of North Vietnamese Army (NVA) troops who'd arrived fresh from the north.

Our company supported this operation from the beginning. We'd been landing in some very hot (under fire) Landing Zones (LZs) and had experienced lots of damage to our helicopters during the first days of the operation. Our missions included returning to those hot LZs with ammo, food, and replacement troops. We often left with wounded and dead, returning the dead to base camps and the injured to the closest Mobile Army Surgical Hospital (MASH) units.

One day we received a frantic call for assistance on behalf of about 100 men trapped and fighting for their lives in an LZ that was being fiercely defended by the enemy. There were NVA and VC units surrounding this group of men in the beleaguered LZ. In some places the LZ's perimeter had partially collapsed. There was hand to hand fighting on the edges of the clearing that was being used for our Hueys to land in.

We could tell from the voice of the radioman that they were in the thick of a firefight. We heard gunfire and explosions in the background as the guy yelled over his radio. They needed a dust off (medical evacuation) as soon as possible. As it turned out, we were the only available aircraft in the sector. We raced to their location, unsure what we'd find when we arrived.

On approach we saw the yellow smoke that they popped to guide us to our pickup point. Red and white tracers bounced off the trees and the ground. Looking back, it reminds me of the laser fights from *Star Wars* movies—the tracers lit up the sky and the ground in much the same manner as the special effects in those films

Explosions from enemy mortar rounds bombarded the LZ. I assumed some in this open meadow were from hand grenades. Smoke drifted through broken trees that had fallen and were on fire. It was a living hell for the men inside that LZ. Total chaos unfolded below—men ran in all directions. No area in this lethal place looked secure or safe from the action.

We flew at treetop level but became an easy target from enemies in the surrounding jungle. The belly of the ship took some hits and tracer rounds flew through the open areas of the helicopter where we'd removed the doors. We rocked and bounced along the treetops. Intermittent, violent upheavals from ground explosions shook our aircraft. I thought it was going to be torn apart by the pounding of the blasts or take a hit and drop out of the sky and into the trees a few feet below.

I had my machine gun fully at the ready but could not pick out any clear targets. The good guys and bad guys were mixing it up in the LZ—there was no way to zero in on the enemy. I sat there while they took potshots at us. It seemed to take hours to travel the last 100 yards to where our soldiers had popped smoke for us to land. As we descended I saw hand-to-hand combat taking place a short distance from us. We would be the biggest target in the LZ, and could not hide anywhere. We needed to load the wounded and get out fast.

I felt dirt and pieces of tree branches hitting my face and body from close-by explosions. Men dropped all around me, ripped apart by automatic gunfire and mortar rounds. The green grass turned red from blood flow. I unplugged my communications line from my flight helmet and jumped off the ship. I ran about 20 yards to the medics who dragged wounded men toward our ship. I pitched in and helped carry the wounded. Bullets peppered the ground around us; some hit the wounded men we were trying to evacuate. It was a miracle all of us were not killed.

The pilots yelled for me to move. Every second on the ground we allowed enemy mortar teams to sight in on our ship. It would take 30 seconds to get us in their range and drop a round or two on the helicopter. Getting out of the LZ as fast as possible was our key to survival.

Then the trees and grass caught fire. A raging forest fire began to engulf the area. It was hot and the smoke made it hard to breathe. I kept returning to load more bodies onto the floor of my Huey. There was nothing gentle in this act as we threw these men in the ship as fast as we could. Within a minute we'd loaded several wounded soldiers on the floor and two more on canvas seats.

By now, all hell had broken loose. The mortar rounds landed yards away; we'd become the focus for all of the automatic weapons' fire. A wall of tracers came at us—which we'd have to fly through. I jumped onboard and looked at the medic who stood watching me as we began to hover and lift off. His eyes were full of tears and some had rolled down his face and turned the dirt on his cheeks to mud. He raised his hand to wave, perhaps to bless his men. It was the saddest goodbye in the world. I sensed he knew he'd not make it out alive. That he'd got his buddies on the ship would be his only satisfaction.

Our eyes connected. I raised my hand to bid him farewell—but it was more than that. I silently sent him my prayers. We were all in God's hands now.

The pilot attempted to rise out of the LZ as straight as possible, but the heat of the day, the height of the trees, and all the extra weight onboard forced us to fly directly over the fighting. We slowly gained altitude, but the tree line came at us and it appeared that we wouldn't to clear it. We needed more room to get enough transitional lift to compensate for all the weight. The pilots continued their efforts and somehow managed to clip only a few branches with the skids.

I looked back so I could get a good shot at the enemy troops with my M-60. I let off about 1,000 rounds into the outer jungle areas where I knew our troops were not engaged. I glanced back at the LZ as we rose above the tree line. The medic with the sad eyes was running for his life. Bodies continued to fall. It was the worst LZ I'd ever seen. I sat back to regain my composure. My heart raced and I couldn't catch my breath.

Then I took my attention to the troops we'd loaded on our ship. I set my gun down and examined the areas where they lay on the floor and seats. I felt sick—blood flowed along the floor. Since the doors had been removed, the wind blew right through the aircraft—and the rotor blades and airspeed made for a lot of wind. Fresh, warm, airborne blood splattered the walls of the ship, our clothing and helmets. The pilots had trouble seeing since so much lined the inside of the windshield. Severed body parts lay in pools of blood. It was all over my gloves and face.

Stunned by reality, I wished we'd had the medic. I had no medicine or knowledge to stop all the bleeding. All I could do was offer prayers and moral support. I checked on each soldier—but every individual was dead. Their bodies were riddled with holes. They'd continued to take hits when we were lifting off.

I became upset about risking all of our lives to bring back dead bodies. I told the pilots to fly to the nearest camp. We did not need to go to the MASH unit anymore.

I sat there looking at these young men. Most had their frightened eyes open. We stared at each other while the ship sped to the closest camp. We needed to dump these bodies, clean the windshield, and return to that LZ. We were their only lifeline, the only link with the outside world that they had. Dazed, I thought about what we had just been through. The eyes of the medic still haunted me, as did all of the dead beside me. I sat there in my blood soaked clothing and knew I'd never forget this scene

Suddenly, something caught my attention. I looked over at one of the young men with his dead eyes wide open. I felt his presence. Then I felt all of them, as if they were still there in the helicopter with their bodies. They were confused and frightened and lonely. I could sense the sorrow of their thoughts and almost hear their cries. I didn't know if I'd cracked up from the horror of the incident, or if I was really sensing the souls of these men.

I sent up a prayer for all of them. My feelings were all locked and controlled. I looked at all these dead men and couldn't find it within me emotionally to even shed a single teardrop—and part of me really wanted to.

I went back to my position behind my machine gun and sat there gazing out at the vast landscape beyond. I felt such sorrow and waste. I felt so much pain within that I thought I would never be able to completely express it to anyone. No one would ever understand what had happened. No one would even want to hear about this experience. I felt isolated from the whole world.

William "Rev. Bill" McDonald Jr.

We finally got to a nearby base camp and unloaded the dead. We took a five-minute break to clean the windshield and wipe some of the pools of blood out of the ship. Then we jumped back onboard and headed back to hell.

One other aircraft joined us from our company on the return trips, so we had some help for the rest of the day. We ended up flying about 15 hours into and out of that LZ, transporting several dozen men, many of them dead. We were only able to save a few for the MASH unit.

The LZ had been a disaster for those men. I felt bad that I was not able to give them better support. I often wondered if that medic ever made it out alive. His eyes still burned in my heart as we went back to our own base camp that night in the darkness.

We landed back at Phu Loi late at night. All I wanted to do was to get that blood-soaked clothing off and to take a shower. I wanted to get rid of the smell and feel of death that was on me and in my ship. When we were unloaded, we were informed that there was no more water available for a shower or to clean up the helicopter. Well, there was no way that I was not going to get cleaned up. My gunner and I decided to use some jet fuel, since that was the only available liquid to clean anything with. We washed out the entire inside of the helicopter and all the seats. It smelled bad and was a fire hazard for sure, but there was no way that we were going to let all that blood stay in our ship.

We took off all of our clothing on the flight line then poured the jet fuel over our bodies to rinse the blood away. We washed our entire bodies with that stuff, including our private parts and our hair. We were careful about not being close to anyone who was smoking, or anything else that might cause a spark.

We walked back to our hooch (term for hut or small home) semi-naked save for our underwear, boots, and dog tags. We climbed into bed smelling up the entire place for everyone else. We did not sleep at all. With the smell of the gas and the thoughts and images of that day still with us, we could not rest.

The next day, with the heat (the temperatures reaching over 95 degrees) along with the high humidity, our bodies began to redden and chafe. We were hurting and uncomfortable as our bodies exploded with a red rash from head to toe that looked as if we had been painted red. We both took a lot of kidding about how we looked and felt, but it was still better than going to bed with all that dried blood over us.

Author's note: During the times I went on Rest and Relaxation (R&R) I took a lot of enjoyment in taking long showers with warm, clean water. I wanted to clean off the Nam and all that blood. Sometimes I still feel the need to wash away those blood stained memories— 'out, out, damned spot!' but those Nam stains penetrate deep into the soul.

VISIONS OF FIRE AND DEATH

There was a period of time when we flew lots of combat assaults in and around War Zone C. We ran a few into the jungles along the Cambodian frontier. We'd inserted small units of men into places that were off our Vietnam operational charts and maps—dropping guys deep into Cambodia; men who did not wear any recognizable military uniforms and who carried weapons made in east European countries. They did not appear to wear dog tags or have identification patches. They appeared to be Americans, but we did not ask any questions because we knew, if we had, we wouldn't have gotten any answers.

Around the base camp at Phu Loi, I started to feel uneasy about a particular helicopter with the tail number 744. Whenever I walked by it on the flight line I got chills and felt uneasy. I mentioned this to a couple of guys and was shocked when they told me they had the same feelings. They shared they were concerned about having to fly in it.

One night, when I arrived back from flying in Ho Bo Woods area I was asked to see the captain about the next day's assignment. I'd had some hairy moments in a couple of hot (under fire) Landing Zones (LZs) that day and was tired and emotionally drained. This was not unusual, since I'd flown about 15 hours that shift. When I finished inspecting and making small repairs to my helicopter I reported to the captain.

He informed me I'd be the crew chief on 744 the next morning for 'hash and trash' runs (taking out food and ammo to troops in the field) to some Special Forces camps. It was an easy assignment compared to what I'd been doing all week. My own aircraft was due for scheduled maintenance the next day, so I was available to fly on any aircraft.

The first sergeant asked me to check out 744 and perform an inspection on it so it would be ready in the morning.

A sinking feeling churned in the pit of my stomach. I even felt fearful as I approached the helicopter. When I reached out and touched the skin of the aircraft I saw a picture of this helicopter crashing into the jungle and breaking into pieces. I saw bodies of soldiers lying in the forest near the wreckage. Everything was on fire. The whole scene was of fire and death and I felt the searing heat. I pulled my hand away from the helicopter, but the inner vision of death, destruction, and fire remained. I knew what was going to happen to that aircraft the next day.

I sat down to think about how to handle this situation. I'd been given orders to fly on this aircraft. I couldn't refuse to go; a punishable offense in the military, probably jail time for refusing to obey an order in combat. I discovered later it could have resulted in a 20-year to life sentence for me.

It was not a matter of being afraid of a combat situation; I *knew* this was a fatal mission for everyone on it.

There was something wrong with the aircraft and became determined to find it. I spent several hours doing the daily inspection and asked for assistance from several crew chiefs. I finally gave up and wrote in the logbook that the helicopter was unsafe to fly. I put a 'red X' in the logbook, which meant that someone else had to officially check it out after I had. I was determined to ground the ship. I hoped someone would find the problem.

The guy doing the follow-up inspection asked me what was wrong and why I had grounded the helicopter. When I tried to explain why, I came off sounding nuts. He checked the entire aircraft anyway and found it in perfect order. He signed off on my 'red X' entry, and the aircraft was once again ready to use for the next mission.

The more I thought about the aircraft being available for missions the more concerned I became. I went to the CO and told him my concerns about 744. I felt the problem was with the rotor blade system, but I couldn't provide any proof. He dismissed my worry and gave me a direct order to be on 744 the next day.

I flatly told him no. I told him to assign me to any other mission on any other helicopter and I would go. But I would not get into that helicopter no matter the consequences of my refusal.

William "Rev. Bill" McDonald Jr.

The CO let me know that I would face charges and prosecution for my actions. He lectured me about facing military prison for a long period in my young life. But I had to go with my own feelings. I had to trust that what I felt was the correct path to take. I made the only choice I felt I could make. I *knew* something was going to happen to 744.

I went back to my hooch (hooch is slang for a hut/home, either military or civilian) and joined the rest of my flight squad. I told them what I'd said, but a few teased me—they'd already heard about 'crazy Mac.' But some came forward and said they had feelings about 744. Quite a few believed me based on previous experiences I'd predicted.

In particular, though, there was one guy in the squad who did not share my view, or respect that I had that view. He thought I was a nut case for sure. Al Durell—Fair Oaks, California, he'd just transferred from Saigon, where he'd left a desk job to volunteer as a door gunner.

Al wanted no part of my insanity. He laughed behind my back. When I went over to him I could feel the heat of fire. I could sense death. I did not know how to tell anyone about this feeling, but I knew in my heart that he was going to be killed the next day. I held my emotions in check as tears formed. Then I looked him in the eye and told him that under no circumstances was he to go flying the next day, and that no matter what, not to get on 744. I told him if he did go out, he would never come back.

Al told me I was nuts and to leave him alone. He said he had no assigned flight gear and hadn't yet had a flight physical.

I returned to my bunk, just across the aisle from his. I tried one more time, sharing that if they were short flight crews tomorrow that he was not to go.

He walked outside to get away from me. I could feel the tension in the hooch. I was either going to be proven wrong the next day and have to face possible jail time, or I would be proven right, which meant others would be killed. I really did not know which I would rather have happen.

I had a sleepless night. In the morning I dragged myself out of bed and faced my buddies. They seemed just as concerned about what would happen that day as I was. I gathered my flight equipment and walked down to the flight line where I had been given another assignment. I would be flying combat missions, but it felt

116

a lot safer than getting into 744. As we took off, the sun peeked over the tree-tops. We pulled around and I saw 744 on the ground. It wasn't going anywhere.

We flew about 12 hours that day and saw little combat; a few rounds exchanged in one hot LZ. We were relatively relaxed on our way back to base, though I still had concerns about 744.

As we pulled around and made our approach to land at Phu Loi, I saw an empty space where 744 should have been parked. My heart began to pound. I already knew it had crashed somewhere and I knew it was too late to save anyone.

When we landed I raced to the flight office to check on the status of 744. I found out that 744 and her crew were overdue.

Apparently they'd needed another helicopter, gathered a crew that after-noon, and sent it off. They'd had one door gunner so the new guy, Al, had volunteered. They could not find a crew chief, since that was my original assignment, so had left with an empty seat.

No one had heard anything from them since the crew of 744 had picked up some soldiers from an isolated Landing Zone (LZ) to take them to another area. No one had arrived at the destination area. Now 744 was presumed missing and down.

I stormed out of the office looking for the CO. When I saw him I asked him why he had let that helicopter go out on a mission. He told me not to overreact and that he was in charge—that he didn't have to justify his actions to me.

No one knew exactly where 744 might be. There were no radio calls to give any indication as to where a search might be effective. It was several hours past the time they were supposed to be back at the base camp before any kind of a rescue effort was put together. Finally, the unit sent out a rescue helicopter and I volunteered to go along. We took off in the vague direction of where we thought 744 might be. There were hundreds of square miles of jungle to search and it was dark. From our high position in the sky, we were able to see a greater distance than if we had flown our normal, lower altitude.

We spotted a flicker of light miles away in the dense jungle.

As we approached it became evident that it was a fire. We flew over the top of the main burnt area and saw broken twisted metal. Bodies had been thrown at random over the jungle's floor. We hovered over the treetops, just out of reach of the flames, trying to see if there was any movement at all, but all we saw were vaguely familiar shapes—the only clue that these were once human beings. These were the same images I'd seen in my mind the night before.

I volunteered to go down a rope to the ground and check the site for survivors, but the pilot did not want to endanger the ship or me. It was too risky; we didn't know if the VC waited below. We circled the crash site several times.

I felt sick about it all. I was mad because no one had done anything to stop or prevent this from happening. The trip back from the crash site was deathly quiet.

When we arrived at base camp everyone knew the fate of the crew of 744. We did not know what had happened, but we knew that they were all dead.

It did not take long before the military justice system kicked into action. An accident investigation team from Army Headquarters in Saigon came to our camp. They'd examined the crash site looking for the reasons that 744 had exploded into a fireball. They could not find any logical reason, other than possible pilot error, for the helicopter to have crashed and burned.

They formed the idea that I must have had something to do with it. They took me into a room and placed me in an interrogation situation—just like the movies.

They repeatedly questioned me about how I knew the helicopter would crash and burn. I kept telling them the same story—about my feelings. They found it impossible to accept the fact that someone could know about things in advance. They tried to get me to confess that I had done something that caused the crash and the deaths of those men. I never moved from my original statement. They became rude and told me that they knew I had done something, but they could not prove it—yet.

The investigation team checked with all the maintenance crews. They found out that I could never have gone near helicopter 744 after I'd turned it over to the other mechanics. There was no way that I could have done anything, but that was not good enough for the Army. When the investigators left they refused to let me off the hook. They said they would be watching me, and that I'd better not do anything like this again.

Some 35 years later, I was able to read the final accident summary—the fault was in a trunnion bearing (related to the rotor).

Footnote:

Helicopter UH-1D 64-13744—Date of Accident 04/06/1967
Incident number: 670406221ACD; Accident Case Number: 670406221
Number killed in accident: 7 total: 3 crew members, 4 passengers
Accident Summary:

The trunnion bearing on the rotating part of the swash plate came out in flight causing loss of control to one main rotor blade. Suspect the trunnion retaining bolts were improperly torqued, allowing the assembly to move in and out, wearing the bolt's {sic} shanks until there was no retaining shoulder. The aircraft fell from cruise altitude. Turbine wheel blade failure.

The following is the crew and passenger information for this incident:

Name: CPT Richard Eric Newton—Aircraft Commander
Age at death: 37.3
Date of Birth: 12/07/1929
Home City: Columbus, OH
The Wall location: 17E-113
Call sign: Tomahawk 26
Started Tour: 01/09/1967
Length of service: 16 years
Married
Race: Caucasian
Religion: Protestant—no denominational preference

Name: WO1 James Leo Darcy—Pilot
Age at death: 22.1
Date of Birth: 02/28/1945
Home City: Helena, MT
The Wall location: 17E–111
Started Tour: 01/11/1967

William "Rev. Bill" McDonald Jr.

Length of service: 1 year
Single
Race: Caucasian
Religion: Roman Catholic

Name: SP4 Alger Edgar Durell Jr.—Door Gunner
Age at death: 20.5
Date of Birth: 10/06/1946
Home City: Fair Oaks, CA
The Wall location: 17E-110
MOS: 11B20—Infantryman
Started Tour: 09/24/1966
Length of service: 1 year
Single
Race: Caucasian
Religion: unknown

Name: SP5 Richard Monroe Dykes—Passenger
Age at death: 27.0
Date of Birth: 04/10/1940
Home City: San Jose, CA
1st Infantry Division
The Wall location: 17E–110
MOS: 63C20—General Vehicle Repairman
Started Tour: 07/29/1966
Length of service: 6 years
Married
Race: Caucasian
Religion: Protestant—no denominational preference

Name: MSG Vincente Medina-Torres—Passenger
Age at death: 42.2
Date of Birth: 01/22/1925
Home City: San Juan, PR

1st Infantry Division
The Wall location: 17E–112
MOS: 13B50—Cannon Crew member
Started Tour: 08/26/1966
Length of service: 22 years
Married
Race: Caucasian
Religion: Roman Catholic

Name: SFC Henry Edward Patenaude—Passenger
Age at death: 37.4
Date of Birth: 10/27/1929
Home City: North Cambridge, MA
1st Infantry Division
The Wall location: 17E–113
MOS: 82C40—Field Artillery Surveyor
Started Tour: 09/12/1966
Length of service: 18 years
Married
Race: Caucasian
Religion: Roman Catholic

Name: SP5 Conrad Earl Poole—Passenger
Age at death: 25.2
Date of Birth: 02/01/1942
Home City: Oneonta, AL
1st Infantry Division
The Wall location: 17E–114
MOS: 13E20—Cannon Fire Direction Specialist
Started Tour: 06/25/1966
Length of service: 6 years
Single
Race: Caucasian
Religion: Methodist (Evangelical United Brethren)

William "Rev. Bill" McDonald Jr.

Author's note: I held onto one of the dog tags of Al Durell, the door gunner, hoping to give it to his family at some point in time when I got back to California. His home of record was listed as Fairoaks, California not far from Sacramento. However, his family had moved across the country and I had no information to go on to search for them.

About 10 years after telling this story in my first book 'A Spiritual Warrior's Journey' and posting it on my website, I was contacted by his niece. Her father was Al's little brother. She was never ever told that he had a brother and knew nothing of him being killed in Vietnam. She confronted her father and learned about her uncle. I sent her a copy of my book along with her uncle's Army dog tag I had retrieved. It was an emotional reunion, if you could call it that.

I felt that my mission was finally accomplished. I had reconnected with his family and given them the full story that the Army never provided. I now feel like I can let this story rest. I am at peace now.

In May of 2015 I got an email from the son of Captain Newton who ran across this on The Vietnam Experience website. He was just 8 years of age when his father was killed in that fatal helicopter crash. He and I talked on the phone the day after he contacted me. It was a conversation that was truly 48 years in the making. I believe that both of us needed to talk and to listen.

I told him more details about the ill-fated helicopter and how I had tried my best to stop it from happening. I had carried a lot of guilt at having failed to save anyone but myself from that fiery death that night. He told me that I had done all that I could have done.

I listened to him about how losing his father affected his family. What it did to his mother and his siblings. It tore out my heart to hear what life was like for them. He read to me a newspaper story that had been written 25 years previous, about his father. The city where he was buried had done an extensive story on how his family had dealt with it. The article was very moving. I could hear his voice cracking just a little to keep it under control emotionally. He needed to talk to me that night (the night before Mother's Day) and I felt privileged and honored to be the one he was talking to. I believe that we bonded at some level that night. I look forward to being there for him in the future.

ROCKETS' RED GLARE

It was a muggy night, which could have been said about almost every night I was in Vietnam, but this particular night it seemed a little worse. Though tired, I was feeling good about having survived another week of being in Nam. My short timer's calendar was filling up; I neared the halfway point in my tour of duty. In a few hours I'd be on my way to Japan for a little Rest and Relaxation (R & R).

My buddy Steve was awake on his bunk above me; everyone else seemed to be sleeping. I was hyped about leaving in the morning—a helicopter flight to Saigon (Tan Son Nhut Air Base) and then a connecting flight to Japan. I lay there in my underwear, trying to stay cool and wishing away the hours.

Sounds echoed in the distance. *Thud-thud.* Not the same as the normal bursts of artillery fire in which our base camp engaged each night. These had a different quality.

My buddy leaned over from the top bunk.

"Incoming!" He shouted what we were both thinking.

As the sounds of rockets and mortars came in on top of our base camp, we called for everyone to wake up and get dressed. As the guys began to roll out of their bunks I felt myself being lifted through the air. I must have flown 15 feet before dropping headfirst onto the cement floor. I briefly lost consciousness—long enough that if I'd been boxing I would have been declared a loser by a Technical Knockout.

It was as if a freight train ran through our small, wooden hooch. (Hooch is slang for a small hut—military or civilian.) My head felt as if a thousand-pound weight had fallen on it; my vision was fuzzy and I couldn't hear properly. I could hardly stand up.

A bump began to form on my head. I struggled to get my bearings and yelled for everyone to get into the bunkers which were just outside the doors at the end of the hooch. That order, however, was too late as everyone had beat it out of the building except for me and one new guy who lay on the floor next to me. He held the back of his bleeding neck. A small piece of metal protruded from a hole below his hairline. He was okay, but concerned because he could not see the nature of his wound. It was his first or second week in the Nam—what a way to start. He crawled out one end of the hooch as I checked to make sure that everyone else was out of there.

My legs had a difficult time staying directly under me so I hung on to the beds and footlockers in order to move around. The rifle rack that stored our M-16s displayed an unusual sight. The barrel of every gun was twisted 90 degrees— steel barrels bent from the force of the explosion. I had never witnessed that kind of brute energy. The gun rack was five feet in front of where I had been standing when the blast went off directly behind me. It had thrown me over the top of the rack.

I managed to grab my boots, but no socks, and then stumbled out the door in my underwear. I jumped into the sandbagged bunker right outside our door and landed in two feet of cold, muddy water, and joined a group of others trying to keep out of harm's way.

We had no weapons and most of us were not even dressed. We huddled together as more explosions rocked and jolted the camp. The whole earth shook each time one hit near us. One of the younger guys (about 18 years old) grabbed hold of me with both of his arms. He wrapped his shaking body as close to me as possible. I held him so that he would not panic or, worse yet, start to cry. I told him everything would be okay and that he needed to relax. I felt like his father, but I was only three years older than he was.

The explosions shook the sandbags on the metal top over our bunker. Sand and dirt cascaded down on us. I looked outside the bunker and saw a night sky bright with red flames. Most of the rocket rounds had hit our airfield and a few helicopters burned. Some exploded. Charlie (from the call sign Victor

Charlie—therefore a slang for the Viet Cong) had known where we parked our birds each night.

I could see from the light cast by fires, and the shadows created from the same, large holes in the earth right by our hooch. We'd taken some close hits from what turned out to be Russian-made rockets. According to an after-battle briefing, that night we were hit with 250 mortars and rockets.

In the misery of the bunker I saw lots of eyes staring at me. I asserted myself and decided to check the bunker at the other end of the hooch to see if the rest of the guys were okay. I counted men in my bunker and then ran to the other one where I took a roll call. Everyone was accounted for.

Then we heard someone yelling about the perimeter being breached by the VC. That meant that there were enemy forces within our compound. We had no rifles, and our machine guns were down by the airfield, close to where the helicopters were burning. That location seemed to be the likely target of the VC as they penetrated our outer defenses. None of us was ready to go down to the flight line to check out our aircraft.

I decided to get out of the bunker and locate the first sergeant (see picture below). I thought he would need all the information. I ran over to his bunker, which was across the company area. I could still hear more rockets dropping inside the camp. When I appeared at the entry to the sergeant's bunker I viewed his pistol up-close and personal. He'd heard the same stories about VC inside the camp, and was not taking any chances. I briefed him then returned to get my door gunner and our clothing—hated the thought of fighting a war in our underwear.

We ran for the airfield to get a couple of M-60s and to check out our helicopter. We found a couple of pilots on the way, and went looking for a flyable aircraft. We mounted the guns in the darkness and did the fastest preflight inspection in history.

We hovered a short distance before the pilot pulled up on the collective and pushed the cyclic stick forward. We tried to scoot the hell off that runway as fast as we could to get out of the rocket fire. We did not turn on any of our running lights since we were greatly concerned that we might be hit from our own troops as well as the VC, and headed for the only spot in the dark sky where there were no tracers coming or going.

William "Rev. Bill" McDonald Jr.

We got on the radio and learned help was on the way. 'Puff, The Magic Dragon' had been summoned for duty. Puff was a converted old Douglas C-47 'Skytrain' (DC-3). In order to make sure we were out of Puff's killing zone we pulled up to an altitude above him. We watched as he flew around the outside borders of our camp, unloading hell on those below. It was as if we were watching the old movie *War of the Worlds*.

In a matter of a few minutes, Puff laid out a blanket of fire across the surrounding jungle. That old aircraft devastated every living thing within its target zone with just a few bursts of fire. And then it was deadly quiet.

We landed and checked to see if our services were needed for any dust offs (medical evacuations). Once the night sky cleared we found that the camp looked like hell, but fortunately only a few helicopters had been destroyed. Most of the rounds had missed their intended targets, but there was a lot of damage that needed to be repaired.

I went back to my hooch. There were holes in my locker, which was next to my bed. There were holes in some of my uniforms and hats that had been hanging in my locker. My record player and speakers had been destroyed. It was a surreal feeling when I realized how close I had been standing to where the rocket hit.

My head throbbed, but my flight was to leave in fifteen minutes. I wasn't about to spoil my R&R by reporting an injury. I pulled my hat over the bump on my head and walked out toward the flight line to find a chopper. I wanted out while I was still in one piece. Nothing would stop me from boarding my flight out of Nam.

The sun's first light sparkled as we pulled off the runway. Smoke rose slowly from residual fires around the base camp. We circled over the camp and I saw the bodies of several VCs across the barbed wire. I looked down at my hooch and watched my buddies wave to me. I wondered what the next night might bring to them.

I would be in Japan later that day. It felt unreal that I lived in a world of such contrast—like a parallel universe.

First sergeant and Bill McDonald of 128th AHC.

R & R IN JAPAN

Hours after an attack on our base—one which I emerged from with a large bump on the head—I boarded a massive, safe, civilian airplane for Rest and Relaxation in Japan. The thought of six days of escape was pure joy, and the fact my mother was meeting me there made it all the better.

My mother had spent her entire life in the San Francisco Bay Area, except for a few trips to Reno (once to divorce my dad) and a couple of years living in Coos Bay, Oregon, when I was young.

I'd purchased her airline ticket and paid for her food and hotel; thought it a nice gesture and an opportunity for bonding. There had always been a lot of emotional distance between us. I was certain she'd not jumped up and down with glee about seeing me, but that the all-expense paid trip would be too good of a perk for her to refuse.

I sat back on the flight to Japan and engaged in pleasant conversation with a grunt from the 1st Infantry Division who was thrilled to get out of the boonies. We quickly formed a friendship and by the time the plane landed he'd decided to spend his days at the Hilton where I was booked.

Also on the flight was a group of civilian workers taking a time out from their overseas jobs—highly paid government contracts related to the war effort. My friend and I made a few rude remarks—loud enough to be heard by a couple of them—about how we were risking our lives for less than minimum wage and they were profiting from the war. In hindsight I'm certain we were fairly self-righteous.

When we checked into the Hilton, these same two men checked in beside us. Instead of being angry, they invited us to be their guests for a few nights on the town. They wanted to pick up the tab and show us a good time. Of course, we said yes. After all, we wanted to help them lessen their guilt. It just wouldn't have been right if we had said no.

My friend and I checked into a room next to the one reserved for my mother. We took hot showers and ordered room service—for me: two tall glasses of cold milk packed in ice. My buddy ordered hamburger and fries. We were in heaven for sure. My buddy relaxed back on crisp, clean sheets and smiled the widest smile from his ketchup- and salt-stained lips. R & R indeed!

I gulped my milk and called to confirm my mother was in her room. When she opened her door we hugged briefly. I didn't know what to say—I'd been almost killed the day before and was currently in quite a bit of pain from being thrown 15 feet from the force of a rocket blast. In addition, there were previous incidents of being shot down and being wounded. Then there were all the guys who were killed and injured. I stood there saying everything was okay and not to worry.

I invited her to dinner with us and soon the three of us were seated at a fine table in the hotel. But again, there wasn't any way to tell her what I'd been doing or what I'd face when I returned to Nam at the end of the week. Long stretches of uncomfortable silence were followed by small talk. We invited her to go nightclubbing with us but she declined; best for everyone.

The next few nights our guilt-ridden government contractors spent a small fortune entertaining my buddy and me. We went to the finest nightclubs in the city. They even paid for women to sit at our table just to talk to us and dance with us. All the young women spoke English and knew a lot about Americans. They were college- and university-educated women who were hostesses at these rich nightclubs—this is the story we were led to believe. It seemed like a high school date with them all dressed up in American-style prom dresses.

I drank lots of beer and almost forgot my pain—almost—my head hurt and I was dizzy much of the time, even throwing up each day. The concussion continued to bother me for months.

We begged my mother to go sightseeing with us in the daytime but she said she was too tired and too old to walk around. Hell, she was only 47 years old, but she behaved like an 80 year old and said she felt like one. She resisted all our efforts to engage her in social activities, only joining us for a few light meals.

Near the end of the week I checked our hotel bills. I wanted to make sure I had enough money. I almost fell over when I saw the room service charges my mother had billed. She'd ordered room service several times a day. I was seriously concerned that I would not be able to pay both bills.

More devastating than the actual finances was the emotional pain I felt. I couldn't understand why she would do this—how could she not understand how little money I made? Her actions caused a further rift between us.

When it came time to leave she informed me she planned to stay on a couple of weeks to visit old friends now stationed in Japan. As I boarded the bus for the airport she came out of the hotel to say goodbye—a cold one. There were no signs of worry from her about my going back—maybe she was just hiding it from me—but I would have felt much better had I seen some concern.

I sat on the bus more depressed for having seen her than I wanted to admit. It was one of those defining moments in my life when I knew that whatever there was between my mother and me, it wasn't love. I felt emotionally orphaned and alone as the bus pulled out. I watched her wave then turn and walk into the lobby—not even waiting until the bus was out of sight.

My head hurt, but my heart broke.

FIRST UNOFFICIAL BOMBING RAID OF CAMBODIA

The day began with a short briefing in flight operations. Normally, I would have been on the flight line waiting with my ship. This day's mission, however, was different.

Coordinates were emphasized and place names were not. I was informed we were taking a small group of men on a single-ship mission to grid coordinates 'such and such'.

When I checked the map for 'such and such' I noticed the shape of the place we were traveling resembled Cambodia. When I pointed that out, I was reminded that we were flying to coordinates.

I checked again and blurted out that it was in Parrot's Beak, inside Cambodia. The two pilots glared at me and restated the grid location; any mention of Cambodia was to be forgotten.

We gathered our gear, loaded the Huey, and did a thorough preflight inspection. Lift off took place just as the sun rose over the surrounding jungle near Phu Loi. I loved flying that time of the day; sunrise through Vietnam's haze painted some amazing colors—sunset too.

We flew to a base camp close to the border between Vietnam and Cambodia and picked up a group of men wearing an assortment of unidentifiable uniforms. No one wore or held anything that would label them as American or even NATO. Their weapons were clearly from eastern bloc countries, AK-47s among others.

It was evident these guys were on a secret mission and their nationalities were purposely disguised, but they took clandestine to a new level; not a word to us, not even a smile.

William "Rev. Bill" McDonald Jr.

We flew to the coordinates at a high altitude. I was used to flying missions at treetop level or even lower at times, but this mission dictated we fly as high as I had ever flown in a helicopter in Vietnam. When we neared the identified area we began a steep dive into the Landing Zone (LZ) and flew into the clearing at treetop level from about two miles out.

I had my M-60 at the ready, but the jungle was so thick I couldn't even see the ground under the trees, let alone any Viet Cong (VC) or North Vietnamese Army (NVA) who might take some shots at us. The tension of our passengers was palpable.

All of a sudden we came upon a clear opening with only the space for our helicopter to touch down and take off again—the only opening in the jungle for miles in either direction.

We bounced due to a hard landing. The men were off before the Huey stopped sliding forward. I gave the pilots the okay to take off. We barely cleared the treetops as the pilot pulled the collective throttle and headed back to get supplies for these men.

The good news was that the LZ was cold (no enemy fire). Our concern, however, was that we not attract too much attention because we'd be returning with supplies. The possibility of having a hot LZ increased the more times we landed.

We returned to where we'd picked up the men and took on a full load: ammo, c-rations (commercially prepared canned meals), medical supplies and, for some strange reason, two cases of toilet paper.

It was a long, boring flight back to the LZ at grid coordinates 'such and such'. I had trouble keeping my eyes open. Then I wondered what one roll of toilet paper would look like if I threw it out from 6,000 feet. Would it unwind and stretch out to its full length?

I opened one of the cases and removed one roll for my airborne experiment.

I pulled about six feet of it from the roll—to get it started—then tossed it out of the helicopter into the sky. It began to unravel immediately.

Within seconds the entire unrolled roll floated like a giant white ribbon then landed on top of the triple canopy jungle below. So impressed was I that I decided to toss another. Well, one good thing led to another. By the time we neared the LZ one case of TP was empty, so I decided to drop that 'cardboard bomb' overboard. I didn't want to have an empty box show up in the LZ.

The LZ proved to be uneventfully safe. We unloaded everything and lifted off, pulling all the way to 6,000 feet and providing a fantastic view of the area below. All of a sudden, one of the pilots yelled. "Mac, what in the hell is all that white crap over the tops of the jungle?"

"It appears like someone toilet-papered the jungle tops. Is that possible?" added the other.

Caught red-handed, I had to tell the truth.

"Yes, sir, that sure looks like toilet paper to me also. We must have had a case fall out when we hit some air turbulence. I assume that all those rolls just popped out of the box and unraveled themselves across the tops of the jungle. Yep, that is what it looks like to me, sir."

One of the pilots began to yell at me but I detected slight laughter from the other; possibly from both.

"Mac, this was a classified mission into Cambodia where we are not sup-posed to be. Now you've bombed Cambodian territory with American toilet paper! It's spread out for miles on the tops of their jungle. Everyone will know we were here," said a pilot.

"But sir, we are not in Cambodia, we are only in grid coordinates such and such," I replied.

Silence. Then over the sound of the helicopter there came laughter from all.

"Okay Mac, if you say the case fell out, then that is what the official report will say. In the meantime, let's pray for some good heavy rainfall to wash all the evidence of our 'bombing raid' away," said the other pilot.

Thus ended the first unofficial bombing raid of Cambodia in 1967; of course, it wasn't Cambodia, it was only grid coordinates such and such. The box fell out. That is my story and I'm sticking to it. And if I tell you anymore, I will have to kill you.

BACK TO THE FUTURE

*C*larification: *In 2010 I experienced a conversation with my younger self, which I then remembered (in 2010) that when I was my younger self (in Vietnam) having 'this' conversation with my future / older self.*

Though it will appear in a future book, I thought it logical to include here with my Vietnam experiences. So, it is written from the future about this past time and place.

But what is the future and what is the past—it all seems like now.

It was one of those warm, muggy nights in Nam when I was emotionally low. It had been a couple of really bad weeks for our unit. I was flying lots of hours and, while greatly exhausted, still had to perform maintenance duty on my helicopter—something we did each night when we got back to the airfield. This meant working late into the night with little sleep and lots of self-induced stress and pressure to fix things. After all, any mistake on my part could cause the helicopter to crash and if anyone would be injured it would be totally my fault. I was not afraid of combat—but I was scared of making a mechanical error that could get someone killed. That concerned me more than anything else because, in all honesty, I was not a very good mechanic—just a very lucky one.

On this particular night events unfolded that I would not fully understand until over 40 years later.

One morning in 2010, around 4 o'clock, I was fully awake reflecting on the problems of family, friends; even the issues of my neighbors. I foresaw all kinds of difficulties for these people. Though I understood karma, and that each person has to work things out for herself or himself, I still found myself 'feeling their pain.' Sometimes I feel and sense too much about others for the good of my own physical health. My heart attacks and the chest pains I've had can testify to this.

While I knew that in the higher sense 'everything' works out, I lay awake and then faded into a semi-dream state.

I drifted back to Vietnam and saw myself as a young man sitting on top of my helicopter repairing it. I vividly recalled a particular day. I'd had some extra heavy combat encounters and our newest door-gunner had been killed in a helicopter crash. He'd experienced less than a couple of hours of flying. I'd personally warned him not to get into that aircraft because I'd had visions of it crashing and burning. I knew that everyone who flew on it the next time it went out would never come back home alive. This door gunner was one of a few whom I tried to warn and protect in Vietnam but all my efforts failed to keep them from their destiny.

Now I watched my 21-year-old self sit in the darkness on the runway working on my ship. My older self of today was also sitting there with the younger me. It was happening to me in 2010 in a real vision-memory, seeing my older self sit with my younger self.

It was then I remembered that back there in Vietnam when I'd been working on my helicopter I'd experienced (at that time) my older self being with me. I remembered my younger self working on that ship and feeling an older 'me' with a grey beard imparting some wisdom. The younger me sat and listened to the older me talk. He heard that 'he' would get out alive. The older me reminded the younger me that all things would pass and so would these terrible times.

Then the younger me reminded the older me that 'we' did not save everyone in combat that 'we' had tried to save—that each soldier had his or her own fate. In this same way, in 2010, the younger me reminded me that I could not save others 'in the future' from their karma, that I could only help assist in their learning process and that I could demonstrate compassion. In the end, I was told that they each had their own individual karma to work through—no matter how painful it was for me to observe.

The conversation played out as if there were two of us.

I totally remembered this encounter from the past and experienced it in real time (2010). The older me thanked my younger warrior self and my younger self thanked the older, wiser me. We'd helped each other to help understand what we needed to focus on. Two conversations separated by time.

When I returned to the darkness of my bedroom, I was alone again, but I understood that I could not help change the karmic paths of all my friends and family. I was not responsible. I also knew that everything would work out for them as well; it always does eventually.

WALKING POINTLESS

In the late summer of 1967, with less than 90 days left on my tour of Vietnam, I began to see and feel 'a light at the end of the tunnel' for me personally.

It'd been a short day of flying and I was one of the first crew chiefs to return. I'd just finished pulling maintenance on my Huey and about to clean up when one of the officers contacted me.

He informed me that since I was the only E-5 (sergeant) around he needed me to organize a few volunteers. We were to go into the jungle a couple of miles outside our base camp at Phu Loi and look for a loaded weapon which had fallen out of a chopper within two miles of the runway.

Thus was born the first and only Tomahawk Short-Range Reconnaissance and Recovery Patrol. I, being the highest-ranking enlisted guy they could find, was tasked with the leadership of this ragtag group. My first challenge was to find enough guys willing to go outside the safety of base camp to walk through the jungle with me as their leader.

I managed to gather a diverse group of men that included a cook, a couple of motor pool mechanics, an off-duty administrative clerk, an avionics repair technician, four helicopter mechanics, another off-duty crew chief, and one actual 11 Bravo infantry-trained door gunner. We made up the Tomahawks own version of the dirty dozen.

What a site we were. An oddball group walking out of the compound past razor-sharp rolls of barbed wire that surrounded the camp. A couple of the guys didn't even bother putting on shirts—bare-chested patrollers, their dog tags became noisemakers clinking together. The cook looked as if he was on kitchen duty—food stains on his clothing and a camouflage steel helmet emblazoned with the words 'Kill for Peace'. Another guy wore cut-off fatigues which exposed his bleached-white hairy knees. Only a couple bothered to take along a flak jacket each; everyone wore a different hat.

We looked like crap but felt like a dozen John Waynes ready to assault the beaches of a South Pacific island. It was as if we were hiking in the American Southwest and a guide had told us to make as much noise as possible to scare off rattlesnakes. I never claimed to be a good military thinker.

To make the scene even stranger we all had M-16s, and one guy had an M-79 grenade launcher that he'd 'found' on one of our missions. He had never fired one before, but he was willing to learn. We took four ammo magazines for each of our M-16s and I carried a red smoke grenade which would alert basecamp of enemy presence. Nothing else: no radio, at least not the communicate with base camp kind—one guy brought an AM version and listened, via one earplug, to rock and roll broadcast from Armed Forces Radio Network out of Saigon. He sang as we walked through the bush.

Several of the men smoked cigarettes and one guy had a cigar in his mouth.

I blew smoke from my mouth and felt I looked every bit the part of my comic book hero, Sergeant Rock of Easy Company: a tough leader, crack shot, grizzly looking character.

It was my job to check for tripwires, booby traps, land mines, and the enemy. Should we happen upon any of them I would be the first to sound the alert or drop dead. I moved along at a good pace as if I were walking through Golden Gate Park in the summertime. The guys were laughing it up, enjoying the outing. None of us had ever been on a patrol. Only one of us had any infantry training.

If the enemy was out there, they would know we were coming.

Most had volunteered so they could get out of the base camp for a couple of hours. They wanted to do something—patrol—that was different than the routine, something they could write home about, and I'm sure there were some enhanced versions. *I'd love to read their accounts.*

After about an hour we figured we'd gone about two miles—figuring and guessing was the tool we used to measure distance—but it occurred to us that if we were walking faster than two miles an hour...

Conversation stopped; even the guy with the radio turned it off so he could listen for sounds in the jungle as we realized we were in the middle of 'Charlie's Country'.

I led the group across an open field, which was not the right thing to do in the first place, but it looked much easier than going through dense jungle. When we were about halfway across the field, my door gunner asked a simple question, "Mac, why do you think there is a plowed field in the middle of the jungle?"

I froze as he reached the question mark. The area featured lumps of grass and dirt turned over and replaced: like divots on a golf course. I tried to think of more than one logical reason the ground would look like that.

A freaking minefield.

I'd walked us into the middle of a minefield. Now I had to lead everyone back without creating any casualties.

There was no chance in that moment of anyone blowing up because no one moved an inch. Everyone had already figured out where we were.

We turned around and, 'inch by inch', retraced our steps exactly, each person placing his feet in the footsteps of the man ahead.

It had taken seconds to walk halfway across the open field, but a lot longer—seemingly a lifetime—to walk out. First one in, last one out: I must have sweated 10 pounds in that 'inch by inch' exit.

We were drenched when the field was behind us.

I decided that we'd sit and wait a half-hour before returning to the base. We weren't going to find any weapon out there on this day or any day, and we knew it. All we were doing was risking injury or death. Everyone was happy to call it a done deal and return in one piece.

We found our way through the trees and brush to the barbed wire perimeter. As we emerged from the cover of the jungle we walked with greater purpose in our steps. When we got inside the wire, no one said anything.

I reported to the officer that we couldn't find the lost weapon. He didn't ask any questions and so I went to my bunk for a late afternoon nap. Not that I did get any shuteye. I remained wide-awake and wired, thankful I'd not be leading any more patrols.

As far as I know, no one in that group ever volunteered for patrols again; I know I sure as heck didn't.

THE MUMMY

A usual day began an hour before sunrise and ended after 12-15 hours of fly-ing followed by post flight maintenance. Only then could I leave the flight line and get something to eat or go to sleep; often this meant quitting time was around ten at night.

One day in the summer of 1967, after returning from 15 hours of flying combat assaults in the area known as War Zone C, I experienced a strange sensation while I performed the required maintenance. It had been a normal day with the exception of finding a small hole in the tail section caused by a single round—probably from an AK-47 Russian assault rifle, though we had seen Chinese AK-47s in the area.

Picking up a bullet hole in the helicopter was not that unusual. I'd previously picked up hits during the long days of combat assaults—not even hearing or feeling anything at the time of the hit, not even noticing any gunfire directed at me. This damage was one of those 'gifts' we found when we stopped to refuel or had the opportunity to look over the body of the helicopter, as I was doing that night.

Always concerned about my flashlight becoming a target for snipers, I worked to keep the glow to a minimum. When I'd first become a crew chief I was not too bright and held the light under my chin so I could free both my hands. Basically that made my head a nice target.

On this particular night I'd considered my 'feelings' to be related to the enemy, but knew it wasn't about me or my flashlight.

I knew something was wrong, but I could not put my finger on it right away. I sat alone in the dark, staring at the star-studded night sky—the door gunner had long gone to clean the M-60s and grab his dinner. Every so often a few tracers were visible at the edges of the camp, some incoming and some outgoing rounds. After being in Nam for more than half a year I was used to seeing this each night.

I considered what I might be feeling was loneliness, but my gut told me it was something else. So real was the 'mood' around me that I could feel the 'something wrong' in the air.

I put away my tools and grabbed my M-16 then walked slowly back to the 2nd Flight Platoon's hooch (a hooch is a term for a hut that can be civilian or military). I focused on how good it would feel to be in my bunk and close my eyes. I could have used and enjoyed a warm shower, but at this hour of night I knew there wasn't any more water. I was totally exhausted.

It's hard for most people to understand how tired one got from sitting behind an M-60 machine gun all day while flying over the jungle. Even though we sat there, we needed to be alert and look for the enemy. Our job was to protect the helicopter from being shot down. The consequences of falling asleep or daydreaming could be fatal. It is a difficult task to be on the edge of a chopper, as long as 15 hours, working to stay alert for those few moments of terror when we were under attack.

The 'something wrong' feeling became stronger when I entered the hooch. I stowed my M-16 in the rifle rack and threw my flight gear onto my bunk. I had my back turned to a group of young men (we were all young men), and felt sick inside; a chilling, painful feeling.

And then I noticed a guy standing next to his bunk bed. He noticed I was staring. The sensation worsened when I moved closer to him. I knew for sure that something was going to happen to him. Something 'unseen' shadowed him. I blurted out my concerns. "You're in great danger and I'm not going to let you fly on any combat missions the rest of the week. You're off flight duty for a few days. Spend the time in the base camp where you'll be safer."

His reply was peppered with four-letter words and unprintable phrases. Basically he said, "Are you nuts? Have you been here so long that you have flipped over the edge or something?"

I could hardly blame him for his response.

The others stopped talking and stared at me. I'm sure they thought the same as the guy I'd spoken to; that I'd flown one too many missions—mentally and emotionally unstable.

The guys went outside to get a beer and I sat alone and wondered about what I'd just said. I didn't know where it came from or why, but I knew for sure something was going to happen to him the next day.

That night I heard the guys talking about me. I knew they'd told some of the officers. Sleep did not come easily even though I was in great need of it. The only thing I was certain of was that I trusted my feelings. I decided to stick by my words and made sure he was out of harm's way.

The next morning, before taking off on my flight, I left orders that he have the day off.

When I got to my helicopter one of the pilots asked me about what he had heard. I replied that I truly believed that this guy was in great danger that day. The pilots winked at each other and smiled. Everyone thought I was ready for a rubber-walled room in a stateside asylum. The thought of that makes me laugh a little now. It's a Catch-22: if they thought you were nuts, you went home; but if you were sane, you remained to fight in an insane war. I guess it made sense to *someone*.

I looked back at the company area as we pulled up to about 50 feet. The guy stood there looking up at me; angry and without a doubt thinking I was nuttier than a fruitcake. I felt the shadows closing in on him—feelings I didn't understand because I had taken him out of danger; a day to relax around camp.

Several hours into our flying—carrying supplies to an isolated Special Forces camp in the hills, we received a call to return to our base camp and pick up a dust off (medical evacuation). There was a wounded man who needed dropping off at the 3rd Field Hospital in Saigon, 15 minutes from our camp.

We sped back, a little confused since there hadn't been any attacks reported. We landed at the medical unit and received a stretcher. On it laid a man with bandages all over his head and face. He looked like a mummy. I helped load him onto the floor of the helicopter and we took off.

Once in the air, one of the pilots asked me to check the man's dog tags. I pulled them out from inside of his shirt and slowly turned them over in my hand. I informed the pilots; didn't have to read the dog tags.

I'd failed to protect him with my warnings. The trip was silent except for the turbine and rotors.

When we returned to base camp we discovered the guy had found a Soviet rocket launcher that someone had brought back to the company area as a war souvenir. He'd been playing with it when it went off in his face.

The rest of the men in the company didn't want to talk to me for several days.

I learned something that day. Another's fate is ultimately in his or her own hands. I did not feel good about what had happened. I felt I had failed him. Looking back, I know it was all in God's hands, and there was nothing I could have done to change it.

LAST COMBAT MISSION

Three days before I was scheduled to leave Vietnam I was ordered to fly one more time—a simple single-ship mission, but we expected to draw some enemy fire—not a milk run or a hash and trash sortie. (Hash and trash is slang for delivering food and ammo.) The assignment involved moving small units of men who were seeking enemy contact. In other words, we'd be looking for trouble.

I felt uneasy about the mission. After all, why should I be taking risks 72 hours before leaving the war zone forever? Old 576 checked out okay, but the feeling of doom about the chopper and the mission weighed heavily on my shoulders and tossed about in my stomach. That Huey had served me well throughout the tour, but it felt like the end of the road for the both of us. I guess it was like saying goodbye to an old girlfriend.

I got up earlier than usual, more than an hour before sunrise, to preflight the aircraft in the early morning darkness. My final mission with my own chopper seemed a fitting way to end the relationship. I held my flashlight close to my body, shielding it from being seen by snipers—one never knew how close the enemy came to the barbed wire; who might be watching for an easy target before crawling back into a tunnel before sunup.

I thought about my first few weeks in the country. My year tour had been filled with adventure, fear, love, hate, pain, fellowship, laughter, honor, horror, death, and bloody memories of places and people. I'd even celebrated my 21st birthday in Phu Loi with a three-hour pass—just time enough to get myself drunk at a bar; not the dream I'd had for a 21st birthday bash.

I'd lost some friends too, but never really grieved. I wondered if I'd let my emotions die in this place? Was I that cold? More important, would I remain that way after 'the Nam?'

I became less fearful of the possible combat and more concerned about going home and what I was going to be like when I got there. I was not the same boy who left Travis Air Force Base in October of 1966 with my high school friend Mike Harrison.

We'd flown to Vietnam together. I wondered if I'd meet up with him and share a 'freedom flight' home. Had he changed too? Would we still be friends?

I sat on top of my Huey and watched the sun peek over the surrounding jungle. I loved this time of the day. I had the whole flight line to myself that morning—plenty of time for personal daydreaming before my pilots showed up.

I savored my last moments of being a Huey crew chief. I didn't even go to the mess hall for any food. All I wanted to do was take the time to appreciate the history of my unit. I knew there was something sacred here that no one else, except those I had served with, could or would ever understand. These men were my brothers, my friends, my comrades. No matter where I went in life, there would always be an unbreakable bond—like a spiritual tattoo on my heart. Forever a Tomahawk warrior.

When my pilots showed up they did a quick preflight inspection and kidded me about being a short timer. I untied the rotor blades and sat down on my worn, familiar canvas seat behind my M-60 machine gun.

We received clearance from Phu Loi Tower and taxied out onto the long runway. We began to build up speed and enter translational lift. The Huey readied herself to jump into the sky and clear the jungle ahead, but when the AC pulled up on the collective, all hell broke loose.

The engine made a loud banging sound—a small explosion. We lost power and dropped the five feet onto the runway then slid several yards because of our forward airspeed. Suddenly the engine became engulfed in flames and smoke billowed into the cabin. I jumped out of my seat and raced to unlock the aircraft commander's door to help him out of the ship. (Our

William "Rev. Bill" McDonald Jr.

Hueys had heavy metal and ceramic armored plates that slid out from the sides of the pilots' seats. The bulky extensions were difficult for the pilots to reach to unlock and slide back. The door gunner and crew chief had the responsibility to open the pilots' doors and slide the armored plates out of the way so they could get out of the aircraft. In a crash this was even more important because of fire.)

After helping the AC, I grabbed the fire extinguisher that was strapped on the floor next to his seat. I completely emptied it suppressing the flames, putting out the fire.

My door gunner had quickly done the same thing for the copilot. He and the pilots got a safe distance from the helicopter while I fought the fire. We assessed the burned engine compartment and noted the precious few yards of runway between us and the surrounding jungle. If that engine had caught fire three or four seconds later than it did, we'd have been at higher altitude and over trees.

The difference between being okay and getting ourselves killed or seriously injured had been 'seconds'.

A couple of airfield fire trucks pulled up to assist. I dropped the fire extinguisher on the flight line and headed back to the company area; relieved and exhausted—nothing like the after effects of an adrenaline rush.

I knew my luck was still with me, even on my last flight. No matter what, I vowed this was going to remain my last flying mission in Vietnam. There was no way that I was going to volunteer for anything more. The only flying time I looked forward to was on a Freedom Bird flight home!

God had seen me through my entire tour; my only concern now was for my high school friend Mike.

The night before leaving for home, I reported to a holding company to get orders for my return flight. And while I was there I ran into Mike. We hugged each other but didn't say much. I'd promised his wife, Donna, that I'd look after him and bring him home alive, but I'd not had the power to do that since we'd been separated during our third week of tour.

He was so happy about going home and seeing his wife again. I was just happy to be getting the hell out of the jungle alive and in one piece. I knew there

146

wasn't going to be anyone eagerly and anxiously waiting for my return, so it was bittersweet and a little terrifying. I envied Mike and some of the guys who would be reunited with their loved ones. What would I find when I returned home? I didn't even know if I had a place to stay. That old familiar feeling—alone—crept back under my skin. Home?

NO BAND PLAYED

It felt surreal to board the plane after spending one year in Vietnam.
A collective shout filled the aircraft when the wheels left the runway and we were no longer on Vietnamese soil. After that each person kicked back into his own world.

I sat next to Mike, just as we had on our flight one year before. We exchanged some conversation, but nothing important, and then drifted off. It seems odd, looking back, that neither of us talked about what had happened to us on our tour.

When the announcement was made that we'd soon be landing, I thought how nice it would be if a small crowd greeted us—even an Army band to welcome us home. *Dream on Mac.*

When we walked down the ramp some of the guys, including me, stopped and kissed the ground.

Our welcome committee comprised several jeeploads of MPs. They marched us into a hangar to search us for drugs and weapons. We were not very happy about it and some of us got pissed off at the treatment and complained loudly. The MPs became nasty; it began to look as if they might use force to get our cooperation. I even thought we might have a small riot between the returning heroes and the military police

It was an ugly welcome. We were herded onto buses heading to the Oakland Army Base. I looked around and noticed a couple of guys trying to hide their tears and anger.

Deflated by the reception, we were made to feel like criminals that society had reluctantly allowed return to America—though through the back door, of course. Not one single welcome mat for returning heroes.

It got worse. Looking out from the bus, people gave us 'the finger' and stared at us angrily as they drove by on the freeway. I wanted to believe that they did not represent the rest of the country. Maybe the world outside Berkley felt different.

It was a cold and foggy day in Oakland which matched our mood. Army personnel herded us like cattle; not a single question as to how we felt or if anyone was having emotional or physical trouble. They just went about issuing everyone a new uniform. It did not matter if we had orders for a new duty station or if we were getting discharged, they treated us all the same.

Once we got our papers, we were on our own. They provided no transportation to any of the airports or bus stations. There were neither airline tickets nor instructions to help us to get to our homes or to new assignments. (I had 30 days of leave before I had to report to Fort Benning, Georgia.)

After enduring hours on a wooden bench the staff offered us a free steak dinner in the mess hall then said goodbye. I don't believe anyone accepted the dinner invitation.

Mike and I walked to the front gate where Karen and Donna had left us the year before. We found a waiting cab and piled in for a ride across the Bay Bridge. There were no special rates for returning veterans. I remember that the cabby charged us a bundle to cross over that bridge.

I had the cab drop me off at my aunt's house in San Francisco because I had learned that my mother was staying there after divorcing my stepfather. Mike and his buddy went on to Sunnyvale and stayed with Donna's folks.

I knocked on my aunt's door and waited for a few minutes. I had looked forward to a Hollywood image of being warmly greeted upon my return from the War.

The door opened and I stood face to face with my mother. She gave me a quick hug—not more than two seconds—and then pushed away. I managed a smile.

I was depressed about the whole homecoming welcome, not just from my mother but from everyone I had met on my return. As always, I suppressed my anger and refused to show or share my true feelings.

I wanted to tell them about what had happened to me and how I felt. I wanted to share some of my experiences so they would understand. I took out my color slides from Vietnam to show them what it looked like. Less than 10 minutes into the presentation my aunt and mother said that they were tired and going to bed. It was not even 8 p.m., and I'd been in their home less than a half-hour.

Rejected and hurt I decided celebrate by myself. I obtained a house key and took a streetcar to Broadway. I wanted to go to some of the clubs and see the city at night, and I didn't want to spend my first night back from Nam all alone. I wanted to share what I was feeling, but couldn't find anyone at the bars who wanted to listen to me. All I really wanted was to get a hug from someone who cared about me. I felt that no one gave a damn that I had returned alive.

One major mistake I made that first night was to wear my uniform. A group of young, unwashed hippies followed me down the street, yelling and taunting me. They chanted a question over and over. "How many babies did you kill?" One good-looking young girl came toward me. I thought she might say something nice, but she spit directly on my service ribbons on my uniform. Her spit dripped and rolled off my 'Distinguished Flying Cross', 'The Bronze Star', and 'Purple Heart' ribbons. It took all my inner strength not to physically react.

It seemed people judged me as if I had just pulled a tour of duty for the devil himself. I could understand their being against the war; hell, even I was against war. I could not, however, understand why people were so cruel and mean-spirited to veterans. We were the pawns of a policy we did not write. We had not declared war on anyone.

What struck me as ironic was that this was October 1967, just a few weeks after the ending of the famous hippy 'summer of love' celebrated right here in this city. Where was the love for me and other veterans? It seemed that whole loving spirit was a bunch of bull crap.

To say that I was lonely that night would be the biggest understatement ever.

I went to a bunch of clubs and wandered around for a couple of hours. I didn't even get drunk. I hailed a cab to go back to my aunt's place. After listening to my tale about the hippies, the cab driver turned off his meter flag and only charged me for a couple of miles. That was the sole act of kindness that anyone showed me on my first day back home. It was just a small gesture, but it still impacts me today. It taught me to believe that even small acts of compassion are always remembered and can alter someone's outlook on life.

I got out of the cab and stood in the cold San Francisco night air, unsure of what I wanted to do. My big night out on the town was a bust. Spending my first night in America alone physically and emotionally was not what I had planned or felt I deserved. I wondered how Mike was being welcomed home.

I went to bed that night in clean sheets and with no fears about being attacked by the VC, but it was still a fitful sleep.

I began to question my whole relationship with my family. I was dying to be appreciated, yet I got so little back from any of them. I felt like an empty pocket with nothing but my own cold hands inside.

All the hurt inside me and still I couldn't shed a tear. All my emotions were dead. I wondered if I would ever find my soul again. I looked forward only to leaving home—again.

The next day I told my mother and aunt that I was going to Sunnyvale to stay with my little sister, Marsha, and her husband. That way I could visit some old friends and be back in my hometown.

My mother did not show any disappointment at my leaving less than 12 hours after returning. She may have felt something within herself, but she kept it a secret from me. My aunt didn't offer me a ride in her big Caddie, so I left on a bus for Sunnyvale that morning.

I walked from the bus station with my duffel bag to Marsha's place, which was about five miles across town. I had already learned that no one really wanted to hear my stories about Nam or any details about the war, so I said little about it.

I met my new nephew, Billy, whom Marsha had named after me. He was a beautiful baby, and he looked healthy and happy. I was honored that Marsha had named her first-born after me.

Except for the bed, I was able to relax at her apartment. Marsha had gotten the bed I was using from someone who had been living the hippy lifestyle. The mattress had bugs in it and I received bites all over my body. I had to go to the medical unit at Moffett Naval Air Station to get medication. All that time living in horrible conditions in Nam only to come home and get my whole body infected by bedbugs from a hand-me-down mattress.

After the bug incident, I went to visit Carol's mother. She was pleased to see me back, and we talked a long time. Of course, I asked about Carol and how she was doing at Cal. Her mother told me how well she had done in her studies, but I really wanted only to hear that she missed me.

I also visited Mike and Donna. They were in love and enjoying being together. I did not spend much time visiting them so that they could enjoy their moments together without having me as company.

Almost all of my friends were away at college or had moved away. In the absence of anyone to visit I gave in to better judgment—couldn't resist going to Berkeley to see Carol. I felt out of place and awkward being there. I think she was happy to see me leave. She was no doubt concerned that I might say something like, 'I love you.' There was a wall between us. I left feeling more depressed and lonely than before.

I was home only a few days, and already I wanted to get away from my family and friends. I felt so much emotional pain that I needed to get some distance between me and a place I no longer belonged to, or understood. Even though I had 30 days off, I wanted to leave before Thanksgiving Day.

I purchased a used 1965 Mustang convertible (a down payment and monthly installments). Since I had only a little money left for the trip to Fort Benning, Georgia, I decided to find someone to split the traveling costs. A community bulletin board held the answer—a young man seeking a ride home to Florida willing to share the cost of gas.

I picked him up at his place in the city. Turns out he was only 17 and he had a friend with him about the same age. They were dirty looking with long hair, and wore tie-dyed shirts and love beads. They piled in the back of my car at the same time as I had second thoughts. I was going to tell them to get out of the car when they told me that they were runaways who wanted to return home to Florida. San Francisco had not turned out to be the place for them in the summer of '67. I felt sorry for them, and it was too late for me to get someone else to help with gas money.

Driving south on US 101 I got to thinking I should check them out. I pulled into a gas station and told them they'd be flushing any drugs down the toilet. I made them go through all their stuff. The search revealed several joints. I then asked them for gas money and they admitted they only had five dollars between them. Not only had they no gas money, but they had nothing for food or a place to sleep

They'd lied in their ad. I took their five dollars for the first tank of gas. I had a feeling that bad times were ahead for them and me.

I made good time on Route 66, and when I got to Texas decided to watch my speed. I'd previously had an issue with Texas law enforcement. When we hit the town of Pecos, I was going five miles below the speed limit. As I cruised down the main street of town, I noticed that people were looking at my car with its California plates and the two longhaired hippies. I began to feel uneasy about this town. All I wanted to do was drive though it and get out of there. When I stopped at a light at the far end of town, some cowboy-types got out of their pickup truck behind me. They walked around and stood in front of my car. They were carrying rifles that they had taken from a gun rack in the back window of their pickup. They motioned for me to pull over to the side of the road. I did not like what was happening. Since it was broad daylight, I hoped the police might rescue me.

I looked in my mirror and was relieved to see a police car coming up the street. I sat inside my Mustang and waited. The policeman, complete with cowboy boots, cowboy hat, and gun in hand, walked up to my car window. I started to get out of my car, and he kicked the door shut on my foot and arm. I got pissed off and asked him what in the heck he was doing.

He called me 'boy' and told me to shut my mouth. He ordered me to get out of the car 'slowly'. He had me put my hands on the hood of the car and asked me who I was. I told him I had just got back from Nam and was taking these hitchhikers home to their parents. He had me lie on the hot street with my arms stretched out over my head. He kicked me a few times and got a big laugh from the crowd of Texans now gathered around my car. The policeman then grabbed the kid in the front seat by his long hair and pulled him out of the car. He threw him onto the ground and called him a girl. He made a bunch of derogatory remarks about the hippies and called them 'queers' and 'fags'.

He pulled the other kid out too—all three of us lying on the hot street. He kicked and worked over the two hippies with a nightstick, then took all the stuff out of the car and threw it onto the street. I assume he was hoping to find drugs or weapons. I was glad that I'd searched the boys; otherwise, they would have been in a Texas jail for 20 years to life, according to the drug laws at that time.

When I began to protest the officer told me to get out of there and not look back or ask any questions. He said he'd keep the hippies, but let me go because he'd seen my uniform with all its medals and awards on it. He wanted to treat me right, since I was a hero.

I gathered up my stuff, jumped into my car, and drove off. The boys remained in my rearview, as did the crowd. Shortly after, a billboard came into view that said, 'SUPPORT OUR BOYS IN VIETNAM.' I feared to think what the fate of those boys might be with a mob of rednecks. There was nothing I could do. Who was I going to call, the police?

I drove for several hours without stopping until I saw a man hitchhiking along the highway. It was Thanksgiving Day 1967—what better reason was there to pick him up? Besides, I was lonely for company and for someone to share a meal with, even if I had to buy both meals. I found out that he was unemployed and had been looking for jobs out of state. He was trying to make it home for the holidays, but was still several hundred miles away.

I bought him a Thanksgiving meal, albeit chicken, and we dined together, happy about spending time with someone other than ourselves. I took him as far as I could and said goodbye. I knew my family back in California would be having a big meal with all the trimmings. Nevertheless, I had fully enjoyed my meal and the companionship it afforded me at that old greasy roadside diner. The pain of missing my family and friends was not as great as the pain of being with them.

I reported in several weeks early to Fort Benning, Georgia, ready for duty.

ALL WASHED UP IN GEORGIA

I n the winter of 1967, I was stationed at Fort Benning, Georgia, fresh from the battlefields of South Vietnam. All I wanted to do was to serve my last 11 months and get out of the Army. The new helicopter company to which I was assigned had only one functional Huey and an old surplus chopper from the Korean War.

There were over 200 other Vietnam veteran crew chiefs in this stateside aviation company, all serving out their enlisted time, as was I. We were war surplus, stored out of the way. They had to hang on to us in case there was a national emergency—none us was ever going to go back to Vietnam because we didn't have much time left in the Army.

The surplus situation fueled a bad attitude about military life. None of us gave a hoot for authority or stateside discipline. It was a challenge for the career officers of the unit to find something to keep each of us busy.

When I went to my new unit I knew I'd face fierce competition in order to keep my flight pay status. There existed one crew chief position, and 200 plus veteran crew chiefs who wanted it.

For reasons known only to God I was assigned to the one Huey. Designated for medical evacuations, it was an old model (also waiting out its days to retirement). But it flew, as did I, and that sure beat hanging around the company, policing cigarette butts all day.

The duty required me to stay in the hangar area to receive phone calls requesting us to medically evacuate someone. Most days were call-less and without visitors. 48-hour shifts included weekends. I slept on a foldout cot, and my meals were delivered from the company mess hall. After shift I'd head over to the company area, shower and change, and go to the PX if I needed any personal items (PX stands for post exchange and is the 'shopping center' for a military area). Following that exciting routine I'd return to standby in the hot and muggy old hangar.

The protocol was that if I received a mission I was to call the pilots at home. They'd drive to the airfield where I'd have the ship serviced and ready to go. They were very trusting. I was lucky if the pilots even kicked the skids and walked around the aircraft to inspect it; expectations were for me to have as much of the preflight inspection done as possible without starting up the engines.

Had they realized how little confidence I had in my own abilities, they might have checked a little closer. The key was to get into the air and to the medical extraction Landing Zone (LZ) as soon as possible. It could be a life or death situation-usually not.

One afternoon we got a call from a Special Forces training camp up on a hilltop in Tennessee. A gas-fueled camping lantern had exploded in a young sergeant's face. He needed evacuating to a hospital. We were the quickest option since the sergeant's unit was in a wilderness area that had no access roads. We were still many miles away, so we got the old bird up and headed north, pushing it for all the speed it could generate.

The LZ reminded me of Vietnam—they'd cut a small area of trees so we could land. It was almost dark when I loaded the sergeant onto the ship and headed back to Georgia. We dropped him at the closest hospital and proceeded to the Atlanta Airport to fuel. We called the control tower and received permission to land next to several large fixed-wing civilian aircraft, with instructions to wait for a large fuel truck.

Adjacent to where we waited was a massive, windowed wall—the area of the airport where people waited to board or met others from incoming flights. It afforded them a great view of the airfield. Our Army helicopter attracted lots of attention and I saw a sea of faces watching us shut down on the tarmac. I strutted around my helicopter sort of checking stuff; thought I looked really cool. I wore a flight jacket and helmet and looked the tough aviator warrior that I was. Several attractive women waved to us and I waved back in a manly-macho way. The pilots suggested that after we'd refueled we should check out the airport and grab some hot coffee and food. That sounded great to me.

When the fuel truck arrived to provide a full load of JP-4 fuel I figured they'd pump it for us, but the guy pointed to the hose and motioned for me to do it myself.

I'd never pumped gas from a truck this size, nor one equipped with high-speed pumps used to fill large airliners. I was used to taking the handle with one hand and squeezing off a few gallons a minute from an Army truck. I reached up and took the handle of the nozzle with one hand and put it in the gas-refueling hole of the Huey—about head high on me. The guy in the truck turned on the pump.

All hell broke loose.

Like trying to hold a tiger by the tail.

The hose pumped hundreds of gallons of jet fuel faster than I could scream stop. It pulled me onto the ground and began to snake around the surface of the airfield with me hanging onto it. Fuel shot up and onto everything around, including the truck, the helicopter, and of course me.

When he turned off the pump I went limp. An ocean of flammable jet fuel surrounded me.

I don't know why I bothered to glance up at the windows at my captive audience. I looked at my two pilots, strapped in their seats and examined the potential dangers around me; around them.

The sounds of fire trucks interrupted my thoughts of wanting to fade away and die of embarrassment.

In a few seconds I was covered in fire-retardant foam. To add insult to injury they followed by spraying it off with ice-cold water. I stood and endured it all feeling smaller and smaller by the moment. And there I stood in front of the anonymous crowd at the window—all those attractive, waving women—and my up-close and personal crew who I knew would tease me mercilessly.

I did not look back at the window again. I hauled my sopping wet body into the Huey and closed the doors as fast as I could.

The coffee and food was just a dream. I wished the entire experience was too.

I AM BACK, BUT NO ONE IS HOME

I got out of the Army November 7, 1968 and drove my Ford Mustang convertible from Fort Benning, Georgia cross-country to California. I stopped only to sleep and get gas. I missed my family and friends.

In Mississippi a drunken lawyer plowed through an intersection and smashed into my car while I was stopped at a red light. He staggered over to my car, reached into his pocket, and pulled out a roll of hundred dollar bills. He peeled off four and told me to drive away, which I did, based on how I felt about the southern legal system and their local police forces.

I made sure that I followed all the laws and stayed on the major highways through Texas and didn't have any car problems until I arrived in Los Angeles to drop off a record player and some items belonging to an Army friend. It turned out to be a good break because his parents allowed me to spend some time there while my car was getting repaired. I used the hundred dollar bills to pay for the repairs and new tires.

When I hit the road again I had only enough money for gas for the trip home. I wasn't worried, though, because every month I'd been in the Army I'd purchased a $25 U.S. savings bond—I had 36 waiting for me to cash—my mother was holding them for me.

I pulled in to Sunnyvale, my old hometown, in the late afternoon only to discover that my entire family had moved. My mother had gotten back together with my stepfather, and they'd moved to another city. I wasn't sure where my sisters were, but I thought I knew where my brother might be.

I decided to stop in at my old friend Karen's house and see her and her parents. I told them about my situation and they offered to let me stay there for as long as I needed. Their kindness was touching and I gratefully accepted their offer. I used their home as a base camp for the next couple of months until I could locate my family, get a job, and look up my old friends.

I discovered my mother and stepfather were living in an old converted motel in the town of Milpitas. When I went to see them and asked for my bonds my mother informed me she'd cashed them all in and spent the money. They also shared they had no room for me to stay with them—not what most sons experience when visiting their parents.

I was broke. I was unwelcome in their home. But I had great clarity. I finally realized I was totally on my own. It was time to begin a new life after the Army and Vietnam.

Me and my Mustang in 1968

PART THREE
AFTER NAM: 1969-2002

The McDonald Family, 1974

"There is a saying in Tibetan, 'Tragedy should be utilized as a source of strength.' No matter what sort of difficulties, how painful experience is, if we lose our hope, that's our real disaster."
Dalai Lama XIV

CHRISTMAS LIGHTS AND LOVE

A uthor's note: When I got out of the service, and finally settled back in the San
Francisco Bay Area, I made a point to visit my ex-girlfriend from high school, Carol.
*She had always been on my mind during the years I was away in the Army. As a 9-year-old
child when I was in the hospital, some seven years before I ever met Carol, I had already
dreamed that I would marry her, so I never entertained any doubts that we would someday
get back together. I only needed for her to realize that I was the right guy for her. She was
reluctant to even date me again, but I persisted.*

I had been waiting to officially ask Carol to become my wife. Timing was important because I wanted her to say 'yes'. I'd hinted before—marriage—but she'd
never burst into a positive. It was going to take a small miracle for her to say yes.
I knew I had a long road ahead of me.

On pure faith, I bought wedding and engagement rings—my first step in
making it happen. I planned to carry the engagement ring with me every time I
visited her. Then if I sensed the perfect time and place I'd get down on one knee
and present the ring and ask the question.

December 10, 1969 was a cold night in San Francisco when I decided to go
to her apartment on Twin Peaks. Her roommate, Beverly, let me in while Carol
busied herself stringing lights on their Christmas tree. She glanced at me and
said something about the lights not working.

These were the kind of lights that if one bulb was burned out or not snugged-
in correctly, then all the lights on the string did not work. In this case, there were
six strings connected together of 100 lights each. All 600 lights were not working. Apparently the two of them had been working all afternoon at getting them

to turn on, but no matter what they did—changing bulbs, repeatedly checking each individual bulb—the result was the same, no lights.

As she explained the problem then asked if I thought I could fix them, I recognized this could be the perfect proposal moment—all I had to do was zap the right bulb (out of 600). When the lights blinked on in all their holiday glory, I would ask her to marry me.

Now, all I had to do was to perform this feat of magic.

I confidently replied that I *knew* I could fix it, and I would.

I stood in front of the Christmas tree and rubbed my hands together. I had already said a small prayer—in my mind—for a double divine intervention; lights and marriage. I figured it was just as easy for God to create two miracles as one.

I reached out and gently touched one tiny bulb then twisted it slightly. The entire tree lit up. All 600 bulbs sparkled and twinkled, illuminating the entire room.

Carol and Beverly stood transfixed. I turned and maintained my look of confidence.

I knew at that moment there would never be a better sign, time, or place to ask Carol to be my wife. I dropped to one knee and asked the question.

She said YES.

Later she told me she wanted some of that 'luck' to rub off on her too. We married within three weeks and remain so today.

Over the years, whenever I see a Christmas tree filled with lights, I remember those miracles on that December night—one small and one huge—when I became the luckiest man alive.

Miracle of lights

THREE UNWISE MEN

Early in my life after serving in Vietnam I managed a scuba diving store in Walnut Creek. In the early hours of one particular morning I received a phone call from the police asking me to go to the dive shop and turn off the alarm—a false alarm according to their officer who'd already checked it out and hadn't seen any evidence of a break-in.

I got up from my warm, comfortable bed at two in the morning and drove 15 miles to the store. When I arrived there were no police around and I went into the dark store alone. Even with the lights out I could see that one window had been completely shattered and the glass display case for the large diving knives had been emptied. I dialed the police from within, while the lights were still off.

Then I heard breathing—more than one person's breath. It came from behind the desk where I was standing. While I reported the situation to the police I looked up to see three husky, young men facing me. They held the diving knives in their hands.

I dropped the phone. For a terrible moment I felt like I did when I was in Vietnam. My adrenaline pumped as I faced a combat situation three years after my tour of duty. These guys had no idea what they were going to be up against that early morning.

I said the quickest prayer of my life: God, help me! Then I decided to attack all of them; a totally insane idea, but I followed my feelings.

I jumped out and blocked their escape route. I yelled like attackers do in old Kung Fu movies. It startled them and they panicked and tried to get past me, but I rushed toward them and knocked them down. I jumped on the closest guy and rolled on top of him while the other two watched. Then I took the knife out of his hand and stuck it into his mouth and down his throat a couple of inches.

If he had moved or tried to talk he would have gagged on the knife blade.

He was lucky that this knife was from the store's display case. I made sure that we had only dull knives on display to keep our customers from cutting themselves when handling them.

He shook violently. I told the others I wouldn't hesitate to cut their friend's throat if they jumped me to rescue him. They leaped over the glass display case and took off, leaving me on top of their friend with the knife blade still in his mouth. He didn't get back up and harm me—he could have; he was about a foot taller and more than 50 pounds heavier than I.

The young man just lay there staring wide-eyed at me. I'm sure he wondered if I was going to hit him again—or kill him. I wondered too. But the fight was out of him and so I knew I'd just hold him there for the police.

The phone had remained off the hook—they'd heard the yelling and fighting and thought the men were killing me. After they took him into custody they caught the other two guys.

Some might label my actions as the results of an adrenaline rush, or even luck, but I believe that God had protected me. But more important, He protected those young men from me. It was God's love that calmed me down in my moment of self-protective rage. No one was killed or badly injured. Thank God.

Author's note: These young men, 18–20 years old, were from wealthy families. The case took almost a year to come to trial. When it did, each had high-end lawyers and they received only probation. I figured they all got off with their lives as well.

Of interest is that many involved at the trial talked about the guys as though they were children and, therefore, not responsible. Their average age was 19, the same as many combat soldiers in Vietnam; I myself was only 24 years old when this happened.

Carol with me in front of SCUBA store, 1971, Walnut Creek, California

SCUBA DIVE INTO DARKNESS

One weekend, when I was a young scuba diving instructor, two instructors and I planned to do a bounce dive to 200 feet and then slowly come back up.

The key to good scuba diving safety is always to stick with the original dive plan because once the diver is deep the diver's thoughts are not clear enough to evaluate changes.

There is an effect called 'Martini's Law' that states every 30 feet a diver descends is equivalent to drinking a double martini on an empty stomach. Basically, a diver gets high from the nitrogen in the compressed air that he is breathing. The deeper the dive, the more dense air the diver breathes—increased nitrogen. The effect is called nitrogen narcosis—aka raptures of the deep.

Most divers begin to have some problems at about 125. Our planned dive would take us to 200 so we needed to follow the plan to the letter since our judgement would be severely compromised.

The other two divers had on double tanks, each tank having 72 cubic feet of compressed air. I went with a single tank and would share their air, if needed, on the way back. In order to do this efficiently, they each had an extra second stage regulator attached, so all I had to do was to grab it—no passing one back and forth between us.

The dive location was off Mission Beach, California, where—a short distance from shore—the ocean bottom drops 1,500 feet down a canyon wall into total darkness.

I followed both of them as they rolled over the edge. It was a surreal experience—inviting in a spiritual way. We dropped off into the darker depths and used our underwater lights. A trail of silt and dirt, kicked up by our fins and the movement of our bodies down the walls of the canyon, produced a cloud of debris behind, so when we looked up we could not see anything except our hazy creation.

We continued our descent, lights shining toward a bottom we'd never see.

At 150 feet I felt light-headed and could tell I was under the effects of the nitrogen. My two friends continued to push down. Our wetsuits were totally compressed, preventing the neoprene (rubber) from providing buoyancy.

Without buoyancy we'd fall like rocks into the darkness below.

A normal wetsuit has so much buoyancy that a diver has to wear a weight belt to drop below the surface of the water. In my case, I had to add 20 pounds of lead weights to my belt. The deeper one dives, the more the wetsuit compresses—no buoyancy. To prevent the diver from 'falling' to the bottom, a buoyancy vest is worn—air is blown into the vest to compensate for the lost lift from the wetsuit. Air is then released from the vest on the 'trip to surface' to prevent rising too fast and getting the bends (the release of nitrogen bubbles in the body's tissues due to a too rapid ascent from a compressed atmosphere). The rate of rise should be no faster than one foot per second or about the speed of a diver's exhaust bubbles when first exhaled from the regulator. The rule is to never go up faster than your bubbles travel toward the surface.

On this trip I wore an expensive vest with a small air bottle attached to it. All I had to do was release some air from the bottle into the vest as I went deeper, and when I was ready to come up, I would release air from the vest as it expanded for a safe rise to the surface.

I looked at my depth gauge as we approached 200 feet, but my friends continued on. All I saw were their fins creating a murky vortex. At this point the wetsuit rubber was so compressed by all the pressure that it no longer afforded me protection from the cold northern California waters.

I realized that I had two choices: I could begin my climb to the surface, and take my chances on having enough air supply to make it a slow, safe ascent; or I could go after them and stop them. Once I committed to either action, there would be no second chance.

If I reached them, I'd need to convince them to resurface with me in order to share their air supply.

I needed all their extra air to allow me time to surface slowly and make a small decompression stop around 20 feet. If I were to resurface without making a stop, I would be impaired for life or perhaps die from the effects of the bends. If I chased them and could not get them to resurface, all of us would continue to drop into the 1,500 foot canyon to certain death.

I had to make a quick decision using a mind that could not be fully trusted. I had a fair chance at resurfacing on my own. I knew they were mentally out of control and without intervention would never surface again.

I took a slow, deep breath and relaxed. I focused enough to say a short prayer. I needed all the help from God that He could give me.

I could not leave my friends. I surrendered myself into God's hands and raced after the fins ahead of me.

I checked my depth gauge as I caught up with the fins.

250 feet!

I reached out, but they continued to sink into the darkness. Seconds later and inches away I grabbed one of them by the arm. He turned around with a wild-eyed look, having the time of his life.

I put my depth gauge right up against his facemask to show him that we had now gone below 280 feet. How far below I could not tell since the gauge needle was stuck on the maximum level. We could have been below 300 feet; there was no way of knowing as we were like three rocks—dropping to the bottom of the ocean.

I took hold of both of their arms and inflated my vest with the last of the air in the attached bottle. It made little difference to my buoyancy so I began to kick with all my strength, pulling them both with me. We made slow progress; their minds weren't engaged in the effort.

Blinded by the clouds of silt and mud that we had stirred up—we couldn't even see each other—we rose. I could only tell that by watching my bubbles float slightly above when I exhaled.

At 190 feet my head cleared slightly. I sucked the last breath off my regulator and dropped it out of my mouth then reached over and began to use their spare regulators while slowly rising.

They both seemed to come around about the 150 foot level. Their eyes indicated a functioning mind. We continued upward, making as long a decompression stop as we could—using all the air but for a few breaths, before surfacing.

Of course, I was angry with them. But the thing about nitrogen narcosis is that it makes the diver feel totally safe. My friends had never felt any danger. They did not realize or admit how close they had been to killing all three of us. They believed they'd been in complete control of the situation. They didn't even realize that I had risked my life to rescue them.

No one goes to those kinds of depths with basic SCUBA gear and survives. I knew God rescued us, even if my diving buddies did not. I have to wonder how many times and in how many different ways God's loving hands have saved others from dangers—dangers of which they were not even aware.

Teaching SCUBA class in Monterey Bay, California 1970

SHARED DREAM OR REALITY?

Early in our marriage, when Carol and I lived in Danville, California, a unique experience shook up her sense of reality and changed the chemistry between us forever.

It happened one hot summer night just after I had finished my usual meditation time. I went upstairs to go to bed, but Carol decided she'd stay on the sofa downstairs where it was about 20 degrees cooler. She was worried about our son's health problems, my job security, and life in general.

I couldn't get to sleep because I kept thinking about her on the sofa, downstairs, alone and worried. I drifted in and out of a state which was unlike any rest I'd had before. I seemed to float in and out of my physical body. I felt light and at peace.

Fully awake, and very much aware of my surroundings, I realized I was floating in the air—at least a part of me. I looked down at my body lying on the bed and saw a silver cord between my conscious self at ceiling height and the 'me' on the bed. We were attached, but I could roam as freely as I wanted—toward whatever I was thinking about.

I drifted downward toward the wall above the stairway, then through it. I floated down the stairs, hovered across the front room, and sat down on one end of the sofa on which Carol lay.

She immediately sprang up. We looked at each other for a few moments. I sat there in my out-of-body state and she sat in her physical body. The sofa raised off the floor a couple of feet and floated freely around the room. Carol's eyes widened.

"Don't worry. I will always be there for you, whenever you really need me," I said, reaching out to her.

She panicked, fearful of what she was witnessing.

It was as if someone had sucked me into a large vacuum cleaner. I was drawn away and zapped into my body on the bed. I landed like a ton of bricks—felt like I'd gained a million pounds in an instant. I opened my eyes and remembered every detail of what had happened. I knew it was not a dream.

I waited until breakfast to ask Carol if she remembered anything from the night before. Normally, she never remembers her dreams, but this morning she stated that she'd had a nightmare.

Before she could relate her 'dream' I explained what had happened.

My story of the night before matched her 'nightmare' to the last detail.

At first she was blown away and did not want to think it was possible. My knowing what she was going to tell me—the details of her 'dream'—made her realize that something had indeed happened. At first she wanted to believe it was just some kind of a shared dream, and that maybe all I had done was to pick up on her thoughts or the dream itself. Over time, however, she came to accept the possibility that it may have been much more than that. One thing was certain; it expanded our relationship in ways that most couples never experience.

Whatever happened is not really as important as the feeling I had from the experience. I knew that Carol was my 'dream lover', and in that state (whatever it was) I had let her know that I would always be there for her. A promise I knew I'd keep.

THE GIFT

I'd spent a great deal of my life searching for a comfortable level of acceptance of my so called 'gift' of intuition.

It troubled me that I'd pick up tragic information about people and events over which I had no control. Knowing who was going to meet a tragic end brought me inner pain and sadness.

The early morning hours of my sleep on December 8, 1972 were plagued with horrible images of an airline crash. I watched the plane turn around and come in for a landing. I saw the plane too low and the wing hitting something— perhaps a tree. In these visions the plane crashed into a row of houses. The city landscape reminded me of Chicago—not sure if that was only an impression or that knowledge was revealed to me in the vision. I knew many people would be killed and injured.

I also had the dark feeling that maybe this wasn't just an accident but that something even more sinister was involved.

I woke up and told my wife about the airline crash.

Later on, when I saw the televised news I discovered, on that same day in Chicago, United Airlines Flight 553 had crashed into a row of homes while coming into Midway Airport on an approach. The loss of life was listed as 43 out of the 61 aboard the plane.

Again, I was overwhelmed with deep sadness over not being able to do anything about an event I'd foreseen. I couldn't understand why I'd envisioned such an event when I could not take action to prevent it. I cursed this 'gift'—felt I'd be better off without it. When I went to bed that night I fell asleep with a feeling of anger toward my intuition.

When I woke up the next morning I felt out of place. The world seemed black and white, and out of focus. Gone were the feelings of having 'insight'— no semblance of intuition. It was as if I had been rendered blind and deaf, and without a sense of taste or touch.

In this darkness I felt isolated from ALL.

It seemed 'not wanting the gift' had manifested—leaving my entire being in darkness. For the first time in my life I was terrified. I had no idea of what might happen or how people felt. I'd been spiritually and emotionally crippled and the pain was immediate and horribly intense.

I did not know how to live my life without knowing things in advance. I hadn't realized how every decision I made was channeled through the 'gift'.

I cried out, after my nightly meditations and prayers, for forgiveness for having treated the 'gift' so casually. Separating me from it was like taking my soul apart. For 2 weeks I begged the Divine to restore my insight.

And then one morning I awoke to Technicolor. Surrounded by the angelic sound of life, the world was more than three dimensional, it was a holograph. I was oneness with light and energy. I fell to my knees with gratitude.

I learned a lot from that loss. Most importantly I have a higher compassion for others when they get depressed and worried. They cannot see the light at the end of their tunnel.

Author's note: Of interest—Congressman George Collins was one of the passengers killed on that flight; later his wife would later be elected to his vacant seat. The wife of Watergate conspirator, Howard Hunt, also perished in the crash. She'd carried a briefcase stuffed with $10,000—speculation was that the money was part of the 'hush money' paid to silence those involved in the Nixon scandal. There was a theory the plane had been sabotaged. The official ruling, however, was pilot error.

SUFFOCATING DELIVERING THE MAIL

I worked for a few years as a letter carrier; in fact, I was once the Vice President of the Oakland Chapter of the National Association of Letter Carriers. I was a lousy union official by my own admission. I didn't have my whole heart into all the grievances. When I was promoted to management I wasn't enthusiastic about that side of the fence either. Neither side wanted the truth or fairness; both wanted to have it their way.

I worked at an office in San Jose, delivering the mail off 1st Street in a new industrial development. Lots of construction went on in the surrounding streets—great trenches excavated in which to put the pipes which had been delivered and left on the sides of the roads.

One day as I made my deliveries I began to feel really lousy. I couldn't catch my breath. It felt as if I were suffocating. As I stopped and began to wonder what might be happening to me I felt great dread and fear come from outside myself.

I fought this suffocation for about 25 minutes. Then the breathing issue stopped. I went on about my business. I considered heading to the doctor, but by the time I got back to the office and punched off the clock I was totally normal.

When I arrived home I greeted my family and turned on the television to the local news which was reporting a story about a construction worker who had been trapped by a cave-in of dirt in the trench he was working—he did not survive. The incident took place one block from where I experienced the breathing issues—and the same time I'd felt suffocated.

I knew there was nothing I could have done to help. I whispered a prayer to the universe and sent him my love. I'd shared a 'knowledge' of his last moments—somehow empathetically connected with him and his experience—and it brought me sadness to know he had suffered.

MESSAGES FROM THE COSMIC RAINBOW

Part One: Home

The evening had begun normally enough: a long meditation left me feeling peaceful and relaxed as I climbed into bed. My guru, Paramahansa Yogananda, smiled at me from a black and white photograph on my bedside table. I was focused on his eyes when suddenly my attention seemed to be sucked into him.

While my physical body remained in my bed, the inner me soared through a vast, heavenly universe, and streamed as a stunning rainbow. Though I couldn't see myself, I knew I was color. And I was not alone. 'We' traveled as a rainbow of souls with no separation from anything around us. We were one with everything we saw, heard, felt, sensed, believed, and thought.

We passed slower moving colors, even colors that blasted along at incomprehensible speeds. Imagine the old television series, *Star Trek*, and the multi-hued lightning streaks of warp drive—our velocity was greater than how that special effect is relayed.

And there was music—lush harmonic strains—all-encompassing melody around and inside us. This music of the universe propelled us lovingly along on our journey.

Negativity did not exist; no fear, anger, or worry. Overcome by a peaceful connection with everything, and happy beyond what I had ever known happiness to be, the bliss wrapped its presence around me as if I were in a rainbow cocoon of joy.

And just as the colors, the music, and the joy were part of us, so did an incredible love engulf us. It was as if I was love itself, and love was the universe, and everything that surrounded us—the traveling souls—was made of love and reflected love. There were no boundaries, borders, separation, or judgment. WE were one spirit and each of us was like a cell or a part of that ONENESS.

As time did not exist, we simply streamed in an infinite present. As we flowed along, I learned something about who we were, and who I was, and the purpose of what was happening. It turned out that I had 'forever' been a member of this 'family' and they had always been one with me. Although I am unsure now about how that worked exactly, or what it signified, I fully understood it then. I was also told (more like remembered instead of being told) that we'd been gathered into a group because we had a united mission. I instantly understood what that all meant.

My knowledge after returning back to my body was limited, but during this voyage of the heart and soul I knew our purpose and my mission, and that time was a rationalized concept—that all is in the 'now'.

I was shown the journey of mankind on this planet earth and that of others elsewhere—more like an instant 'KNOWING' than 'shown'. In that timeless-dimension I understood the big bang and the creation of LIGHT and LIFE and that there is a plan; nothing is random. The Creator does allow all of his dream creations the use of their free will.

I traveled along, reawakening memories and reviving an understanding that already lived inside me. I did not have to ask anything because knowledge came to me before I could register wanting it. It was a homecoming in which dreams and creation danced together in cosmic harmony. I was home.

My 'downfall' came when I had a thought about my earthly family and when images of my wife and children jumped into focus inside my spiritual heart. That 'thought' was all it took for me to lose the other worldliness filled with color.

I felt the downward force of a physical earth pull me back to my body lying on my bed.

I fought the return trip with all the loving intentions of my soul. I longed for my cosmic escape to continue because it seemed I was being asked to return to a prison. A sudden explosive release of energy and light separated me from the rainbow.

I felt several tons heavier, the spectacular rainbow dissipated and I felt a profound loss. Tears began to stream and roll freely down my face. I was already homesick!

Part Two – Home Again

I began to weep, overwhelmed with a sense of loss at having to return to the physical me. My wife, Carol, rolled over and asked me what was wrong. I had great difficulty talking, let alone explaining what had been the most enlightening spiritual encounter of my lifetime.

Carol and I talked; but I mainly sobbed uncontrollably and my words did not make any sense. I knew what I'd experienced was real, but why it happened I did not know. There was no way for Carol or anyone to fully comprehend the myriad emotions at work in all the various levels of my being.

My journey in the rainbow seemed to have encompassed thousands of centuries, an eternity really. But when I glanced at my clock, I saw that only a little more than an hour had physically passed. In truth, for what had happened to me, time was totally meaningless.

I was already lonely for my other family with whom I had been reunited and then abruptly forced to leave again, and yet I became 'earthly' joyful and blissful.

Significant and life-changing would all be understatements to what transpired that night. In the truest sense, it was a spiritual journey of my soul. All my notions about reality and the purpose of life were shattered as I crossed from my physical world into a consciousness of light. I felt that the very fabric of my spiritual DNA was altered.

Even though I am not able to recall or remember all the details and wisdom imparted to me, I have retained the spiritual memories of the journey itself. I sat down and recounted the elements of the journey I felt I could share. Some of what I experienced can never be shared—not because I do not desire to do but because I feel I have not been granted permission to share and therefore there has been a selective erasure of memory. However, I know that I will be able to recall what I need when there is a real need to know.

My impressions and beliefs of the experience are:

- I was a part of a family of color, light, music (vibration/sound).
- I have always been a part of this family and always will be.
- I traveled with this group at the speed of thought.
- I felt as one with this 'family', and this family was one with everything including the music, the colors, and the light around us.
- Love was everything! There was nothing else in the universe. Light and colors and music were expressions of love.
- I felt no stress, worry, pain, anger or negative feelings while 'traveling' in the rainbow of beings.
- I felt there was a purpose to this 'family unit,' some mission this group (team, family) had. I felt I was told about it, but I have no memories (only awareness).
- Time was meaningless in the universe where I'd traveled. There was neither beginning nor end. It just was.
- I was loved beyond any measure of what anyone might imagine. Love was what this whole journey was about. Love traveled with us and was a part of us and surrounded us. Love was the only reality in the universe. Everything was just a reflection and a manifestation of that love.
- I came away realizing that we can never be alone. We have a 'family' looking after us and helping us to evolve and progress spiritually on our journey.
- I felt I received certain information about events and things and, when needed, I would remember. I came away with a message to always follow my intuition.
- I know all that happened was not a dream, and that I was never asleep. I was fully conscious at all times.

I still reflect on this one supernatural voyage as a turning point in my life. It has influenced all of my life decisions since. I know now that I am never alone and that there are unseen forces and energies at work in our lives helping us. I know this happened to me.

LOVE is what this universe is made of!

Years later, I still feel and believe all of these things I've recounted. I believe what we call life is nothing more than a dream.

Author's note: A couple of decades after this experience I happened to read what is referred to as a 'rainbow body experience' by Tibetan monks who have left their body in death in a wondrous blaze of rainbow light. I also came to the realization that I was never traveling in that experience - although it seemed like travel - but it was really expansion of the consciousness - thus, I was able to 'travel' in all directions at once.

SPHERES OF BRIGHT LIGHT

I sat in my meditation room enjoying the peace after a long meditation. My mind was blank. All of a sudden I became aware of someone watching me and that the room was brightly illuminated with white light.

Up above me to the left a sphere of light danced and flowed just out of reach; it's light so bright it should have blinded me but didn't. I looked directly at it, wondering what it could be or mean. It moved slightly, never losing its intensity.

It was almost hypnotic and I remained fascinated as I stared and felt surges of energy run up and down my spine. Though I felt a message of abundant love and being abundantly loved by this presence—it truly seemed an actual living, intelligent consciousness—I did not entertain thought about communications.

I didn't entertain any thoughts at all—blissfully blank, but for love.

It was as if a part of me already understood who or what was present. The light infused every cell in my body with a radiant peace. I absorbed all it offered; at times felt the sphere and I were one.

After a period of time (I had no clock as reference) the LIGHT burst into sparkling white energy like fireworks on the Fourth of July. A sonic boom—like that of a jet—filled my ears. I expected the entire neighborhood would run over to my house to find out what happened. As it turned out, no one heard any sound except for me.

I sat in wonderment, a bit of a spiritual stupor for several minutes. I did not wish to break the moment and lose the feelings I had just experienced.

William "Rev. Bill" McDonald Jr.

Thirty years later, I attempted to recall the 'LIGHT' from my memory in order to write a reflective poem. At that moment I realized I'd missed a golden opportunity to find out more about it, and I'd a mental list of important questions that I'd ask if the event reoccurred.

Then I felt someone watching me. I looked up and to my left from my computer keyboard and that same familiar ball of white blazing LIGHT hovered over my head.

I was calmly elated to have the visitor back. I watched it once again, as I had done some three decades before. I tried to focus on it to see if I could learn more. It danced around in the space above me in a dazzling display.

Time seemed to stand still. There were no thoughts about any of my questions. Just as before, there were no thoughts about anything; only contentment and total love. All my plans I had made to ask the meaning of the visit were forgotten. Nothing mattered except LOVE in which I was bathed.

When the sphere exploded into a light show of billions of white sparks they appeared like shards of glass that penetrated deeply and painlessly into my entire body and soul. My spine tingled as it had before.

The sound almost knocked me out of my chair. Surely someone heard it this time.

Eventually I went downstairs to ask my family if they'd heard an explosion. They looked up from watching the television. No one had heard anything. I'd had my own personal sound-and-light-show.

I'm unsure what to make of these spheres. Identical in size, shape and intensity, they both exploded and spread light into the entire room. Each time I felt loved and was left in great awe. But there seemed no messages or any material evidence that anything had ever taken place.

It is one more mystery in my long journey.

Next time, I will ask questions—for sure I will. I'll have a long list so I can remember them. Well, that is my intention.

Author's note: This has happened twice that I can remember: once shortly after my 'cosmic rainbow' experience, and once again about 30 years later when I was writing about that original experience.

OUT OF THE MOUTHS OF CHILDREN

A family outing with old friends and their children entailed a rafting trip down the American River—not too far from downtown Sacramento. After a good dose of summer sun we pulled over to a beach to rest and have lunch. As we did, shouting reached us from a beach up-stream.

Our friend Beverly, who'd been ahead of me, rushed to the scene where she discovered a group of young people had pulled a young man from the water. They'd gathered around him, heads bowed.

The youth's face was white and bluish, his body motionless. He was not breathing. No one moved or did anything to help revive the drowned boy.

Beverly, who'd just completed a Red Cross CPR class, readied herself for action, willing to do what she had been trained to do, but not totally confident since this was real life. I'd been a certified, proficient lifeguard in my last year in the U.S. Army, and had some life-saving experience. I'd also taken refreshers over the years.

I knelt and took the young man's head in my hands.

He appeared dead, having been on the beach for several minutes. I began mouth-to-mouth resuscitation. I felt his chest swell each time I pushed my air into his lungs.

In a separate focus my thoughts traveled to why the others hadn't done anything. Able bodied teens with their heads bowed. No action. Anger stirred as I continued to force my air into the victim's lungs.

All of a sudden he coughed violently, shooting a stream of vomit right directly into my mouth and up my nose. I gagged, and stopped briefly to clear myself of his vomit. He continued to throw up violently so I turned him on his side to allow him to clear his lungs. At least a cup of water poured out of his mouth and then he gasped and sat up.

As his color returned, he coughed and spat. When fully alert, he stood and his friends came over to hug him. Though in a daze, he looked very much alive, no thanks to 'them'. My annoyance over their lack of attention bubbled over and I told them how I felt.

They remained calm as I lectured them that I thought they should have been doing something besides staring down at him.

And then one of them made a statement. "We *were* doing something. We were praying to Jesus to send us someone who knew what he was doing to come and save him," he said.

"Well, what good did that do?" I muttered arrogantly.

"You came, didn't you? And you knew what to do. Can't you see, you were the answer to our prayers?" said the same spokesperson.

I stood there speechless. How could I not see that these teenagers had actually done something? I was there at the right time and the right place, and I knew what I was doing.

I left feeling humbled and blessed. My only thought was that of a passage I had read in the Bible: *"Those whose glory above the heavens is chanted by the mouth of babes and infants."* Psalms 8:1-2.

FAILED PREDICTION

S ometimes I get intuitive messages in the form of visual clues.

In 1981, repetitive images appeared in dreams of President Ronald Reagan surrounded by dark storm clouds. I saw a man with a gun and heard at least half a dozen shots fired. The president was shot in the chest and the bodies of three other men fell. These intense dreams continued for several weeks.

I had mentally connected all the dots that March 30th would be the fated date. I shared this with some of my closest friends and a couple of neighbors.

Well history did prove me wrong on that fateful day. The President was indeed shot in the chest, as I had foreseen. Three men around him were also shot. There were a total of six shots fired on March 30th, as predicted. However, my intelligent analysis of the visions was very wrong in one major detail: the President was not killed. He was wounded—a bullet in his chest near his heart. Though I was not upset that the President lived, I was angry with myself that I'd jumped to the wrong conclusions.

The lesson I learned was that sometimes, even with the right information guiding us, no one is ever one hundred percent certain. It is in our *rush* to connect the dots that we filter, or even alter, what we intuitively sense. When we add our minds to the process, things can go wrong. My brain figured that if he was shot in the chest that he must be dead.

I had been partially wrong about the JFK Assassination as well. Though I was much younger when I had those visions, they were just as real. I correctly saw him in my dreams/visions getting shot in Dallas. I was right about where and when, and the fact that he was killed; however, in those intuitive experiences I saw more than one assassin. I saw someone shooting him from the grassy area by the road. But I also sensed that there were others involved beyond what I was seeing in my dreams and visions. Now history has provided evidence through many government committees and hearings that there was one assassin, Harvey Lee Oswald. That was yet another time I *thought* I was correct.

Anne Wilson Schae
"Trusting our intuition often saves us from disaster."

ESTES PARK DAM

It was one of those wonderful summer trips that I took annually with my children when they were young.

I had several weeks of vacation time each year and I would take the time all in one bundle. This allowed me enough time to roam around the country with my children to see state and national parks. Meanwhile, it gave my wife, Carol, a stay-cation—she'd remain at home and be free from the usual routine of taking care of kids and husband.

It worked great for both of us.

This particular trip, July 1982, I took the children to Mitchell, South Dakota. It happened that neighbors of ours were there visiting their parents and settling an estate sale so we decided to stop in and visit for a day or two.

Instead of finding a campsite, we pitched our tent in the large yard of their parent's home. The children had captured a jar full of lightning bugs and let them loose inside the tent. It was an exciting night. I loved sharing in their enthusiasm.

I did, however, become uncomfortable about the winds, but not enough to pack up. A violent thunder and rainstorm ensued and heavy winds buffeted the tent about, and rain poured inside.

The next morning we heard the reports on the news that tornado-like winds had knocked the local movie screen down at the drive-in theater. Other buildings had been damaged as well. We packed up, having decided to make our way to the border and enter Minnesota; the kids wanted to reconnect with other friends there.

I began driving down the highway and that uneasiness visited me again. I abruptly changed directions and headed west toward Colorado. Later we heard a news report that the road we'd been on—to Minnesota—had been washed out by a flash flood. Had we continued on that same highway we would have encountered some dangerous issues or at the least, major delays.

We ended up in Colorado and headed to Rocky Mountain National Park. We rented a hotel room in the small town of Estes Park—I'd briefly thought of camping in the Aspenglen Campground below the dam, but had gone with my gut that the hotel was the only decision. The kids thought the hotel pool and a pizza dinner totally outranked the tent. Life was great.

The next day we visited the lake which was formed by an 80 year-old earthen dam. We rented a rowboat but I immediately felt uneasy, again! So uncomfortable was I that we rowed back to shore earlier than we'd planned.

I knew that the sooner we left the area the better, so we hit the road, and headed for Rocky Mountain National Park.

Once again, a breaking news story reported that a disaster had occurred in Estes Park—the dam above the lake where we'd been boating had collapsed. A 30 foot wall of water had rushed down the canyon and, following the Roaring River into the Fall River, flooded the Aspenglen campground where four people had been swept away to their deaths.

The city of Estes Park had six feet of flood water on its main street. Damage caused by mud and water would total over 15 million dollars.

I listened to the news story and kind of felt a chill at the thought that we could have been in that campground. We had been on the lake.

I realized that on this trip I had dodged a tornado in South Dakota, avoided a flash flood in Minnesota, and evaded a dam burst in Colorado. We'd escaped great dangers. I was grateful I'd listened to that inner voice; my children were safe. Someone was surely looking after us.

VISUALIZATIONS AND TROPHIES

When I was in my 40s and fairly out of shape, some of the younger, athletic guys working for me at the post office began to trash talk about how old and un-athletic I was.

I challenged them by telling them that even at my 'old age' and in 'bad' shape I could put together a basketball team and not just be competitive, but win the city championship. It created a good laugh for the employees.

I then made up my mind to prove what I had said.

I gathered a few of them along with some neighbors and friends and registered the team for the upcoming season in the city league. I even found a sponsor to pay for t-shirts and fees. I told everyone that we were going to win the trophy at the end of the season and we would do it with me as a starting guard. All 5 feet and 6 inches of me!

The season began. Most of the teams we played were bigger and more talented. Their players were in their 20s and early 30s. However, each week's games brought us more victories. We never won by much, but it frustrated the others to be beaten by a bunch of mostly old, out of shape guys.

We made the championship game. If we won we'd receive the trophy I'd predicted. This final game I listened to some rumblings from the team saying it was too important a game for me to be coach and starting guard so, bowing to pressure, I sat out and started one of our younger guys.

When we had fallen 19 points behind—still in the first half—I got off the bench. I pointed to the scoreboard showing how much we were behind. I reminded them we were going to win then I injected myself into the game.

I then went out and hit two quick baskets, closing the difference to 15 points. The other players improved their playing—perhaps they were embarrassed by me—they were on fire. By half time we'd closed the gap to 5 points.

During the half time break I repeated that we were going to win.

We played fairly evenly with the other team for most of the second half, but toward the end they were frustrated we were so close. They attempted to play us one-on-one and forgot about passing the ball around. It was inevitable we'd tie it up.

Then in the last minute we sunk a couple of baskets. Victory!

It was exactly as I had visualized all season long. The trophy was in my hands at the end of the game.

But I wasn't holding the trophy because I was any kind of a great, or even good player. I knew we would win all those games in spite of talent or other evidence against it happening. The power of visualization created a force. I pictured each game before we played it and always saw myself at the end of the season holding the championship trophy.

I continued with this team and went into several other open leagues around the area winning in Sacramento as well as in my own town of Elk Grove. The results were always the same. In the end, after several years and a room full of trophies I decided to load my pickup truck and donate them to a local charity to recycle them.

I had visualized my computer room completely filled with trophies. When that vision was realized, I no longer had a desire to have them. Mission accomplished.

THE MIDNIGHT PHONE CALL

It's the thing most parents dread: an emergency phone call at midnight from one of their children.

I was sitting on the sofa watching the news which showed footage of a car accident in which those involved had suffered serious injuries. Lights and emergency vehicles lit up the television screen as my daughter, Daya, a sophomore in high school, entered the room.

She asked me if she could borrow the family car, a little four-wheel-drive convertible, to take her friends out.

Her request hit me like a ton of bricks. Even though she was a new driver, I usually allowed her to use the car, but it didn't 'feel' right. I had visions of her in the back of an ambulance with car wreckage across the darkened roadway. I sternly relied, *NO* to her request.

She pleaded with me to reconsider but I stood firmly by my intentions not to let her be the driver of any car that night.

Alternate plans were that her friend would drive her own car, so I felt I could not object to Daya going out. I asked that she ensure her seatbelt was fastened and that she must insist her friends fasten theirs too. I told her that I did not want to get a phone call from one of her friends at midnight telling me that she was involved in a bad accident like the one on the television screen.

She thought I was overreacting to the news story, but I told her my feelings were independent of the coverage. I asked that she assure me she'd do as I'd asked. She said she would, so I let her go.

I felt extremely uncomfortable about her being out that night, but I didn't mention it to my wife; didn't want her to worry given I could be overreacting, as my daughter had thought.

We were in bed when that phone call came in at exactly midnight.

I jumped out of bed, knowing already that the caller would tell me about an accident involving my daughter. Now the only questions were, was she safe, where was she, and had she followed my instructions?

I picked up the phone and a boy's voice told me that Daya was sitting in the back of an ambulance out on a country road. He said he couldn't get close enough to talk to her because the road was blocked by so many emergency vehicles; even a medical evacuation helicopter sat on the road next to the car wreckage.

My wife woke and asked about the phone call. I told her to go back to sleep, that I needed to go help our daughter who had been in an accident. 'Nothing to worry about', I told her, even though I knew it was much worse. I dressed and was on my way to the accident scene minutes after hanging up the phone.

Red lights flashed and rotated all over the country roadside There was no way to drive close to where Daya was being held. I looked down the road and saw her best friend's car, upside down and mangled. My heart hurt because it was obvious the others were badly injured.

I walked to one of the ambulances parked on the roadside and heard my daughter's voice. She was upset and talking fast. When she saw me she began to cry and yet managed to tell me she'd made sure her seatbelt was tightly fastened. She told me that when she asked her friends to do the same they had laughed at her. They wouldn't put them on even after she warned them her dad had told her to make sure they used them.

I stayed with Daya, but looked around. Lots of blood. Broken windows. I saw where one of the girls (later discovered she was 14) had been thrown head first through a side window and landed 50 feet away after breaking through three strands of barbed wire fencing. Her neck and back were broken. She would never again move her arms or legs; would be a captive of a wheelchair the rest of her days. Her face, once a beautiful vision of her youth, was jaggedly torn.

Another passenger, who did not get ejected from the car, was tossed around inside as it rolled three times; she had suffered a head injury. It must have been like being tossed around in a dryer. It took three weeks for her to regain consciousness—also a fourteen year old.

The driver, my daughter's best friend, had been changing music tapes. When she looked up and saw that she was going off the road, she'd overcorrected the steering and flipped the car. She was able to grip the steering wheel tightly to keep from being tossed around. Other than some bruises and bumps, she was okay physically. But the emotional and spiritual damage took its toll when she realized what she had caused. Even though it was an accident, she put a lot of guilt and blame on herself.

My daughter told me that her seat belt had held her when the car was rolling over. She'd been hanging upside down when the vehicle came to rest on its rooftop. She saw that the other girls were hurt and tried to help them, but there was nothing she could do.

I took her to the hospital before bringing her home about four hours after getting that midnight call. My poor wife was worried, but grateful our daughter was okay.

The crash made the next day's front page news—multiple photos. Then it dawned on me: they matched the images I'd had in my mind the day before.

Had my daughter not listened to my demand for her to buckle her seat belt, she would have ended up like her young friends. If the others had listened to her that night, their lives could have been spared so much pain. I had known that something was going to happen that night. I had tried to do what I thought was the right thing. Once again, I found it is difficult to alter other people's destinies. I feel blessed that I was able to warn my daughter and that she did listen to me. We had a special bond, Daya and I—as well as sharing the knowledge that guardian angels looked after her.

Author's note: My daughter since reminded me of something else that happened on that night that she felt important I document: Right after the car crashed and rolled to a stop upside down on the side of the road, the person who reported the accident—who lived at the closest farmhouse—came outside where she met a man standing along the road who claimed to be the young driver's father. He waited along the roadside for the emergency crews to do their jobs. The man spoke softly to the woman as she stood transfixed in horror at the upside-down vehicle. Dust and smoke hung around the crash site like a misty fog in the cold night air. Rock and roll music could still be heard coming from inside the wrecked car along with the screams of the two young girls still inside.

The man claiming to be the driver's father remained until the emergency crews had finally arrived and all the girls were being treated. The woman who'd reported the accident said that she wasn't sure when the driver's dad had left the scene. Several others stated that they had seen or talked to him as well.

The witnesses told the young driver that her father had been there checking on her to make sure she was okay. When the driver responded with a blank stare, they went on to describe him—an accurate description. That would be strange enough by itself, but the fact was that her father lived in Florida—3,000 miles away—at the time of the accident.

Daya, age 2, in Daddy's army boots

PARTY WARNING NOT HEEDED

M y daughter, Daya, and I have had many unusual experiences. This one began as a quiet, normal weekend night for my teenage daughter.

Once again, I sat on the sofa as she arrived with a request: could she go to a party that night. She explained it was in a 'good' neighborhood, that she knew the people giving the party, and that the parents would be home.

By all indications, it would be a quiet, safe party.

But, once again, that 'everything's not right' feeling bubbled up inside me. I shared my feelings and said she could go but to promise to leave by eleven. I felt if she stayed longer something would happen to her or her car. Unclear on the specifics, I simply knew she should not stay later than that time.

"Am I going to get into a car crash or something?" she asked.

"No," I replied. But I did feel her car was in some kind of danger.

She prepared to leave and I reminded her about leaving early to avoid danger. She gave me that 'oh Dad' look that teenagers do so well, and left the house.

I continued to feel uneasy about the party, but I knew I needed to allow my daughter to live her own life and experience her own karma. I just didn't want her to get hurt in the process. It was always hard for me to know if I should force myself into her life when I had these feelings.

Though I'd warned her, but I wondered if she had really listened.

It was about quarter to midnight when my daughter called, asking for my help. She told me that a gang had vandalized her car, and she needed my help to get it back home.

It turned out that the nice neighborhood party had been visited by a local gang who were upset about not being invited. The gang members fired a couple of rounds into the air, then proceeded down the street with baseball bats, smashing the windows and windshields, denting hoods and knocking the mirrors from more than 20 cars.

By the time the police arrived the punks were long gone and the street was littered with broken glass.

When I arrived I discovered my daughter had not left the party at or before eleven. The gang had shown up around ten minutes after eleven. I reminded her that had she left when I told her to, she would not be looking at a damaged 'brand new' Honda.

It took a while to clear off the debris to get into the driver's seat. I gave her my truck keys and asked that she follow me.

I didn't feel a lecture would be any more effective than her seeing what happened when she failed to heed my warning. But I also knew I could not spend my entire life cautioning her about events and dangers; this was something that she needed to develop and to handle herself.

I felt that up to this point in our relationship I had in some ways enabled her by telling her too much. I vowed from that time forward to step back and let her get in tune with her own intuitive abilities, which I knew she had. We both learned a lesson that night.

SWAMI'S ADVICE

During a spiritual convocation in Los Angeles I sought guidance with a monk with whom I'd developed a personal relationship.

The question he and I discussed was when to use one's intuitive gifts and when is it improper to do so. He opened up an area of thinking that had eluded me. The specific issue was about when to say something and when to withhold information because people need to deal with their own karma—there is a fine line that exists between a sacred right to privacy and trespassing into a zone that interferes with the spiritual growth of another person.

I listened, at times teary eyed, ever so thankful for his authenticity. I came away with the following lessons of how to use my gifts:

- I shall not become one who entertains and amazes with predictions. Sharing information about others or events is not about providing amusement; nor is it to serve my ego or self-aggrandize.
- Having knowledge about someone or an event is not about power, but compassion.
- Successful message delivery is often better delivered in stealth mode—people need to connect their own dots and so it's best to only provide the tools. This way they will obtain the message themselves and learn from the experience.
- Sometimes the best thing to do 'as a knower-seer of events to come' is to support others emotionally and spiritually.
- People do NOT need to know everything that will happen to them. How does that make them better people? It is best to direct others to handle their own personal issues. DO not tell them what to do, or

how to do it. Allow them, with assistance if needed, to discover their own path.

- Realize that no one, except for GOD, is one hundred percent certain of any outcome. Some visions can be misinterpreted by one's own emotions and belief system. The truth is always filtered through the eye of the beholder.

- Prediction/telling what will happen is not the goal. Preparation for their karmic goal is a much better intention. Too much information does not help another person make beneficial future choices.

- It's okay for me to have the information to help understand others— there's no requirement to pass it to anyone.

- Unless one is God (or an avatar) there is no deciding of a time of death.

- Compassion is more important than providing overzealous support which renders the person 'enabled'. Everyone needs to walk the highway of life independently, with their cheerleaders at roadside.

- Be casual and just share. Tell a story. People like stories. People learn from stories.

- Follow my heart always. Do with love first and foremost.

- Do not lecture anyone. Allow others to have their own truth without berating them. Truth is ever-evolving and changes with spiritual growth. In the end, the truth is whatever it is; it matters not what everyone believed it was.

- NEVER use intuitive gifts for ill purposes. Not gambling, or eavesdropping on minds or hearts. Respect the privacy of others.

- My gifts are NOT my gifts. ALL comes from the DIVINE. I am not the source. I am a channel through which God's love flows to others. Be that open channel.

- Be very careful about physically healing others. There are many karmic laws involved and big consequences when you upset the balance of karma. Disease is a way for karma to be worked out for the soul. Taking away that source of spiritual cleansing may not be the right thing to do. Sick people should visit doctors and attend appointments with others who deal in health. I need permission from the Divine before proceeding with any healing. The key is to not interfere unless I am instructed to do so.

AMAZING GRACE

It was during the summer of 1994 that a most wonderful and unexplainable event transpired in the lives of my daughter, Daya, and me.

I went to Los Angeles for a church convocation, and stayed in a downtown hotel in which the classes and meetings were held.

One afternoon, between events, my old friend Bob invited me to lunch at a local Indian restaurant a short walk from the hotel. We enjoyed a delicious lunch over great conversation then set out on our return trip to the hotel.

Many homeless people hung around the downtown streets. As we stepped around one corner, a man with a wild look on his face jumped up in front of us. He thrust a filthy finger at Bob as he shouted out a date, including the month and the year. Bob froze, and when I asked Bob the meaning he replied it was his birthdate and year. We were dumbfounded the man knew. He looked much like all the others who were without homes, except for a strange look in his eyes.

We continued to the other side of the street, still in shock from the episode. Outside the metro station steps there stood an old black man. He held a tarnished saxophone in his weathered hands and his beat-up instrument case lay open on the sidewalk, a few coins scattered inside.

I felt compelled to engage him and asked if he accepted requests. He said he did, so I asked if he'd play my favorite hymn, *Amazing Grace*.

He nodded and hinted a smile; said he'd give it a try. He lifted his dull sax to his chapped lips and softly played. As the music flowed, people stopped walking. Cars slowed, and drivers and passengers rolled down their windows. The music spilling from the instrument was unlike anything I'd ever heard.

Tears formed in my eyes. The old man gave the traditional hymn a jazz styling.

The remarkable thing about the music, however, was its effect on all those who had been running about. People coming up from the Metro station stairs stopped to listen. No one moved; all of us transfixed. And even the other men who were homeless seemed transported. It was as if we had all come together in a chapel.

When I looked at the musician, I noticed that a change had come over him as he played that song. His once dirty, street-hardened face and hands appeared softer. His eyes sparkled with a moist, far-away look. He held the saxophone tenderly, as if it were his child. As he finished the song he glowed—became radiant—a soft light came from him.

I placed a donation in his case. It felt as if I had put it in the collection basket at my church on Sunday.

He boasted a knowing smile across his ebony face. I asked him to play it again for me then I listened to it all the way back to the hotel. *Amazing Grace* bounced off the tall office buildings surrounding us.

When I boarded the plane to return home to Sacramento, that old man's face was etched in my mind. The sound of his music played within me. The memories of the song caused tingles up and down my spine, almost as if I were in love or being loved. I sat on the plane, completely at peace with myself and the world.

When I returned home, my daughter came to visit me. As I began to tell her the story of the old man and the song, she interrupted and asked if it had happened that past Thursday. I replied that it had. She asked if it had taken place about one in the afternoon. I confirmed that too. She then told me about her experience, the same day and time in Sacramento while I was still in LA.

She and her boyfriend had been driving around town, and she was trying to find some music on his car radio. As she was turning the dial, she happened upon the sounds of a saxophone playing *Amazing Grace*. She explained that it sounded different from anything she'd heard before. She described the style 'kind of like jazz'.

The song was so moving that they pulled off the road so they could listen to it with their full attention.

I was moved by her story. I found it wonderfully strange that a radio station could have been playing that same song, at the same time as my street musician was playing it for me in LA. Also, both versions of the song were played by a sax and both had that soft jazz sound to them. The reactions of my daughter and her boyfriend were just as emotional as mine and Bob's.

After we exchanged stories it was time for me to take my daughter to pick up her car. When I turned the key over to start my pickup truck, the radio was already playing *Amazing Grace*. It was not the same version, but it brought us a moment of reflection over all that had happened.

Then a blissful wave of love engulfed me as the impact of what had happened thoroughly sunk in.

I do not know how any father and daughter could ever feel any closer than we did at that moment. We will never be able to fully understand what happened, but we will always cherish the memory of *Amazing Grace*.

I continued to experience a deep sense of peace whenever I heard the hymn played or sung. I knew then, and know now, that God loves us and blesses us in so many ways.

> *"Amazing Grace! How sweet the sound*
> *That saved a wretch like me!*
> *I once was lost, but now am found,*
> *Was blind, but now I see."*
> John Newton

IF YOU BUILD IT—
THEY WILL COME

I built a new meditation room in the attic space above my garage. It had a pull-down ladder and a skylight that opened up for fresh air. I had tiled a small area next to an altar and added a carpet to cover the rest of the sanctuary. It held only two chairs comfortably, one for me and one for my guest, usually my tabby cat who sat as long as I was up there.

When it was complete I invited my daughter, Daya, to come see it. She kidded me because I used the phrase 'if you build it they will come' from the movie *Field of Dreams*. I told her that now that I had built it, *they*—angels or spiritual beings—would come.

We were alone in the house as my wife had gone shopping; she'd locked up before driving out of the garage, and closed the garage door too. She knew we'd be up in the attic space and had secured the rest of the house out of habit.

Daya and I sat in the new meditation room when the sounds of people walking to the door (that leads to the garage from inside the house). We remained quiet and peeked down the hole of the pull-down ladder. We heard the door open and saw light shining from inside the house onto the floor of the dark garage. Daya and I knew that no one else was in the house, so she thought that we might have an intruder. I reminded her once again of what I had been saying, 'if you build it, they will come.'

She quickly climbed down the ladder and rushed into the house, hoping to find whoever it was that had opened the door and made all the noise. She ran around inside the house for several minutes, checking under beds and looking in all the rooms while I enjoyed it all.

William "Rev. Bill" McDonald Jr.

When she returned she remained baffled that all the doors were still locked from the inside, and that no one was in the house. She and I smiled at each other and considered what I'd been saying.

I did build it, but did they come?

Author's note: The connection with my daughter remained strong, but I told her less and less. I wanted her to develop and trust her own intuitive feelings, which I already knew she had.

My daughter, Daya, on her wedding day, June 2002

MY DAUGHTER'S NEAR ACCIDENT

Both my children inherited psychic abilities to differing degrees. As the years passed I watched my daughter, Daya, become trusting of her gift.

On one occasion when she left West Sacramento on Highway 80 to drive to Fairfield she sensed something was going to happen. The feelings became stronger the closer she got to the town of Davis. As her senses became more intense she slowed her car.

Then it happened.

In her field of view a truck appeared to drop through the air on a collision course with Daya's vehicle. (On the other side of the divided highway—which she couldn't see because bushes were planted to separate eastbound and westbound traffic—the impact of a car striking a pickup had sent the truck airborne over the highway divider). She had, moments before, taken her foot off the gas.

The truck landed on the highway several feet in front of her car; momentum allowed it to slide into the other lane and created a clear path.

Her heart pounded as the scene unfolded before her eyes. Had she not followed her intuitive feelings to slow down, the truck would have landed on top of her car.

At that moment I was home, feeling uneasy about events—the evening and my daughter. Though I didn't know what kind of danger she was in, I felt something happening. I sent a silent prayer her way. Then I received one of those midnight calls.

"I didn't do anything to kill him. He was dead already!" Those were the first words I heard—not the most reassuring statement a parent wants to hear from their child.

My heart beat faster, in time with my daughter's rapid, breathless account of this man's death. She related her memory of his face during the accident, and went on to describe his body when she'd gone to him.

One of the first people to stop and help her at the scene of the accident was an off duty California Highway Patrol officer, a friend of my son's—someone she knew. Grateful was I that he'd given her his emotional support.

My daughter had saved her own life by listening to her inner voice. Learning to trust our intuitive feelings is a matter of great faith. That night she passed a major test of her faith in that ability!

ATTACKED IN THE CHURCH

The Sacramento Meditation Center, in the heart of Sacramento—where many homeless people congregated—offered a Friday night meditation. One particular rainy, winter night I volunteered as an usher, and welcomed a number of people who wanted to be out of the cold. Though they did not want to meditate, they were not discouraged from taking shelter.

One of the visitors was a young, muscular man who stood about 'six-six', weighed well over 250 pounds, and used a heavy wood and metal cane. Chills ran down my spine as he entered the building and glared at me. His stare was bone chilling; an evil eyed look. I felt like I'd been stared at by the devil himself.

Closer, he looked down at me but said nothing, then briskly pushed me aside with the cane and found a seat in the chapel. So heavy were the vibrations of hate, anger, and actual evil, I could not shake them off. My inner alarms sounded. Something was wrong.

The service began and I moved from the vestibule area to a lone seat at the very back. I sat next to the doors and had a full view of everyone inside. I watched the man who'd pushed me aside. He was restless, as if he was 'casing the joint'. I thought perhaps he was looking for something to steal. My guard was up.

The visiting Minister led the group meditation at the altar, but his briefcase had been placed near the back of the chapel. The evil stranger kept looking at the case, then moved over to it and opened it. When he put his hands inside it I quietly rushed over and gently touched his arm and requested to speak to him. I asked him to follow me out of the chapel. No one else saw this. No one saw us leaving out the door.

William "Rev. Bill" McDonald Jr.

When we reached the vestibule area and the doors to the chapel closed behind us he grabbed me by the throat with his huge hands. He lifted all 5 foot 6 inches of my 150-pound body off the floor, about a foot in the air. My feet dangled loose below. The rage registered on his face let me know he wanted to harm me.

I looked into his face as he took one hand off my neck—in order to grab his cane and raise it; his intention to strike me in the head. I said a silent prayer for protection knowing I was overmatched and overpowered.

His face was void of any love or compassion—the face of evil. He cocked the cane and swung the cane toward my face.

A total calm filled me; almost blissful. In that great peace I smiled at him while he steadfastly restrained my neck and had already released the strike.

Then suddenly he stopped. Mid-air assault to halt. He released my throat and set me back on the floor. He appeared to be frightened of someone standing behind me, and began to yell at 'both of us' that we were crazy. He insisted that there was a huge man behind me. He said the two of us caused him trouble then raced out onto the street, screaming that we were trying to kill him.

I was watching him as he made his way through the rain when a couple of men from the group came to check on what was happening. I explained as best I could. They shook their heads in wonder—I should have been hurt. One of them suggested that the man had been frightened off by one of my guardian angels.

My thoughts, exactly.

FATHER JACK

Thanksgiving 1990 saw my wife and me traveling to Santa Clara, in the San Francisco Bay Area. We'd decided to spend time with my wife's sister and her husband, Richard, who was fighting (and losing) a long battle with cancer. Usually we'd stay home for Thanksgiving, but it 'felt' right to visit and provide moral support.

We kept it casual. I wore a pair of clean, blue jeans and a nice t-shirt. Richard and I were relaxing on the front lawn when a large motorcycle pulled onto the driveway. The biker was a Catholic priest who dismounted and walked directly to me and asked, "You're a priest aren't you?"

I looked at him directly and decided to tease him with a totally Eastern response: "Not this lifetime, but in the past I was a priest." (Something I'd believed for most of my life).

"Yes you were. And *I know* who you were," he said.

I smiled and said nothing. It turned out the biker, Father Jack, was from my brother-in-law's neighborhood church. He'd ministered to Richard for some time, and came by that day to wish the family happy Thanksgiving, but on having found me there his focus had changed. Though casual with his question-statement—you're a priest aren't you—he was actually a little animated, as if he had discovered something and was excited to share it; which he did, though indirectly and cryptically at first.

He pointed to my right leg and stated it was shorter than the other leg—I'm not even sure my in-laws knew that; in fact my own children and others who know me don't know it. Yet he told me, not asked me, about my leg.

"That's true," I said (of the shorter leg).

He pulled out more facts from his bag of tricks.

Of course he had my attention; he was reciting facts about me. Then he dropped the bomb: he'd spent most of his adult life looking for me to give me a message.

He asked Richard if there was a place where he, Father Jack, could speak to me privately. I wondered about the good priest's sanity as we headed to a back room—his visions might be nothing more than delusion. He did seem a little odd, but I was curious enough to listen.

He began by telling me that as a small child he lived in a Catholic Children's Home in New York. It was there he began having dreams that were more like visions. In them, he saw me as I looked at this time in my life. Since he was about five months older than me we were both children during those times, yet his visions showed my likeness at 44 years old. He went on to explain that he saw these images throughout his life and had been on an active quest to find me— decades of searching.

He shared that he'd traveled to places that he 'felt' or 'sensed' I might be. He went to Vietnam and visited the same parts of the country that I had, but only after I'd left. He went to Sacramento and worked there for a few years, but I'd been in the Bay Area then. When he moved to the Bay Area, I had moved away. He'd missed me until we ended up at Richard's house this particular day—a time of year, Thanksgiving, when I'd usually be home.

When I asked him what the important message was—one that had taken him on an extensive search—he quizzed me first, asking about the dreams I had as a child and as an adult.

He asked if I'd dreamed about building schools, colleges and homes for single-moms—a specific kind of question to throw out there, but I had had those kinds of dreams as a child and as an adult.

He asked me what college I'd attended and, when I replied that I'd graduated from The University of San Francisco, he asked me if I knew it was a Jesuit University run by The Society of Jesus.

I nodded and asked why he'd raised that point.

He then went on to explain that I resembled the founder of the Jesuits: Saint Ignatius of Loyola. He suggested I take a look at drawings and paintings of the man. He then shared that Ignatius had one leg shorter—the same side as me—from a war wound. Father Jack went on about the similarities between me and Saint Ignatius; a long list.

At last he explained that it had been revealed to him that I, Bill McDonald, was the reincarnated soul of Saint Ignatius of Loyola. He had been instructed to inform me; thus he'd spent a lot of time looking for me.

I wanted to be cautious about what Father Jack had said. It could have been a strange dream—I had sensed his thoughts might be confused, but he did appear genuine in his declaration. Ultimately, the claim was something I could choose to explore on my own.

When I went to tell my wife, Carol, the priest had already let the cat out of the bag at Thanksgiving Dinner. My brother-in-law, Richard, wasn't sure what to say as his ultra-conservative beliefs did not include reincarnation. Hearing his own parish priest telling him about reincarnation placed an orthodox Richard in the middle of an assortment of baffling faith-based questions.

That week I decided to go to a Catholic bookstore and pick up some material about Saint Ignatius of Loyola. When I discovered his autobiography Carol and I were stunned when we saw Ignatius' image. Yes, he looked like me—or I looked like him.

The real surprise came when I began to read his life story. Our lives seemed to have paralleled in interesting ways: likes and dis- likes, mannerisms, temperaments, where we traveled, and our outlook on life.

Besides the short leg, and both of us being warriors wounded in battles, Ignatius' travels across Europe took in many of the same places I felt compelled to visit when I was a young man.

There was a reference about him climbing out a window of the Notre Dame in Paris to meditate on the rooftop of that church. I had done exactly that in 1965, having discovered an old stairway that went up to a window which I could open and get out onto the roof—certainly not something that many people think about doing.

As well, when I'd visited Vatican City it felt like a reunion—so at home did I feel, and perhaps others perceived me at home, that I'd wandered around for hours before someone asked who I was and what I was doing.

Ignatius had even tried vegetarianism as I had. There were many things we had in common and yet doubts lingered—the messenger, Father Jack, perhaps slightly unhinged.

I also experienced a bit of wondering—an egotistical kind of wondering—and that frightened me.

The thing is, even after I let the 'knowledge' go, others—as in several dozen—who were not connected with each other or with Father Jack, have suggested the same connection: Saint Ignatius and I.

When I first met Yogiraj Gurunath Siddhanath in August 2008 he called me 'The General'. At first I thought this had to do with my military experience, or even in reference to my lifetime as a warrior. Then I read that Ignatius went by that nickname; taken from his title of 'Secretary General' of The Society of Jesus. Those who worked with him all called him The General. I do not know if Gurunath was tuning into that connection, or not, but it was another piece of the puzzle.

Although I have joked that I'd have to be one of the biggest fools ever to start believing that any of this was possibly true, and that there can be a danger to believing these kinds of things, I know one thing for sure: I know who I am today in this lifetime. And this lifetime is enough of a challenge.

In studying the life of Saint Ignatius I have found him to be someone I would love to emulate in my own spiritual life; truly a great spiritual warrior and lover of God. I am honored to have shared his dreams.

Author's note: Some time after meeting me, Father Jack chose to be initiated in Kriya Yoga meditation technique as taught by the Self-Realization Fellowship. He had to get special permission from the President of SRF because the organization did not want him to be breaking his own vows to his church.

He had a very rough and rocky relationship with his own church leadership. They finally ended up retiring him from all his official church duties when he fell victim to one of those African Scams on the Internet that involved others in the church community losing money.

IGNATIUS

A Quote from a lecture and an article titled:
"An Ancient Sage With Eternal Wisdom"
BY:

—— PAUL COUTINHO, S.J. IGNATIAN SPIRITUALITY, SOUTH ASIA, GUJARAT, INDIA

" Ignatius is one of those Great Seers (Rishis) who attained Enlightenment (Satori in Zen Buddhism) on the banks of the river Cardoner. It was here that 'the eyes of his understanding began to be opened, not that he saw any vision, but he understood and learnt many things, both spiritual and earthly and this was so great an enlightenment that everything seemed new to him'. From this moment on Ignatius was convinced that 'if there were no Scriptures to teach us these things of faith, he would be resolved to die for them, solely because of what he has seen'. Ignatius found his own secret religion that helped him to scale mystical heights and also led him into constant conflict with people in power and institutions of his time."

AN EXORCISM

There was always a solid bond between my little sister, Marsha, and me.

I remember playing mind-reading games with each other when we were children. One of us thought of a short sentence or phrase (Mary had a little lamb; Twinkle, twinkle, little star; Happy birthday, and others) and repeated it in our mind. The other had three guesses as to what it was. It was not too challenging for us; our success rate was high. We'd do something similar with cards from a deck of 52. One would look at the card and send the information to the other. We did not count it as correct unless we got both suit and value correct. We limited this to one 'guess' only. We far exceeded what would be considered 'random' luck of the draw; often 30 out of 52.

As with many people who grow up in abusive and dysfunctional families, her life 'after leaving home' has had its difficult patches. Given my soft spot for my sister, she knew she could count on me when needed.

One particular situation was beyond anything I'd ever encountered.

My sister had many good reasons to believe in a powerful, negative force in her life. I listened open-mindedly to her list of 'concerns' and found myself asking her if she'd asked a Catholic priest to perform an exorcism.

She shared the details of a first request to one particular priest. She'd approached him and shared the story of the strange happenings, to which he responded that he'd help her. The following week she discovered he had 'quit' the priesthood and left town. He never contacted her again.

Her second request was to a priest who also agreed that it was a case for an exorcism. The following week, after agreeing to perform the rite, she contacted the church and found out he'd died of a heart attack.

At this point she made the decision to ask me to help her rid her family of this evil energy. Though she was fearful of what might happen (to me), she was desperate for help.

She was the most afraid I had ever seen her, providing a list of improbable happenings that included a child's doll spontaneously bursting into flames. One of her children reported seeing 'bad people' in the house.

I knew that she needed a strong spiritual and emotional anchor to hold her life together.

It was then she dropped the bombshell, explaining about a possible connection to Daddy Bray. Daddy Bray—a man from my past when I'd lived in Hawaii in 1964—had been kind to me but also had showed me ways that spiritual power could be used in negative ways.

The reason she believed it might be related was that apparently our mother had forged an affiliation with 'Daddy' Bray in 1967—she'd dropped in to meet him in on her way back from meeting me when I was on R & R in Japan. My sister explained that my mother and a group of Daddy's followers had formed a secret group in California and Nevada.

This was news to me and I was stunned.

I decided I needed more information, including help with how to go about this so-called 'exorcism'. I knew something about these kinds of supernatural forces, but I wasn't an expert. I chose to visit Father Jack, a Catholic priest I knew in the Bay Area. He told me all he knew of the process, gave me a large container of holy water, and wrote some prayers for me to give to Marsha for her to use.

At first, the trip to Marsha's was a regular drive. But when I exited the freeway and headed down a country road I encountered a blanket of fog; strange because the rest of the valley was clear that night.

It became difficult to see a few feet ahead, but the outline of a dead dog on the road was clear and I drove around its body. Just ahead of that there appeared a dead rat on the asphalt. I continued to push through the fog and came upon another dead creature: a cat. A few yards later the body of a blackbird, then a squirrel, a raccoon, and an opossum. The excess of animal carnage was other worldly. More animal carcasses presented themselves within the thick soup through which I drove.

William "Rev. Bill" McDonald Jr.

I recalled Marsha's car had broken down on this same stretch of road the week before. She'd told me she'd driven into a blanket of fog and that the car had simply stopped running. She'd become frightened, but had been able to start the vehicle and continue.

I was in this same area, and saw more dead animals, collectively, on the road than I had ever seen in my whole life. Even the gallon of holy water didn't do much for my courage.

My concern peaked when the next animal I encountered was the symbol of my spiritual energy: the beloved owl.

I asked myself if it could be true; if that's what I had truly seen. Of all the road-kill I have ever seen I'd never witnessed a dead owl on the road. The body count was in the dozens; a freakish and frightening occurrence.

I'd gotten into helping my sister, only halfheartedly believing Marsha—I believed she'd emotionally created a great deal of what had happened to her. Now, as I drove through the fog, I became convinced something dreadfully evil was afoot.

I arrived at Marsha's apartment and unloaded everything I thought I'd need to change her situation: the gallon of holy water, the written prayers, incense, and some holy pictures to put around her apartment. I had no clue what I was doing, but put together a ceremony that combined what I had been given from Father Jack and from what I remembered from my studies under that old kahuna, Daddy Bray.

The unfamiliar territory called for me to make it up as I went along. But my theory was solid—good overcomes evil.

I remembered watching Daddy Bray use chants as a weapon against evil. He'd told me about the great powers that come from the vibrations of sound.

I used a form of chanting along with my prayers. I did the best I could and trusted that something would work. When I finished my ceremony I instructed Marsha to use the holy water I had given her; splash it liberally on her windows and doors for the following 40 days. I asked her to burn incense and maintain a daily routine of meditation and prayer. Then, exhausted, I stumbled out of her house and returned home.

Home: my sanctuary. After I'd finished my meditation, I looked into the darkness of my backyard. I more than felt a protective energy surrounding my home and guarding my family; I saw it. A dome of energy like an inverted glass bowl covered my entire property. The protective cover was as real as the moon and stars.

Then my physical and spiritual eyes saw demons attempting to break through the energy field.

Though it was frightening to see the potential invaders—I'd never truly believed in devils, demons, or evil spirits—I also felt the strength of the protective dome.

I realized at that moment that people who do not have real spiritual energy and power should never attempt to perform a ceremony such as I had. The results could be dangerous to them physically, mentally, and spiritually, as had been proven in the situation with the two Catholic priests Marsha had contacted. I went to bed, concerned about Marsha's situation and I wondered about Father Jack's fate.

Before the end of the week I received a call from Father Jack. He had been admitted to a hospital in Mountain View. His superiors believed he was having an emotional breakdown and had committed him for observation. He slurred when he spoke to me—from the drugs he'd been given. Apparently his talk about reincarnation had concerned those in the chain of command. If he wanted to remain a Catholic priest he had to submit himself to an evaluation process which included hospitalization.

The scorecard registered three priests' careers ended or interrupted. But that was the worst of it for everyone involved.

Happy was I that my sister's life began to change for the better. Though I remained confused about all that had transpired, it pleased me that her lot was improved. I've put it down to one of many mysteries of my life.

EBONY ANGEL

It was around 1991 when a series of events took place that got my attention; the kind that moved me to rethink some of my beliefs about children and making judgements about them.

The phone rang well past ten o'clock at night. Usually I'd be in bed by then—most people I knew understood this and never called late—but I was still up and dressed.

The voice of an experienced social worker from a local foster home—where I'd mentored a 17 year old boy the previous year—was calling me for advice. Strange, because we'd never met; she knew about me from the boy.

The agency had a full staff of counselors and so there was no logical reason she'd call to consult. I'm not even sure if she realized how unusual the initiation of the call or the following conversation was, but she spoke to me as if I were an old friend and colleague.

Since I subscribe to the 'everything has meaning and purpose, there are no accidents' school of thought, I listened to her concerns.

She told me a 17 year old girl was in great physical danger from her stepfather who had pulled a knife on her and threatened to harm her. The social worker described all the problems facing the girl. Then she asked me what I thought *I* could do to help her.

The question at first floored me, since she could have called any number of qualified sources, but she called me, a total stranger, for assistance. It was clear to me there was a higher power at work—after all, the social worker had an entire department at her disposal.

The young girl needed help; I knew I had to provide that help. She gave me the address where the girl was hiding from her stepfather. I reassured the social worker, and promised to take care of it.

I wrote down the address. Even though I knew I'd written it correctly, I knew it was wrong. I headed to Sacramento on a cold, foggy December night—the week before Christmas.

I spotted the outline of two police cars through the fog as I drove up to the address—a shopping center parking lot. When I shared my intent and reason for visit they offered to help. They punched the address into their computer and discovered it was a wrong number. They volunteered to help me find the girl by going door to door down the long street of apartment buildings.

When they had knocked on the doors of a half dozen apartments they found her and brought her to me. She was a large, athletic-looking young girl with an innocent, child-like look. She trustingly climbed in my pickup and I pulled out into the fog.

Once we were headed toward Elk Grove she introduced herself and stared at me while I drove. She told me she'd been dreaming about me ever since she was a young girl; she'd seen my face many times in her dreams and knew it would be okay to go with me.

I was a little stunned and considered it might be a 'foster-kid con job' but the tone of her voice and her body language suggested honesty. I remained silent.

We arrived home around midnight, but everyone was up waiting to see her. My daughter welcomed her with a hug and my wife made her hot chocolate and served some cookies. We listened to her as she explained the problems in her life; her birthday had just passed—not that she'd celebrated.

I wondered about leaving her alone in our house while we were off at school and work the next day but, as soon as I thought that, she said "I know what you are all thinking about me, taking your things if I am alone in your house; please trust me, I won't do you any harm." Her voice echoed that of having been previously labeled, that of race and age (teenager).

I was impressed that she could pick up my thoughts, since I hadn't given her any indication of my concern, but thought it was perhaps a logical guess.

My wife and daughter said their goodnights and the young woman and I sat in the family room. She relaxed in a big, soft easy chair and I sat on the long sofa—the other end occupied by our old, fat cat. All of a sudden she stopped talking and looked directly at the cat whose hair stood straight up. The cat focused on a spot between us on the sofa. The young girl pointed to the cushion, which was pressed down as if someone had just sat on it.

"There's someone sitting on the couch with you. Can you see anyone?" asked the girl.

All I could see was the cushion pushed down and the cat freaking out with its eyes fixed on the spot. A slight breeze passed, sending chills up and down my spine. I didn't move as I tried to shift my attention back to this young woman sitting across from me. The conversation continued on, but every once in a while I glanced sideways to observe the slightly crushed sofa cushion and the alert cat.

Her conversation style was simplistic. It was like talking with a child of seven instead of 17, yet we discussed deep principles of Zen and yoga as well as various spiritual concepts. Though she did not use big words she was intuitive, easily grasping what I was saying. It was as if she was a spiritual savant. It left me wondering about her identity.

The spare bedroom downstairs had been my personal meditation room for 20 years. The room would be quiet and peaceful. When we spoke the next day I learned the room was also a place for visions. She told me that, when she had gotten into bed, my mother had come to her and tucked her in. She described how a dark-skinned, long-haired woman wearing an orange robe made her feel safe and at peace.

I stood there listening to her and wondering if she was talking about my guru, Paramahansa Yoganada. I grabbed a copy of his Autobiography of a Yogi, which has a color photo of him with long black hair and wearing an orange robe. I asked her, "Did she look like this?"

"Oh yes, that is her," she said excitedly. "She was there last night and helped me get to sleep. Was that your mother?"

I had to explain to her that *she* was actually a *he*. That it was my guru—she had described—that had helped her get to sleep. My mother had passed away the year before, and did not fit the description.

We engaged in a long conversation about reincarnation, forgiveness, karma, and a host of other subjects. I was so surprised that this young girl had been gifted with a visit or a vision of my very own guru. She took it all in stride as if it weren't anything out of the ordinary.

She spent three days with us before the Sacramento County Child Protective Services called. They wondered why the girl was at my house and why the foster agency had called me instead of them. They told me that I had no legal right to keep this young girl at my home; they were sending a police car to pick her up later that day. I knew in my heart that she needed to go, but this was just a few days before Christmas. I hated to see her spend it at the children's shelter.

When I broke it to her that she couldn't stay with us any longer, she began to cry. She had really enjoyed her short stay with us, and it was killing her to have to leave. She told me a story of what had happened to her that morning when I was at work.

She said that she had been sitting on the edge of the bed looking at an old photo (Again she'd thought it my mother. It was a black and white photo of my guru taken minutes before he died. It shows a much-aged guru, and that is why she did not relate it to the photo of the young man in the orange robe she'd seen the day before.) She said that when she stared at the photo she'd become relaxed and felt at peace, after which she felt something pressing on her upper leg. When she pulled up her pant leg she saw the impression of the face of an owl (like the impressed lines one gets when sleeping on textured fabric and it leaves lines on the skin).

She said the owl's face made her feel loved.

I explained my lifelong history with owls and symbols representing owls. It seems that whenever something very special and spiritual is about to happen in my life, or when I need a sign to refresh my faith, an owl visits (in some form). Sometimes it might be a real owl flying across my windshield, or overhead. Other time it is a hooting or screeching outside my window. It might be a photo of an owl someone passes to me; any number of serendipitous deliveries, but an owl nonetheless.

When this symbolic visitor shows up in my life, I know things are okay, and that was what I told her.

She sat there crying, both for joy and from the sadness of having to leave me. Soon it was time to go. The police arrived and took her, making her sit in the back seat as if she were under arrest. It was so sad for me to see. She reached up and pressed the window with her hand. I touched it on the outside. I looked at her for that last time as the police pulled away; tears flowed down her checks. I could hardly see her face through all my own.

I watched her leave, feeling as if I had lost an old friend.

Who was this young 'ebony angel' who spent a few days in my life and who has never left my mind since? Why did the group home call me out of the blue? Who was on the sofa with me and my cat? Why did she see my guru? What caused her to have an outline of an owl's face on her leg? Did she really dream about me for years as a child?

I still do not know the answers. All I know is that there are no accidents in life. We served each other for some purpose, and I am grateful to have had those few days with my ebony angel.

THE HITCHHIKER

For several days a feeling kept reminding me someone special was waiting for me. As if I had an appointment. It got to the point I couldn't get it out of my mind. Hebrews 13:2 played like a mantra—constantly: *Be not forgetful to entertain strangers; for thereby some have entertained angels unawares.*

I went to the local bookstore and picked up one book—Linda Goodman's Star Signs. It was stacked on a lower shelf; I had to stoop down to see it there. I'd reached down and pulled it out among dozens of other books. It seemed to be a magnet—I felt drawn to it. So intense was the feeling that I opened the book immediately. The Bible quote from Hebrews 13:2, which had been present in my mind (all week long), jumped out.

I did not know what specifically I was to do or whom I was going to run into. I trusted my inner feelings would lead me to 'an appointment' at the right place and time. I relaxed and let the thought go.

Later in the week while working in downtown Sacramento I got an urge to leave work early and head home. The feelings were too strong to ignore. As I headed south on Highway 99, the Bible passage returned. I knew something was about to happen, so I became alert for what it might be. The feelings became stronger the further south I drove.

When I passed the South Sacramento Kaiser Hospital, only about five miles from my house, I saw a young man hitchhiking alongside the highway. It was illegal to hitchhike there—he wasn't near an on-ramp and was standing where it was unsafe to pull over. It was obvious he didn't have a clue how to thumb a lift.

It didn't feel like an option; I simply pulled over—he had to run about 100 feet to get to my pickup truck. By the time he was at the side window I saw his youth—later I discovered he was only 22 years old. He wore a short sleeved shirt, and he didn't even have a jacket. He had taken a pair of white socks and had fashioned gloves over both of his arms. Beaten up by the weather and life in general, soaked from sleeping in a field (the night before) by the highway, the rain had continued to dampen him and his spirits all day.

He looked in at me through my truck window, but pulled back with a strange look on his face when he got a good look at me. I asked him where he was heading. He replied that he was trying to get to Texas, to find his stepdad. I told him to hop in the truck and I would take him a short way.

He smelled like someone who had been living out on the streets for weeks. His rancid body odor filled the truck cab. He was filthy and he was so chilled he shook. When I took the turnoff, I asked him to stay in the truck. I took him to my home so he could warm up and eat.

When we got home, my daughter's expression was a 'what the heck?'

I showed the young man the bathroom where he could take a hot shower and gave him some of my clothing, then tossed his rags into the garbage. When he was clean and freshly dressed I took him to the garage and pulled out the camping gear; if this kid was going to survive he needed some basic equipment.

I filled a backpack with essentials including a waterproof tarp under which he could shelter. I added a wool blanket and some comfort items from the house and added underwear, t-shirts, sweaters, socks, jeans, and most importantly: a jacket. I also gave him an old Oakland Raider's baseball cap and a bag to carry extra food and clothing. This boy was fully equipped.

He was grateful and polite when I made him lunch, but he looked at me in the same way he had when we first saw each other on the highway. I asked him what he was thinking.

He told me that he had left his grandmother's house up on the northern coast of California because she had died. He had no one to turn to and no place to call home. He told me about all his time spent in foster homes and about the lousy life he had been living. He'd decided to hitchhike to Texas to see if his stepfather would take him in.

He went on to tell me how he got to that place on the highway and what had happened to him the night before—the rainstorm had drenched him. He'd been unable to stay dry because he'd had no tent. His sleeping bag had been ruined so he'd thrown it away. He had no jacket or spare clothing.

He continued talking, and it was easy for me to see that he was desperate and depressed. The night before, he'd felt that he had absolutely nothing in his life for which to live. There was nobody in his life to help him or care about him. The inner pain he'd felt had been tremendous, he said.

I could empathize since I'd felt this way many times during my younger years.

As he talked about his night of despair, I could tell how close this young man had come to thoughts of suicide. He had felt so unloved and unwanted; even the weather was against him.

At this point in his conversation, his eyes got that fixed look on me again.

He told me that at his lowest point of despair, the night before, he had some kind of 'real-life dream,' as he called it, while he was totally awake. He saw a man who looked just like I did: same clothing, same beard, hair, eyes, and voice. He believed I was the one who had been in his real-life dream the previous night. He did not understand how or why. He went on to say that 'this man' came to him with a smile on his face as he reached out and said something.

I stopped his story at this point. I opened a kitchen drawer, reached in and pulled out an opened pack of sugarless chewing gum. His eyes opened wide.

'Some people have said that I have a special psychic gift. When I hand you this, you will understand more fully what happened to you last night,' I said.

He stated that in his real-life dream the man who looked like I did had put the package of chewing gum into his hands. Then, the man in the dream went on to say something to him.

"And the man said that everything would be all right. God loves you." I finished his sentence for him.

The young man let out a gasp. He said that was word for word what the man in his dream had said to him. Those were the exact words that the night before gave him enough hope to continue his journey to Texas.

My daughter, who had been watching all this transpire, couldn't believe all that she heard. The kitchen was very quiet for a few moments as we tried to figure out what had taken place. We had just witnessed something incredibly special. We did not have a clue as to how or what had happened, or why.

I gave the young man a hug. We got back into my pickup truck, and I drove him to the best spot to catch a ride heading south on Highway 99. I put a few dollars in his pocket and handed him a raincoat so he would be comfortable. He got out of my truck, and I watched him walk away down the road. He turned one last time to look back at me, sitting there in my truck.

"Thanks," he called out.

"Thank God," I replied.

He walked over to the on-ramp for the highway to continue his journey. I started up my truck and turned around to head home. My eyes were beginning to tear; figured it must have been all the rain, but I knew this was much deeper. I knew God had given me a special gift that day.

That happened back in 1991, and I have been sending out prayers for this young man ever since. I do not know his name or where he is, but I know that in some strange and wonderful way our paths had crossed. Our lives have been forever changed because I listened to that voice within me. How many more strangers are waiting out there for others to discover and help? How many are 'angels unawares?'

GOODBYE, BECKY

My sister's oldest daughter was a wild teenager; no virgin to the life of drugs and sex. Her anger toward the world could throw her into mean and abusive moods. However, when Becky lay dying a slow and painful death, all of her transgressions meant little to me. Instead, I pictured the toddler with a huge smile and healthy laugh. I remembered the innocent little girl I once took to Marine World to ride an elephant.

I will always remember her as an angel.

At 30 years old she should have been starting her life, but she'd already suffered a decade of illness with HIV—now she had full-blown AIDS.

I'd watched her change over the years from an angry person to a helpless skeleton. My heart broke for her and I wondered if someplace along the way I'd missed a connection to help her. I searched my mind for a moment in the past when I could have done more to help her as her uncle, as another human being?

When Becky was down to her last few days of life she was at her mother's home—my sister Marsha's apartment. I witnessed that physically she was stiffening, as if slowly dying from the feet up. I couldn't move her legs; they were locked in place.

She could barely talk, and when she did make a sound it was impossible to tell what she was saying. It all sounded like a muffled crisis call.

I worked hard to control my emotions so as not to give her any fears, but inside I was repulsed and sickened by the vision of the dying soul in front of me. Her eyes were sunken into her skull. Inwardly I compared her to a victim at a Nazi extermination camp.

But I held her cold hand and knew there was no more hope. I believed she was holding on for her six-year-old daughter, Marcella—such a beautiful child.

I celebrated that Becky had been able to take a trip to Hawaii with her daughter that fall, creating memories for the whole family—that's where she wanted her ashes taken. And as I worked my way through 'being' with Becky I gave her permission to go 'home'.

So strong was I in front of her, and yet each time I left the apartment and got into my car I couldn't hold back. I'd sob for Becky and for her daughter and for my sister. The pain I felt from seeing Becky in pain was overwhelming—but nothing compared to what she suffered.

I returned each day to offer support but felt so inadequate. I'd never had any experience dealing with this kind of killer disease.

It also hurt me that others seemed to be afraid to go and visit Becky—God help them if they had to touch her. Sadly that was the curse of AIDS; people were so afraid of it and therefore afraid of those who suffered from it. In addition, the lack of compassion based on the 'origin' of AIDS was unfair, unwarranted, and unbelievable—she got it from her 'lifestyle' and therefore it was 'her' choice. My heart broke a thousand times when anyone said that. Not just for Becky, but for all the Becky's, and for the very condemners as well. My soul ached because of the absence of compassion and my mind beseeched it—had basic kindness absconded with sensibility? Were we all to be cast out in an ocean of dismissal?

Yes, all of us. I was forced to examine my own thinking. Had I been less than sympathetic toward people with AIDS? What about those with lung cancer who happened to have smoked? *They* all created their own health problems. So had all those overweight people dying of heart attacks. Could I generalize about more sub-groups and categorize them? Judge them? Had I reduced my level of compassion based on a scale?

Watching Becky dying taught me as much about my own self as it did about others.

When Becky died in the early morning hours a week before Christmas Day, relief flooded into all the cracks of my broken heart. She suffered no more.

In the days, months, and years that followed my attitude altered, my capacity for compassion became category-less.

Though it is unfortunate it took her death to educate me about compassion, her legacy is a gift which I treasure.

Author's note: This was the hardest story to write. I realized how terrible the disease of AIDS really is and how little compassion there is for people who have it. The death of my niece, Becky, taught me some hard lessons about life and myself.

Becky as a toddler with her brother, Billy

CAT ANGEL

We once had a chubby and lovable tabby called 'Critter'. She belonged to my son before he went into the Army and eventually off to the Gulf War. That is how my wife and I became the caretakers of this furry feline.

It didn't take long for Critter to take over the house—she was simply full of love. She knew how to get anything she wanted by turning on the charm. The cat was not a fighter but definitely a lover. She got along with all the neighborhood cats and dogs, allowing any of them into our yard.

When I went into the garden she followed, stopping where and when I did. She lay or sat at my feet as I weeded or planted, sometimes causing me to trip over her. She was a people cat—loved to be around us all the time.

I had a room built into the attic space above my garage ceiling; my sanctuary, a quiet place for prayer and meditation. I put a couple of chairs right under the skylight I'd had installed. I'd sit in one chair and old Critter often wandered up the pull-down steps and hopped up onto the other chair (it had a soft cushion on it).

No matter how long my session of prayer or mediation, she remained with me—purring. She left when I left and we went into the house together. If I left the pull-down stairs extended she'd often wander back up and sit in 'her' chair.

The time I most enjoyed her company was bedtime. Her nightly routine began by jumping on our mattress and pouncing along from the foot of our bed up to our pillows. She'd circle around a few times, rubbing her furry body into our faces then settle between our heads. I loved to pet her soft body, which started her purring like a small motor. But in order to get any sleep I'd have to nudge her toward our feet where she'd then curl up into a ball and rest until about four in the morning. At that time she demanded to be let outside.

Once, when I was away on business, my wife called me with some bad news. Stray dogs had run loose, entered our yard and attacked Critter. Though my wife was not home when it happened a neighbor had stopped the attack and rushed Critter to the vet. Sadly, Critter did not survive her injuries. Though my wife and I were spared the pain of seeing her bloody body or hearing her cries for help, not being there created an emptiness inside me; no closure.

Not long after Critter's death, on a cold Sunday morning when I decided to sleep in, I felt a familiar bounce at the end of the mattress. It was followed by the pouncing of little cat-like feet walking up the bed toward my head. I felt the touch of fur on my neck and the back of my head. I could hear the purring and feel the warmth of breath in my ear. I reached behind my head expecting to stroke my cat but, when I did, there was nothing there. No cat.

A gentle current of energy flowed up my spine as I realized what had happened. I knew Critter was gone, but I knew the sensations were real. She'd returned to say goodbye in the only way a cat angel could. Peace returned. I had closure.

VOICES, THUNDER, LIGHT, DEATH, AND HEALING

It was one of the strangest and most difficult of times for my relatives and family. Our son was in Saudi Arabia with the Army as part of Desert Storm. My wife and I were concerned for his safety. My brother-in-law was nearing the end of his long fight against cancer; and I was 3,000 miles away from home—in Washington, D.C.

My family really needed my presence at this time, but my job demanded that I leave home for three weeks.

The first day away I received a phone call informing me that my daughter got a speeding ticket. The second day another call—my daughter had a skiing accident and her knee was injured so badly she'd need an operation. A few days later my wife called to tell me she'd given permission to a young boy—whom I mentored at that time—to move into our house (because he'd turned 18 and had to leave his group home).

Days later, I received word that my brother-in-law had died.

And so this was the background for my first two weeks away from home.

In the meantime, my temporary home was a small hotel room which contained a desk and overhead lamp. I'd put a photo of my guru on the desk so the light could shine on it when I meditated. The problem was that the light did not work, no matter how many times I fiddled with it. The photo remained under the non-working light.

Around four in the morning, on the day my brother-in-law had passed away (information I learned later), a thunderous sound shook me wide-awake. "It is only a dream!" The words thundered through the room then the light came on by itself, lighting up the photo of my guru.

I knew then that things would be fine. After all, life is but a dream.

When I arrived home my daughter was on crutches with a temporary cast on her leg. She told me that she needed an operation on her injured knee, but I informed her that there was nothing wrong with it.

She gave me a look of disbelief and said, "What are you talking about, Dad, are you blind?"

I asked her to come with me to my old meditation room on the first floor of the house and lie down on the rug. I held her knee with both hands and began to concentrate on pushing energy into the joint. I tensed up and my whole body trembled as I visualized energy and light moving into her knee. The session lasted about three minutes at which time I asked her to stand up and walk.

She did just that, leaving the crutches and temporary cast on the carpet.

Later in the week, I took her back to Kaiser Hospital to see a knee specialist. He examined her and stated that there must have been a mistake in the first medical review of her condition. Nothing wrong with the knee—operation?

A footnote to this healing took place about a month later at my house when my daughter fell down a full flight of stairs. She cried out in great pain, and the foster child in our home saw it happen and ran to get me. When I reached her she continued to writhe in agony. I moved her knee back and forth and felt small pieces of cartilage or bone moving around inside her kneecap. The entire joint seemed to have exploded and was now much worse than the first time she'd injured it.

I told her nothing was wrong with it.

I got her into the meditation room and placed my hands on her knee. The pain stopped and she was once again able to get up and walk. She told me she was 90 percent better; just a slight stiffness and soreness remained, but nothing that would prevent her from doing normal physical activities.

For some reason, she had to go through the injury and healing process twice. Maybe that is what she needed to believe that the first time was not an incorrect medical diagnosis but an authentic healing.

FOUR FUNERALS

My Father-In-Law

I loved my father-in-law very much despite the fact he'd become a totally different person when he drank alcohol. At those times he changed for the worse—not a happy drunk, rather vulgar and crude. He used profanity and became verbally abusive, and loud.

My wife and I had lived through our youth dealing with drunks and emotional abuse. It was something to which neither of us wanted to expose our children.

One Christmas Day, we were at his house sharing the holiday with him and my wonderful mother-in-law. We noticed he'd visited the garage more than a few times during the morning—not hard to figure out he'd gone to have a beer, or two, or three. An expert at storing a supply of alcohol amongst his tools, he progressively got smashed but did not think anyone would notice.

When his behavior escalated to cursing and speaking vulgarities to my wife (his daughter) and our children, I asked my wife to pack up so we could leave—I'd had enough. When I looked at him, all I could see was a drunken rage on this otherwise beautiful Christmas Day.

I explained to my mother-in-law why we were leaving then looked directly at my father-in-law and pronounced I'd never be back in their home until he was sober or dead. The words came from deep inside me.

We packed up the kids and left for home. My intention had been to shake him up enough to take personal action toward sobriety. Booze totally consumed his life and affected those around him in ugly, negative ways. It was also physically killing him—my deeper concern, as it wasn't about him being drunk on a holiday as much as it was about his health and a premonition he needed to stop before the alcohol killed him.

The following week I received a phone call from my father-in-law's next-door neighbor. He informed me he'd found my father-in-law dead on the garage floor; a beer can clutched in his hand. His last conscious act in his human body involved alcohol.

I put the phone down and registered a shiver down my spine. It had only been days since I vowed to never return unless he was either sober or dead— now he was dead.

My words were a warning, but one which did not reach him. I felt that my words should have come sooner and perhaps more forcibly, but a part of me knew that this was his karmic destination.

My Stepfather

We all called my stepfather 'Eng'. Even my sisters—his biological daughters called him that. None of us children ever called him dad, father, or pop. He didn't want it. There was never that kind of closeness on his part toward us. His friends called him 'Eng' as well—a nickname for his last name of Engelking.

Eng was an extremely violent and angry man most of his life. He'd recounted many times how he'd robbed and killed a man with a knife (in England) during the War. He'd admitted to having thrown a US Army officer off a troop ship crossing the Atlantic Ocean because he did not like him. He admitted to several contract killings (after the War) for money.

He was truly a loner and had little compassion for others or himself; decades of drinking, fighting, and being a nasty son-of-a-gun had managed to destroy all of his family connections and relationships.

There was a period of time after Eng and my mother divorced when he disappeared from the radar—15 years off the grid. Then one day as I drove down Highway 101 in San Jose I looked out the window and there he was, hitchhiking. I knew instantly it was him—more intuitively than recognizing him, as I was driving fast. I made a decision to pull over and offer him a ride.

William "Rev. Bill" McDonald Jr.

He looked surprised (but not happy) that it was me who had stopped. He then proceeded to direct me to drive him some distance off the freeway to where he was living. He said very little about his own life, or what he had been doing, and he never asked any questions about mine. He didn't know I was married or had children, or that my house was three miles from where he lived.

I dropped him off and gave him my phone number.

I heard from him a couple of weeks later. He got down to business immediately—wanted to borrow $700.00 to buy a car. I told him my budget was tight and I could not give him anything, but I invited him to meet my family and see my house. He told me he wasn't interested and hung up.

A few years passed without contact. My brother, Gary, let me know he'd located Eng through some relatives in Oregon—Gary had visited Eng, who lived in a one-bedroom cabin near Mount Shasta in northern California. He relayed the address and contact information.

Like some kind of a Pollyanna optimist I took my family up to his place for a visit. I brought along photo albums to share with him. It was an awkward visit to say the least. He drank vodka like it was water, consuming an entire bottle as we sat at his small kitchen table. The funny thing was he could still function. According to his neighbors, he drank at least a bottle every day.

Needless to say the visit was not very satisfying at any level. I'd so wanted him to see the parts of my life he'd missed, but I felt bad for having dragged my family up there to witness his disrespect. I drove back home feeling a great sadness for the things he'd missed in his life.

A couple of days later I received a friendly phone call from him. He wanted me to buy a car in Sacramento and then drive it 300 miles to his place. He said he'd eventually reimburse me. Nothing was said about how I'd get home or pay for the gasoline to get there. He assured me that when he got his Social Security check he'd send me a check, but he needed the car now.

I didn't have to think about my response. I told him if he sent me a check for the car then I would pick it up and drive it up there for him. He said that wouldn't work and ended the conversation. He then called my brother Gary with the same request. Of course, my brother said no. I never heard from Eng again.

One day, after a deep meditation, I wrote Eng a long letter that explained how much he was missing out on the lives of his beautiful daughters and grand-children, and his stepsons. I shared he had isolated himself from all of the family and that he needed to reach out and mend relationships with his family before it was too late. I predicted in no uncertain words that if he did not change things he was going to die alone and no one would be there to care. Not even his so called friends and drinking buddies were going to see him at the end of his life when he was ill. I predicted that no one would come to his funeral. I told him that I loved him and would be there for him but that he had to ask me.

The sad fact is that he took that heartfelt letter I wrote and read it to my siblings who all had dropped by to visit with him a few weeks later. He laughed out loud at 'Crazy Bill' making predictions. He ranted about how self-righteous I was. He tore up my letter in front of all of them. I understand not one of them defended me, or my actions. I only sent him that letter to tell him that I still loved him. I would be there for him if he wanted me to be. What I got back was a huge slap in the face. I truly believed it would end that way for him and it sad-dened me.

Less than a year later, when he was put in a rest home, the staff contacted me to say no one was visiting him. I was told that they (the staff) were sure he wanted to see me.

I asked the caregiver to put him on the phone. I heard her put down the phone and call out to him: *your son, Bill is on the phone.* I clearly heard him tell her to say he was sleeping, that he did not want to talk to me. It was obvious that it was the nurse's idea to call me. She may have meant well but it hurt to hear him saying that he did not want to talk to me.

The next time I heard from the rest home was late one night—he didn't have long to live and I should drive up to see him, and make arrangements for his funeral. I asked them to put him on the phone; I was willing to go if he asked me. There was a long silence before someone returned. The caller stated that even though he wouldn't come to the phone she was sure he wanted me to come up and take care of the arrangements (like paying his medical bills and funeral costs).

Weeks later, I received a call from a funeral home where his corpse had been taken. They 'told' me I was responsible for his expenses. I gave them a firm 'no' and they threatened me with legal actions. I informed them I'd been his stepson years ago but after he'd divorced my mother he'd not contacted me for decades—there was no relationship legal or otherwise. He was NOT my father!

In the end, no one, not even his own two daughters, or my brother Gary, attended his funeral; nor did anyone pay for one. He was cremated at the funeral home and his ashes mixed with others in some nameless place.

No one came to pay his or her respects while he was dying; and no one was there when he was cremated. He died alone and no one marked the occasion of his passing.

It tore me up to know his fate and then see it unfold. Even though he never wanted to see me and only wanted money from me, in my heart I still loved him. I sent him loving prayers and said good-bye to him from my own home.

No one is totally evil. I could still see some goodness and love in him, just as I could in all people.

My Mother-In-Law

Sometimes you get really lucky. Maybe it's good karma. I had the most wonderful mother-in-law. I always knew that she loved me; which truly counted in my world where I got so little of that growing up. She was most always upbeat and loving to her grandchildren. After my father-in-law's death she had some health issues. Never ill enough to be in the hospital, people said she was in fair health. She took some medication for blood pressure and other ailments, but functioned well.

I remember certain feelings the week before she had a major stroke. I kept asking my wife to call her and talk. I, myself, made a point of having a nice long conversation with her just four days before she was rushed to the Emergency Room. I did not realize at the time that would be our last communication, but I recall that I hadn't wanted to hang up the phone. After my wife and I told her how much we loved her I could feel a darkness closing in. I felt like we were going to lose her.

On Easter Sunday, while at the Catholic Mass at her local church, she collapsed in one of the pews. People worked hard to keep her alive and rushed her to the closest ER.

She never regained consciousness.

We were told that there was nothing anyone could do for her—she'd remain 'alive' through artificial intervention only. Her brain had been severely damaged, she would never talk, feed herself, sip a drink. Nothing.

This presented my wife and her sister Darlene with a moral question—continued life support or natural course. They knew their mother had always been clear about this situation; never would have wanted to be kept a prisoner in a mind that did not function. The joint decision was made: stop the machines.

Carol and I went to her bedside to tell her of the decision even though she could not respond. I remember placing my hands on the top of her head and fully tensing up my entire body while mentally visualizing a current of loving electrical energy charging from my fingertips to her brain. I held my hands on her head for about 45 seconds then stood there as she sat up and opened her eyes and looked at us. She looked directly at me and then slowly reclined.

That was the last time she ever opened her eyes or made any kind of meaningful movements.

It took almost a week before she took her last breath and died.

It was the hardest decision our family ever made. We were at peace with it because we respected her views and carried out her last wishes. It still hurt—emotional pain for all involved.

I've always thought it was karmic in how she was struck down in church on Easter Sunday, sitting in her regular pew, while my father-in-law died in his garage holding onto what was most important to him—a can of beer. An interesting detail is that when her husband collapsed on the cement floor years before her own death she was down the street attending her neighborhood church services.

Almost 25 years and I still miss her.

My Mother

Of all the funerals and memorial services I have ever attended or at which I officiated, none was so emotionless as my mother's. Neither did any of them hold such profound sadness.

For over 40 years my mother had told all of us that she was dying. She said it so often that one wondered if she really ever wanted to live. Doctor's appointments were a regular occurrence; whenever she felt a symptom she'd go get a prescription. The cumulative side effects from numerous prescriptions must have contributed to her declining health.

My mother was also extremely depressed. It was as if being ill gave her an excuse for not doing things and not living a fuller life, and people had to take care of her needs—the latter was perhaps motivation to remain 'ill'.

I have no medical data to show what her actual health issues were, if any, but I always felt that she used her illness as a way to manipulate the family.

On the day she died she'd seen her doctor to complain about her health. He wrote her off as a depressed neurotic who protested too much about imagined health issues. He'd told her that if she took her medicine as prescribed then she should be okay.

She left his office without new pills or a dose of empathy.

Two hours later she died in her bed. Her final moments took place not long after she'd had 'another' verbal argument with others in the household.

My sister, Marsha, called me soon after my mother's death. I volunteered to pay for the costs but was told that it was not necessary. It was going to be a simple open casket viewing in a 'rented casket' followed by cremation in a cardboard container (the next day). No minister, no flowers, no service, no newspaper obituary, no friends—immediate family only to pay last respects—not much of a send-off.

Marsha explained to me that our mother had not wanted any fuss. I decided I couldn't let it happen without some recap of her life and what she meant to us. Once decided—good intentions—I had difficulty coming up with notable positive attributes. It seemed impossible to come up with pleasant memories. I tried hard to recall what others had told me about her life. I suddenly realized how little there was to share that was positive and uplifting. Engulfed by sadness—for her empty life—I pushed myself into deeper thought, which only made my task more difficult. She'd lived a life void of joy.

My mother never sent cards, gifts, or made any phone calls to my children, let alone to my wife or me. We used to send her photos of the kids but when we visited her we never saw them displayed; only photos of my Marsha's children only. She never remembered birthdays, holidays, or graduations, nor did she attend celebrations for my kids. All those years she'd never once reached out; she'd only lived an hour or so from us.

My son Josh was away in the Army. We did not ask him to come home for this. My daughter was busy with school. She hardly knew her grandmother. She only had some old memories of meeting her when she was younger. There was nothing warm and sweet in her memory box. My daughter felt no emotional pull to attend her grandmother's 'viewing'.

As sad as that was for me to see how my daughter felt, I understood and allowed her the freedom to make her own decision.

The open casket viewing was in the evening for two hours. My siblings and their spouses and Carol and I attended. Marsha brought a couple of her children with her.

The room was devoid of emotion.

I got up and walked to the casket then turned and did what I thought needed to be done. The words I spoke were more about the spiritual realm and for-giveness—I tried to make it uplifting—rather than ramble an account of our mother's life. Everyone at the small gathering knew her personal history and attached their own truth to their relationship with her.

Not one teardrop. Not from anyone. Profoundly sad.

I told myself that when I died I wanted to matter to someone. I wanted to be missed by someone. I wanted to be remembered for having loved others.

A couple of weeks after my mother's death her mattress was taken out of the house. My sisters discovered several weeks' worth of medication stuffed between the mattress and box spring. She hadn't been taking all her pills. I won-dered if her death was a form of slow suicide or an attempt to get more attention from being ill.

It took me almost a decade before I could grieve my mother's death. I felt she'd missed so much by not allowing me to share my family and my life with her. I had wanted to see her enjoy her life. Now the best I could do was to pray for her and send her my love. She was gone and all the opportunities to mend and heal these relationships were gone as well.

Despite her bizarre ways, that included cruelty and manipulation, she was my mother. She gave me life and helped make me who I am today. For that, I am forever grateful.

PRODIGAL SON
(A CHRISTMAS STORY)

S everal years ago I asked my son Josh, a police officer, to do a kind deed then tell me about it—a story—instead of gifting 'something material' for Christmas.

My son had been patrolling in his squad car along U.S. Highway 101, just up from the Golden Gate Bridge. It was raining and cold as he cruised along looking for anything out of place on Christmas morning—not a happy camper to be working the holidays, but that was the job. Suddenly he noticed a young man walking along the side of the freeway—dangerous and illegal.

He put on his lights, pulled over, and called the young man to the car. When the man stood close Josh could see they were about the same age. When he had the dispatcher run a check he discovered the man was 22 years old and on parole, having been out of prison a couple of months. Now he was drenched and very dirty. He told Josh he'd been living along the freeway, sleeping under overpasses. He had nowhere to go.

My son didn't want to cite him or give him a bad time, especially since it was Christmas morning. He drove the man a short distance off the freeway so that he wouldn't be in danger of being hit by passing cars.

As the young man got out of the car, Josh looked at the report from the dispatcher and noticed the address listed for the young man was only a few miles from where he'd been sleeping on the freeway. When asked, the young man replied that this was his parents' home; they'd had no idea where he was or what had happened to him in the last four years. He confided he was afraid to go home because he'd been in so much trouble (and spent time in prison). He said he'd rather live on the streets alone than be rejected by his parents.

My son was not going to let the possibility of a reunion on Christmas Day slip away. He had the man sit in the back of the car and drove to the address in the upscale neighborhood of Mill Valley—million dollar homes were the norm. Josh pulled up to an exclusive home. The young man wanted to leave, but my son left him in the back seat and knocked on the door of the luxurious home.

Unsure of the outcome, he knew he must try—he'd dealt with cases where parents had thrown out their sons or daughters and never wanted to see them again. He wondered if these people might be upset with a 'cop' for attempting a reunion. If they called his sergeant, he could be written up for not following procedures.

Josh told himself it was Christmas Day. He had to attempt this. He couldn't bear thinking this guy—around his own age—would be sleeping rough on the holidays. He placed the outcome in the hands of God and knocked once more.

It was about seven in the morning. Lights came on inside the house and door latches clicked. An older man stood looking at my son in his police uniform. Josh got to the point and watched the man's eyes grow teary. The man called for his wife to come to the door. He nodded to affirm to Josh that he should leave his son with them.

The parents stood in the doorway, looking at the young man who was looking out from the back seat of the police car.

They had been sad for the past four years, not knowing if their son was alive. They didn't care about gifts or money; they missed their son. Their prayer for the holidays had come true.

My son opened the door to let out the young man. He walked slowly toward the house. My son watched from the curb as the family joined together in a hug. He could see the love and joy as the three of them cried. They disappeared inside.

Josh had great faith it would turn out well. He sat in his patrol car for a few minutes.

Merry Christmas, Dad—know you'll enjoy unwrapping the gift.

SURROUNDED BY LOVE

On the morning of August 15, 1998, I reached what I thought was the end of my rope. I could no longer endure the pain and suffering alone.

I sat at my computer in the early hours of the morning and sent a message—a cry for help—to my closest church friends. With the click of a mouse they'd see a different side of me.

I've always been a pillar in crises. I was raised to suffer quietly and alone, never asking for help. I was always the giver—the one who did for others: the visitor to the sick, the one who prayed for those in need. In Vietnam, during the war, I remained calm under fire and took risks to aid the wounded. I never showed soft emotion—men do not cry and do not need hugs.

But now I sat in pain and opened a part of myself I'd never explored. I was going to proclaim to my friends that I was weak. I was going to tell them I needed their love. My tough guy image would be ruined forever.

E-mail messages of this type went out that morning:

Friends,

My skin cancer treatments have become very aggressive and painful. I want to ask you guys for supportive prayers. My face is extremely raw and painful this morning. I feel like I need a group hug to keep going. When you do your meditations please take a few minutes and send me loving energy. I must admit that my inner child wants to cry this morning, but that macho guy on the outside will not allow that.

I rose after poor sleep and showered. It took all my strength to stand the pain as the water hit my face. I forced myself to stay there while the water ran for over an hour so that it would take away the old scabs and skin. My face bled; throbbing and aching in the process. It bleeds still as I write this.

I cannot breathe without the movement of inhaling and exhaling causing pain. My face feels like it is in a frying pan—the soreness from five weeks of treatments. It no longer seems to have any surface skin, but resembles raw, bloody meat. I am unable to continue this treatment because it is just too painful to do so, but I know I must see my doctor as soon as possible.

I feel like such a wimp this morning. Me, the guy who faced 500 North Vietnamese with an M-60 machine gun on my hip and a few thousand rounds of ammo. Me, who is not afraid to jump out of an airplane. Me, a man who is not afraid to face troubles head-on. Now I am admitting that I am in so much pain and discomfort that I no longer care about curing this cancer. I just want the pain to stop.

I sure hope that this does not destroy my image, but this morning I just feel like rolling over and saying enough is enough.

Okay, I know it is the lack of sleep and this is the pain talking, but this tough guy is listening to his inner child this morning, and that child wants to sit down and cry his little old heart out.

I'm feeling sorry for myself this morning and I'm reaching out for some hugs. Even tough guys want to be hugged once in a while. I needed to share this and I hope none of you mind being part of my coping process. I just wanted someone to listen to me. I guess I am still a little boy on the inside. It just seems to be easier to handle this pain if others care about you. Thanks for listening to me this morning.

Your friend, Billy

I had been battling skin cancer since 1980, but it was getting worse. When I went to the dermatologist in July, she told me if I didn't immediately engage in aggressive treatment I might lose my nose—surgically removing all or a large part of my nose. The thought of dying never bothered me, but having my nose cut off—being disfigured—depressed me. Call it vanity or ego, I kind of liked my nose just the way it was, right in the middle of my face.

I began the treatment during the hot summer of 1998. As the Sacramento Valley was having record highs, chemicals slowly burned my face. I said I was willing to endure whatever I had to do. By the third week of treatment, my face had blistered and had begun to bleed. When I showered, pieces of my flesh fell from my face—including from my nose. It was extremely painful, but I continued doing what the doctor told me to do. Since the treatment was to continue for three months and this was only the third week, I knew I was in trouble.

What the doctor did not know was that by week three my face was totally diseased with two separate infections: a bacterial infection and a herpes virus. I could barely open and close my eyes.

I kept calling my HMO to see my doctor, but the advice nurse kept telling me I was okay and to continue the treatments. I continued to phone and the nurse repeatedly told me the doctor was satisfied with the treatment—to continue.

By week five I looked like I was wearing a Halloween mask. I went to work but had difficulty concentrating on my job. Finally I reached that weekend when I lost control of my tough-guy image and sent out the e-mail message. After that, all kinds of things began to happen.

The reception I received from close friends and people I hardly knew at the following Sunday's church service amazed me. My friends had shared my message with other concerned and caring people. It was a precious moment—more caring than I'd felt in the previous 52 years of my life. This gift continued to grow—has never stopped.

When word got around that I'd asked for prayers, people sent letters, made phone calls, and fired off emails. Though I remained in great pain, wondrous things took place within me. The healing process was going to begin inside first, with my emotions and spirituality. I was to heal from the inside out.

The day after the service, I demanded to be seen by a new doctor. An early morning appointment was set up.

The moment she walked in, a young, beautiful doctor of Indian origin, I felt absolute confidence. She took just one look at my face and said she knew what the problem was. Though she cut away some flesh (for testing) she was certain I had a viral and a bacterial infection. She stopped my previous treatment altogether and gave me medication for the infection. She instructed me not to return to work. Had I waited much longer I could have been disfigured.

I went home to rest and recover. My body was completely exhausted. It took several days for the pain to decrease to the point I could sleep, but I knew I was on the way to recovery.

The following Tuesday I received messages about a healing prayer service at the chapel that night. Two dozen members of the Sacramento Meditation Center got together for the purpose of praying for me and sending me healing energy and love.

I was deeply touched. I had never had other human beings do anything like that for me. I reached out to them that night as I sat in my own home, allowing their love to flow my way. I felt surrounded by so much love coming at me at once. I felt loved and as if the entire universe was hugging me.

So powerful was the energy sent from the chapel 25 miles away that I forgot about my pain. I only thought about it the next day when I looked into the mirror. I made a decision to ignore the mirrors and the pain.

Over the next few days I felt like a small child wrapped in the arms of a loving mother. I felt great peace and joy within. I began to have newfound insights about myself and the illness. These thoughts helped come to a realization of what the cancer might be about. Before the cancer treatment I had been a giver—never a receiver. It was as if I was unworthy of 'receiving' gifts.

The love expressed by others and directed to me showed me love is a cycle. In order to complete the circuit the love has to be given willingly and willingly received. Not receiving breaks the cycle of love.

During this time of realization I opened childhood wounds and explored my past (in the safety of a place of peace). I discovered that my healing was not for me alone. From the communications I received it became obvious that others were touched—people opened up and shared parts of them that had been hidden from me.

The door was open for healing to come to many of the group. Many who had sent me so much love and healing energy were now enveloped in a healing process.

Each day during my convalescence I heard stories about how my illness and healing affected others in positive ways. It was amazing how it unfolded.

William "Rev. Bill" McDonald Jr.

The pain eased in a few days, and over time I began to heal. Some of the messages I sent to those praying for me included these observations:

Prayer Circle,

Last night I felt so loved and full of peace. Those of you who have been praying and sending me energy have succeeded far beyond your realization. I felt as if I was in a cocoon of love all night long. I had a great sleep and awoke this morning with my face looking even better than yesterday. It is okay to look in the mirror now. The infections are losing their battle to all your energy and the power of your love.

You guys are better than family; no, you guys are family in the real sense. I feel so much closer to all of you.

I am filled with awe and joy this morning. I wanted to share this with all of you, so you can realize how powerful your prayers have been. We are not talking just on the physical level but deeper within me there has been great healing. You are all a part of this drama and all a part of my "good karma."

Billy.

I learned so much from this experience. Yes, there was intense discomfort, but in the end I found that the hurt was 'spiritual growing pains'. I can honestly say that I would not have changed anything that happened to me. I would not give up a minute of the pain if it meant giving back all that I had learned and experienced.

Being loved by others is truly the greatest healing gift God can give us. The love that surrounded me during my illness made me feel that God's own loving hands had caressed me.

THE END OF THE RAINBOW

Few places on earth can surpass the breathtaking scenery along the Columbia River Gorge.

I'd been married to Carol for almost 30 years when we decided to take an early autumn trip to Washington and Oregon. We packed my pickup truck with clothing and items for the trip. Carol, in her established tradition, made sure we had plenty of snacks and drinks for along the way.

We spent time exploring waterfalls and hiking in the rain forests. We headed north, driving along a road that took us toward Mount St. Helens National Volcanic Monument. It was rainy outside as we wound through a landscape of contrast: destruction and regeneration. It reminded me of nature's own life and death mosaic.

It was symbolic, as I'd just spent five months off work fighting to recover and heal from skin cancer. This trip was taken, in part, to help regenerate the joy I've always felt for life.

As we drove up one particular hill we saw a deeply hued rainbow that stretched across the horizon—the entire horizon—as far as we could dream. I thought that this was an exceptional, mystical vision—hope illustrated.

I felt differently about this rainbow than any I had seen before.

I thought about how destructive the skin cancer had been to my face and how I must have looked to others. I could hardly bear to look in the mirror because I had become so disfigured by my battles with the disease. My face was much like Mount St. Helens, having been almost destroyed, but now in a regenerative state—I had started getting new skin and overall renewed health.

William "Rev. Bill" McDonald Jr.

I studied the rainbow—a promise of hope and second chance—when the strangest thing happened. We reached the peak of the hill and saw the end of the rainbow hitting the road just ahead of the truck. Stranger yet is that we drove past and under the rainbow. It was suddenly behind us.

The end of the rainbow is for lines in Irish fairy tales and wishful prose. I've never known anyone to actually 'find' the end, because there is no end. As for traveling under one? But on a rainy day on the road to Mount St. Helens volcano we experienced an incredible moment.

Scientifically, droplets of rain split light and cause a rainbow. Spiritually, that day, the light was ahead, around, over, and then behind us—unusual refraction.

In the 'sign', the 'rainbow moment' I knew real healing was taking place within. I felt renewed with joy and peace about my own life. I knew that rainbow was a gift to my own spirit.

GOING POSTAL

A uthor's note: For years, the United States Postal Service had so many workplace kill-ings and suicides that a phrase was coined: Going Postal.

During more than thirty years of working in management for the United States Postal Service I witnessed many incidents—complications between workers and supervisors; human communication. And in my last position as a safety manger I became involved in transformation.

I remember a supervisor in mail processing who had the reputation of being hard to work for. It was said he was a womanizer, and if one believed all the rumors he may have done drugs and was a hard drinker. The more I heard about him the worse he sounded.

When I received orders to go to Los Angles for a week of training I discov-ered another manager was being sent with me—the idea being that two people with individual styles of communication would evaluate the class on 'communi-cation skills' and then decide if it merited sending others. In order to save money he and I would share a hotel room.

It came to be that the other person was the supervisor about whom I'd heard the bad things. I then decided there was another reason for our being paired—a more important purpose why we were attending together.

I remained open minded even after many other supervisors wished me a 'good luck-watch out'. My wife and his wife meet at the airport when we were leaving. He demonstrated nothing but kindness and grace to his spouse. I remained hopeful he'd maintain this pleasant level.

The entire week we took classes together and then spent time outside class taking walks in the evenings and enjoying late night discussion about the purpose of life. His language was clean, he never went to the bar or brought drinks into the room. I found that he was hungry to learn more about spirituality. I was delighted to share stories and views and beliefs.

He began to share his heart with me. Telling me how for the first time in his life, that he was seeing things much differently. What was so important before to him no longer held his attention. He had truly fallen in love with his wife and family again. He wanted to talk about God and things divine.

He told me that since the beginning of the trip—perhaps even before, when he'd been notified—he was a different man. He confided he was someone completely different—not his old self.

His questions continued. We talked about reincarnation, karma, compassion and the purpose of life. I knew nobody was going to believe me when I came back to work and talked about his exemplary behavior, nor that we were now best of friends.

I truly enjoyed his company and felt a divine spiritual connection, as if I was there to answer his questions and witness this transformation. But I also felt a deep impending doom.

I could not shake that darkness around him, even when he smiled and laughed. I knew his time was slipping away. What I did not know was when and how. Images of violence had obscured an otherwise wonderful week together.

When we landed in Sacramento my wife picked us up and we drove him to his home. His whole family came out to greet him and hug him. He was as warm and loving a father and husband as anyone could ask for. He looked the picture of happiness. Even my wife liked him and enjoyed his family. He said he wanted to get back together soon to do something with us. We drove away with waves on both sides, huge smiles from them, from us.

That would be the last time I would ever see him. When we were half-way home a thought came to my mind and I fought hard to get rid of it.

The darkness I saw was his death. There was nothing I could do to stop it. The following week the television news broke with a tragic story of a shooting at the mail processing plant. A supervisor had been killed. The reporter used those words, that phrase: a disgruntled worker had '*gone postal*'.

My wife asked me if I knew who it might be. Though I had no official knowledge of the shooting I told her it was the new friend with whom I had shared the previous week at the course.

She asked me how I knew.

It was a simple, yet complicated answer—I just did. I also knew that we were supposed to spend that last week of his life together. We are destined to have those wonderful spiritual conversations. He was awaking spiritually and in love with life and his family. I was glad that I honored his spirit in the way I did.

It was a profoundly sad funeral.

BASKETBALL AT THE YMCA

In the summer of 1989 I found a sponsor for my team to enter the big YMCA basketball tournament in Sacramento—a four day event with games all day and into the late night. The event was a double elimination—teams played until they registered two losses.

I went to the organizational meeting a week before to get the rules and register my small team—I still needed a couple of players. Having to play several games a day would take some creative planning to conserve energy. 64 teams from all over northern California would be participating. One of those teams was from San Francisco and was the favorite to win, but I'd always fielded successful teams in the area—winning open leagues in Elk Grove and Sacramento. I was confident we'd be in the hunt.

As I sat listening to my friend 'Snake' run down the rules, I thought about how I still needed players, especially a tall center. A 6 foot 8 inch lean man of African American descent sat next to me. I asked him if he'd like to play on my team for the tournament. He smiled and said he was already on another team. I replied that if it didn't work out he'd be welcome to play on mine.

After the mandatory team meeting my friend Snake asked me what I was talking to Ricky Berry about. It dawned on me I'd been sitting next to the NBA rookie for the Sacramento Kings basketball team. Though I was a little red faced about asking him to play, we laughed about it. Ricky was not just any player. He'd had a fantastic rookie year and scored 34 points against a high ranking Golden State Warrior team that season. Much was expected of him for the coming season.

Ricky had been at the meeting, and involved himself in the YMCA program to help support others. He did not come with a huge ego and spent several days hanging with the young kids, teaching them basketball skills. I was immensely impressed with him as a person; but there was a sadness and darkness which I picked up on when I was close to him. He'd smile, but my intuition felt an inner pain he was not expressing. Something wasn't right but there were always people around so I could not have a private conversation.

During the week I learned lots about him. I discovered he did not do drugs and didn't drink much alcohol. He lived a rather clean life and had a beautiful wife named Valerie. What I saw was totally different to what was hidden in his heart. I sensed his relationship with his wife might be troubled, but in public everything seemed okay.

My team made it to the championship game which did not start until midnight. Some of my players had to go home! My best guard had a graveyard shift at the hospital. That meant the little, old, fat man would play a lot. I was one of the oldest players if not the oldest—certainly the shortest. The team we faced had won every game by over 30 points—a semi-professional group stocked with two guys seven feet tall and one former LA Lakers (played in their preseason games before being cut) and several All-American college players as well. They were loaded with talent.

I had to start myself in the opening lineup because we had so few players. I faced off against their six foot five star who had great outside shooting. I held him to seven points in the first half yet failed to make a single point myself. I spent every ounce of energy playing defense on him and I was exhausted.

We lost the game by seven points—the smallest margin they'd had in all of their games. It felt good that we took home the second place trophy for our sponsor.

Ricky presented the awards and spoke to us. Then Snake told me some of the guys were going over to Ricky's house for a small party and wondered if I wanted to go with him. I declined. I had to work a few hours later. A part of me wanted to go, but not for the party, I felt there was something terribly wrong with Ricky.

The black cloud, like an aura, that I'd seen surrounding Ricky was like those I'd seen in Vietnam during the war. A fog of death clung tight around Ricky's head and heart. I could not shake it off.

William "Rev. Bill" McDonald Jr.

A few hours later, on my way to work, I turned on the radio and learned Ricky had put a gun to his head. A self-inflicted gunshot to the head had taken his young life just a couple hours after we'd all said good-bye.

He was a baby—23 years old. He had fame, money, a wonderful wife and home, a promising career. Seemingly, he had it all and yet he'd taken his life. The only information given to the public was that there'd been a minor argument between Ricky and his wife and that she'd left to stay at a girlfriend's home. He left a suicide note, but there were many unanswered questions, and abundant sadness.

When I spoke to my friends they said they'd not seen any evidence of problems. They'd left his home in the early hours of that morning without a clue as to what would happen next. After all these years no one is any closer to why it happened. I used to think that had I said something maybe things would have turned out differently. But now, I am not sure what I could have said to have changed or altered it.

Suicide is never an answer, and it always hurts those left behind.

LIFE FORCE ENERGY

The pain in my shoulder had been excruciating. I'd reached the point where the pain and lack of movement made it difficult to function. I'd seen HMO doctors and tried physical therapy; even entertained their suggestions of shoulder surgery, but I didn't want to go under the knife unless all options had been exhausted.

I discussed this one Sunday afternoon at the meditation center with a friend who was an acupuncturist. He suggested he might be able to help.

I wasn't a believer in acupuncture at all, but I had read it could be successfully used to relieve pain. I agreed to try a treatment or two for what was now a 'frozen shoulder'; if nothing else it might help manage the pain.

The following week I met him at his office and was shown into a treatment room—I wasn't sure what to expect. He told me he'd be inserting thin, steel needles into various meridian points on my body—a relatively painless procedure.

Shirtless, I reclined on a treatment bed then he applied alcohol to clean the sites where he'd insert the needles. I guessed he pushed more than thirty needles into me. I felt like a giant pincushion—a live voodoo doll. Then he asked me to remain relaxed and he'd return in 40 minutes to remove them. He reiterated that the time should be spent in a relaxed state—there would be no pain.

When he closed the door I began to feel streams of pain running through my body—like my nerves were on fire. It was uncomfortable to the point of actual 'hurt'. It felt like each needle was being heated up and was on fire. I squirmed around to deal with it but I did not call out for him because he'd said it was painless and I didn't want to sound like a wimp—he'd only been gone a few minutes.

I decided to do some deep breathing and then focus on a meditation to deal with the discomfort—more than discomfort—but was still fighting with the pain when he returned.

I told him it wasn't so pleasant as he'd said it would be. That the pain—which had started after he left—had become worse and was still increasing.

I can still see his look of total disbelief. He told me no patient he'd treated over the years had ever complained about pain. But there I was squirming about suffering what felt like multiple electric shocks to my system.

He began to remove the needles from my body but found it difficult. He had to make an effort to pull each one. When he'd extracted several he stopped and looked at the medical tray that he'd thrown them into. He brought it to me and showed me the needles he'd just removed. They were all bent—some of them in a letter S shape and some in other multiple directions and a few just angled over. The bottom line was that none of the needles he removed was straight.

We looked at the tray and all of the bent needles wondering how stainless steel could become bent like that just by inserting and removing them from my skin. He told me it was a first for him, but he had heard about this kind of thing happening. He told me he'd preserve the needles and in the future he'd give a talk about this to members of his association.

When I rose I felt frustrated at having gone through electrical torture. I grabbed my t-shirt and put it on. Then I realized I was using my shoulder and there was no pain. It was no longer frozen and I was able to move it around.

All I'd hoped for was an outside chance at managing the pain. It was clear to me that he was surprised. He was not expecting instant success either.

When he asked if I had any other physical issues I mentioned my killer migraines and he requested I come back the next week.

When I returned he emphasized that the previous week had to have been some kind of glitch—a lightning never strikes twice in the same place kind of thing. He assured me this would not be a painful experience—could not be.

He inserted a few dozen stainless steel needles in and around my head and face. Once again he left me alone in the treatment room to rest and heal.

And, once again, the electrical pain increased until I felt like my body was plugged into an electrical current. I twisted and turned and my head felt like it was going to 'cook'. As the heat rose so did the level of pain.

When he returned he could see I was suffering. As soon as he started pulling out the needles he became excited about how they had twisted and bent. He placed them on the tray as if they were gold nuggets he'd just panned from the river. He beamed with scientific enthusiasm about what had taken place inside me.

Though I did not share his joy in that moment, I sensed my migraines were going to get better.

Exhausted from the anomaly of the procedure, I wondered how the energy in my body could bend steel needles and asked him for his theory.

He believed that the energy—energy that was being blocked in my body and causing me to have the physical issues—had built up like water does behind a dam. He theorized the needles released this power and the energy had engaged the steel and caused it to bend.

He asked me if he could test something on me to check on how unusual my receptivity was to energy and electrical and magnetic currents. I reluctantly allowed him to try.

He pulled out a tiny magnet—one he'd used with some patients in a wrist, arm, or leg band which they'd wear next to their skin in a treatment that 'over several months' would heal certain conditions.

He took my hand and pressed the magnet into one of my fingers. In seconds I felt my left ear burn as if an electrical current had been run through it. I complained about the feeling and pulled away to stop the pain. He was delighted about what I said about my ear.

He went on about how theoretically that was the part of the body that would be affected by this magnet, but he'd not met anyone who responded to it. He had purposefully not told me what part of the body this would affect or what he was trying to do. That was his way of testing me. I did not need to be tested any further and packed up my stuff, got dressed, and told him I had seen enough.

He told me later that he felt that I conducted energy in my body better than anyone he had ever worked on. He said that when my energy gets blocked it truly becomes a big issue for me to deal with physically. Well, I was not interested in furthering his research and that was my last treatment with him.

Years later I did engage in acupuncture treatments, and interestingly enough those painful effects were never duplicated. As we remained in touch, he explained he felt I'd had about 50 years of blocked qi (energy) and his treatments released a massive amount—which, he felt, caused the needles to bend.

I feel that whatever ESP abilities I have may be directly related with how my body handles and processes high levels of qi (energy). My body has always been very sensitive to energy, like broadcast radio signals. When I was younger I was able to pick up AM and FM radio stations from time to time when I was in the shower and had some water in my ear, or even sometimes in times of total quiet. I have heard of people picking up radio stations from their fillings in their teeth, because of the metal, but I have not yet run into anyone who has picked up radio stations as I have done.

The thing is, in the end, we are all energy.

CAR CRASH THAT
NEVER HAPPENED

I remember the moment as if it was yesterday, but I still do not understand what happened or why. If there had been no other witnesses to what happened, I would be questioning myself about what I 'thought' I saw.

My work as a senior safety specialist with the United States Postal Service (USPS) took me to the little valley town of Modesto, California. I went there with my friend Sam, a fellow safety specialist. Sam headed down a busy street at about 45 miles per hour in our government staff car on our way to one of the post offices across town. Everything seemed normal and ordinary that morning.

When we entered the middle of an intersection, a huge recreational vehicle turned directly across our path.

It must have happened very fast, but at the time it all seemed to be in slow motion, as there was no time for Sam to reduce our speed.

I remember looking directly into the eyes of the RV driver, just a foot or two from impact—a frame by frame experience as we neared the front section of his traveling home. As a safety expert, many years of accident investigations dictated this would be in the serious collision, multiple injury category.

I froze in anticipation of what was supposed to happen next. But I seemed to have had plenty of time to think, and all I could think of was God's love.

When we reached the point where the two vehicles should have impacted, the RV disappeared from our view—yes the 24 foot motor home vanished. We passed directly through where it should have been on the road, and were instantly transported past the point of collision.

We looked back and registered that the RV was on the other side of the road.

Sam pulled a U-turn and headed to the parking lot where the RV driver was parking. We pulled up next to him and stared at each other for a few moments. When we got out and spoke to the shaken driver he confirmed what we had seen—or not seen. The driver said he saw us; in fact, he had been looking directly into my eyes. The next thing he knew was that his RV was out of the way. It was as if we had passed directly through where he was.

We all agreed that we should have hit in that intersection, and there should have been serious consequences. But there we stood, bewildered but unscathed.

Sam and I knew from our training and experience that the incident was unexplainable. However it had happened, there were powers at work in the universe that saved us.

I felt that God was once again protecting me, and I felt blessed to have been gifted the experience.

YOU CANNOT TAKE IT WITH YOU

I was invited to a potluck lunch hosted by a fellow postal manager who was leaving his secure job, after 20 years, to try a new career.

I applauded the young guy even though in my gut I knew that the risks were more than he realized. One of the postmasters at the get-together talked about the real purpose of life—to make all the money you could in 'go for it, grab it' style. He encouraged the young manager to risk it all and never look back.

I sat listening about virtues of money and career success; that working the extra time and days and giving up experiences with family and friends was the price one had to pay for greater success and more money. My body language gave away my disapproval of that life path. The speaker—postmaster—saw this and began to make fun of me. He told the small group that Bill is 'new age' with his outlook on life. He stated he'd outlive me and bury me with all the money he made.

I had an instant image of him in a grave. So powerful was the vision I looked directly at him—in real time—and expressed he'd better do something other than just making money—that he needed to look after his family and spiritually related issues. I explained he didn't have all the time he thought. I asked him to imagine what he would do differently—now—if he knew he'd die the next month. I was serious.

He roared with laughter, as did the table of postal managers.

For me the words were not from a 'what if' category. I *knew* it was fact. I tried to get him to rethink what was really important to him, but he kept citing how crazy I was; that *I* was the one missing the whole point of life. Money was the mother's milk of life, therefore success.

Just over three weeks later I received notification that this same postmaster had fallen in the administrative office stairwell—an apparent heart attack. Several of the managers planned on visiting him as soon as he stabilized. But I knew he was never coming home alive. This was his final week.

His ex-wife and kids got all his money. He couldn't take it with him.

As for the young man who'd left to a new venture: he lost all of his investment money, was high and dry without a job within one year of leaving.

TWO ENCOUNTERS WITH TIBETAN MONKS

Author's note: I feel I've had a special bond with my first grandson, Spencer, since before he was born, picking up his energy prior to his birth. Shortly after his birth—they had just finished cleaning him and placed him a bassinet—I looked at him and he turned his face toward me. We made eye contact and held it for the longest time. It was like acknowledging an old friend returning to the family. The two instances in the following story may appear to be unrelated to this 'note', but my feeling is that they are connected somehow.

One: Sands

There was an art show I wanted to attend in San Francisco, featuring paintings by a famous European artist. Fortunate was I that my sister-in-law invited me to it.

At the end of the row of exhibits there were several Tibetan monks working on a sand painting of a holy symbol. They'd spent a couple of weeks on the design and estimated it would take two weeks more.

When I saw the scene I immediately flashed to a dream I'd had that week. In this dream there was a wild, crazy woman who jumped up on the monks' platform and messed up their art. I saw it in my mind at that moment, as I had in my dream.

We left the museum while the monks added grains of sand to their sacred work.

The next day I read in the newspaper that a woman had acted in a fit of insane rage and jumped onto the platform, destroying the religious sand art. She'd had to be physically removed from the platform and restrained. The story went on to say how the monks simply swept away the old sand and began to rec-reate the symbol. Her protest hadn't seemed to upset them.

Two: Of Time

Several years later my wife and I drove to Truckee to return our 10 month old grandson after he'd stayed at our place for a couple of days. We stopped at a rest area to change his dirty diaper. A picnic table made the perfect change table, but we chose one far from the others at the rest stop so as not to offend.

During the diaper changing I felt someone was watching us. I looked around, then down the hill at a group of four Tibetan monks wrapped in traditional orange robes. One of them faced my direction but focused on my grandson, Spencer. When he noticed I'd seen him he bowed slightly with his hands together as if he were in prayer.

A necklace of wooden beads hung from his neck (used by the monks to count their repetitions of prayers or their mantra that is chanted silently or aloud). His head was clean-shaven and smooth. But his eyes caught my attention; they radiated love. Smiling eyes. We stared at each other for several comfortable moments, then I reciprocated the folded-hands gesture.

He raised a hand—a goodbye, a blessing perhaps. I looked at my grandson who was now standing up on the tabletop and holding onto my wife's hand. Spencer was focused on the monks down the hill and returned their smiles.

As we drove off I could not shake the good feeling that something special had just happened. It was all very gentle and causal, as if it were normal. But how often do you meet four traveling Tibetan monks at a roadside rest area on your way to Truckee?

Once in a lifetime for us.

Spencer surrounded and protected by his parents

SHARON AND THE BUTTERFLIES

*A*uthor's note: One of my best friends from childhood was Bob Brooks. Our association began in fourth grade in Sunnyvale, California. We went through school together as friends and then went our separate paths for a while; he to college and me to Vietnam. We remained friends even when we did not see or hear from each other for years at a time. I also knew his sister, Sharon, and became great friends with her in the last decade of her life. No recalling of my life journey would be complete if I did not relate some of the experiences that I shared with this family.

We were connected to the Brooks family in the 1950s—common ground between some friends of my mother. I knew Bob from elementary school, but it wasn't until my final year in high school that I paid attention to his little sister, Sharon (she was only one year younger).

The first summer out of high school I moved to Hawaii. I'd been there only a week when Bob, Sharon and their parents traveled to Oahu. I was working my butt off for minimum wage in contrast to Bob's family who flew in on free airline tickets and then booked into a ritzy hotel. (Mr. Brooks worked for United Airlines as a pilot.)

We got together on my time off and toured around the island. My impression at that time was that Sharon was incredibly bored. This was my impression of her until a family crisis brought us together years later.

Bob and I remained friends and went about our lives. It came to be that Sharon began working for President Jimmy Carter in the White House.

The Brooks' family crisis arrived by way of Mrs. Brooks taking an overdose of several poisons in a suicide attempt. Though she didn't die right away, she remained comatose; her death a slow process for everyone involved.

I spent most of my time at the hospital—day and night—with Mr. Brooks. That week we became closer than I ever expected. He confided in me things which he was uncomfortable talking about with his children. He knew that his shared information was safe with me. (I continue to honor his wishes.)

Mrs. Brooks' actions changed the chemistry of the entire family. Life changing for Bob, Mr. Brooks, and Sharon. Sharon and I spent a lot of time talking after her mother's death. She often invited me to come and have lunch or dinner in the White House. Though I couldn't afford to fly there and back with my family, we continued our correspondence, and then it trailed off and we went back to our separate lives.

The next time I saw Sharon was at her father's funeral in San Jose. Something very special happened that day.

When Mr. Brooks' casket was in the church, and the pastor gave a talk about him, a large Monarch butterfly floated high by the stained glass windows near the ceiling. The early morning sunlight filtered through the windows and cast spotlights on the dancing butterfly.

The minister paused from his prepared speech and pointed out the butterfly to those who had not already become aware of it flying so angelically and free above everyone in the church.

Later, at the gravesite, we noticed another large Monarch butterfly patrolling the skies around us. I tapped Bob on the shoulder and pointed it out to him and Sharon. Soon everyone was smiling and feeling good about the funeral as they watched the butterfly.

After the funeral we went to Mr. Brooks' house for refreshments and to talk. My wife and I and a small gathering of close friends from high school were there with Bob and Sharon and their families. To my amazement and delight another butterfly flew around in the house. It came and sat on my shoulder. Chills traveled up and down my spine. I put it on my finger and sent it off to fly around the room. Eventually we were able to see it out of the house and watch it soar to the heavens.

Time passed, and out of my concern and that of others—including my friend Karen—for Sharon I flew to Washington, D.C. after she quit working for President Bill Clinton. Sharon's depression had consumed her. I spent a week trying to change her fate. When I confessed that I believed she was thinking of taking her life she said that she wasn't. I could feel the end coming. I knew it was going to happen, and yet I was helpless to stop it!

I felt terrible knowing that she would take action. Weeks of uncertainty—not if, but when.

And she did.

(Fast forward a number of years—I'd already retired and had further adventures) And then I was sitting next to Karen, at the Carter Center in Atlanta, Georgia, listening to President Jimmy Carter talk about our dear friend Sharon Brooks. Bob and his family were there among others in this private ceremony which included a guest I'd brought along—Robert Reese with whom I'd traveled to Vietnam a couple of months previous.

President Jimmy Carter honored Sharon's memory by naming and dedicating the only lake at Carter Centre to her. He spoke of her incredible value to his administration and her wonderful qualities.

I sat thinking about Sharon and the fact that I could not stop her suicide. I felt a great sadness. She'd ended her own life almost 20 years after her mother's suicide.

When I looked up, her brother, Bob, addressed our group and spoke to President Carter who now sat with his wife in front of me. Behind Bob, and out of his sight, a large Monarch butterfly flew gracefully over the lake and around the back of Bob's head. I smiled and poked Karen who was sitting next to me. She was already smiling.

I knew then that everything was as it should be at that moment. I sat back and sent Sharon my prayers.

Author's note: At the memorial service in California that Bob had given for his sister Sharon, there was a comforting event that took place. We had pulled into the parking lot where the service was to be held. I was with my old high school friends Karen, Mahaila, and Linda. I had been explaining to them about the importance of owls and their symbolism in my spiritual life. I'd cited a few examples of how they've appeared to me to give me comfort, a message, or reassurance that what was happening would be all right.

As we stood next to the car in the parking lot I focused on the tall chapel bell tower. There, up high on the ledge, was a huge owl, hooting for her partner. He appeared. They began to mate right there in the broad daylight on the ledge.

We were fascinated by the possible spiritual connection. We wondered why owls would be out in the daytime having sex.

It occurred to me that sex represented the creation of life and this was perhaps Sharon's way of letting her best friends know that she was eternally alive. I shared this thought. Mahaila fully agreed. We watched the owls for several minutes until they disappeared inside the bell tower. I felt at peace and knew intuitively that Sharon was okay.

SHARON'S SUICIDE

I stare at my monitor screen
Still expecting you to answer
My last e-mails.
I am hesitant to delete
Your e-mail address,
It would leave me without
A gravesite or place of entombment
To kneel at and whisper
To you my words
Of poetry and love.
You never answered
My last e-mail.
Were you already fading beyond
Into that darkness?
I wish I could have held you
Just once more,
To tell you
How much we all loved you.
But you had already
Bought a ticket out,
And you did not want to wait,
So you left us all a note
And so many wonderful memories.
But I would
Rather have you here tonight.
Notes are such a lousy way
To say goodbye
Forever!

For Sharon Brooks

EARLY RETIREMENT

My body told me it was ready to retire long before the official date. 30 years in management at the Post Office neared. I watched the calendar. Physically I had been deteriorating, and mentally I worried I might not reach the magic number in order to retire.

Injuries suffered in Vietnam haunted me. In July 1967 I had been thrown to a concrete floor via the impact of a direct hit by a rocket. The old concussion had grown to be troublesome. I'd been diagnosed with epilepsy and prior to retirement had several seizures a week.

When I felt one coming on I'd sequester myself inside my office, after which I'd try and function as best I could for the rest of the day. Enduring the seizures and the secret became exhausting. Clear thinking was difficult. I kept a low profile, greatly concerned that my seizures would prevent me from driving to work. I made sure never to drive when I had those feelings.

At this same time I ignored the signs that my heart sent me. Sometimes I'd get sharp pains in my chest and I'd have to sit down and rest. If that wasn't enough, my doctors had told me I was pre-diabetic—but since I'd had that diagnosis for 15 years I never gave it any serious thought.

In the end, though, it was my back and hips that prevented me from walking on the cement surfaces of work areas in the mail-processing plant. (Back and hip issues which were a direct result of my time in Vietnam.)

I was physically miserable.

The goal was to reach my 55th birthday in order to retire early.

Those last few years went slowly for me. I counted the months and days. I went from being an award-winning manager to being thought of as someone who goofed off, waiting to retire.

During my last months on the job, I went in to work at four in the morning. This allowed me to check over the safety issues of the graveyard shift as they worked the last three hours of their workday.

One morning, as I walked into the administrative office tower to go to my office, I felt compelled to look up above the door. In the darkness I saw two small owls sitting on a building ledge. They watched me with their big eyes. I stopped and acknowledged their presence; knew from experience they had a message for me.

As I walked inside the building several dark flashes came across some of my fellow managers. I saw that death was closer to them than they realized. I foresaw four of them dying within a short period of time. I knew there was nothing that I could do to stop it from happening. By this stage of my life, I had come to realize that I could not change that final exit date for people. But it saddened me to have this information. I was never really sure or comfortable with what to do with that knowledge. (It came to be that two died prior to my retirement, and three passed away shortly after I retired.)

None of these individuals were into new age or what might be termed spiritual. In fact, they each had a rather negative outlook on life. I knew starting a conversation with any of them on this subject would not be well received.

But there was one supervisor whom I did approach, visiting him at his home and taking him a book. Not long after my visit he discovered he had a terminal illness—cancer in its last stages. I was at the hospital when the tumor was removed from his abdomen and his doctor told him he had six months to live. And that is how long, to the day, he lasted.

He took a disability retirement and got his life in order, mending his relationship with his daughter. It seemed to me he made peace with dying.

The Postal Service provided me a good income and benefits for my family. Retirement from the Postal Service offered me an opportunity to do things I really wanted to do with my 'real life'. I was not rich but my needs would be met. Certainly, I was not the same young man who'd started there, but I had dreams and plans for my life and—with my battered body—I welcomed the next stage with open arms.

SUICIDE HOTLINE

O ne of the first things I did when I retired was to volunteer to man the Suicide Hotline.

I signed up for the training, took it, and was assigned the shift no one wanted—2 a.m. to 7 a.m. weekdays.

I reported to a large office building in the Sacramento area which was totally secure—the kind where one goes to the back entrance, is viewed through a screen, and then buzzed in. In my case, the next step was to walk down a hall to an unmarked, locked office. Beyond the door was an 'outer office' that featured four doors—one of which opened (with a key) to an operations room with a bank of phones operated by volunteers.

Normally there would be one or two people on a shift but the early hours were hard to staff—there was only me.

The phones did provide complete privacy to the callers. Contrary to what people might have chosen to believe, there was no way volunteers knew who was calling, let alone from what location. An additional phone line existed in order to call the police to the person in crisis while still on the line. It was possible that a volunteer might have incoming calls on both lines. A volunteer had to have the ability to perform triage.

If two calls came in at once, and only one volunteer was available, one option was to ask the person to call back at an arranged time—sometimes that was a good option—the crisis caller knew then that someone cared to 'make time'. Sometimes an emotionally distraught caller needed to be heard immediately, and that is when it was hard to be alone on the job. But I had a flair for handling the situations and used my intuition to guide me.

Many callers wanted attention—someone to listen to them during the lonely hours of the morning. For some, the conversation was enough of a connection with another human being so they could get through another day.

One morning I took a call from a suicidal young woman. I knew she was on the edge and ready to take her own life. I determined that she had the means and the way to kill herself and she was in a very dark mood. Out of nowhere, I stopped the conversation and asked her if she had a view of a lake outside her window. She became quiet. I asked her again, stating that I simply had a vision of a lake in my mind and that I felt it was outside her window. She meekly replied that, yes, she did.

I asked her if she lived in Lake Tahoe. She affirmed she did and asked how I knew any of that.

Then I asked if that longhaired cat that was sitting on her lap was black and white? She became spooked. I had her full attention—which is what I wanted.

She asked me how I knew these things and I brushed it aside by nailing a couple more observations about her surroundings. Then we talked—I mean I talked. I spoke about her situation without her needing to share anything.

When I had finished she said she was blown away that I understood her situation so well. I gave her some suggestions on how to handle the personal crisis in her life. We stayed on the phone with each other a couple more hours; meaningful conversation that would lead her to make better choices. The other phone remained quiet until we'd finished. When I knew she wasn't going to take her life we prayed, and then I wished her well.

I had many such calls while volunteering that first year of retirement. One morning, as my relief volunteer replaced me at seven in the morning, I was informed that I should come to a special luncheon that day in downtown Sacramento.

Though I was really tired I agreed, because they emphasized they needed some 'real' volunteers there for a National Suicide Prevention program. When I got there I was pleasantly surprised that they had me lunching with actress Mariette Hartley, and also with my personal hero, California Legislator Jackie Speier. (Later a successful member of Congress.)

Mariette Hartley gave the first keynote talk for the group, which also included United States Surgeon General, David Satcher. The talk by Mariette focused on her life struggles with mental illness, depression, and her suicide attempts. She was totally involved in and dedicated to helping with the national efforts on suicide prevention. It was a great talk and she was very kind and considerate to me and allowed me to take a photo with her. She listened to me about what I had been doing locally.

The highlight of the day for me was getting to meet Jackie Speier. I'd read all kinds of stories about her courage. She'd come into national news in 1978 as a staff member to Congressman Leo Ryan. They'd traveled to Jonestown, Guyana to check on the welfare of some of those at the compound of a religious cult where the Reverend Jim Jones had built a community; brought his People's Temple followers to South America.

When Ryan's delegation arrived to investigate, cult members killed six of their party on the runway. Speiers was shot five times and lay unattended and bleeding, in pain for 23 hours before help arrived. The full tragedy unfolded as she lay on the runway; over 900 members of the temple were involved in a murder suicide.

The incident was truly a test of her character and I wanted to hear about it personally. What I really wanted to know is how she turned such an attack into a life of public service. I was not the least disappointed in what she shared.

Eventually my volunteer work at the suicide hot line came to an end.

My health became a concern—chest pains and other medical issues. Being alone in a locked office where no one could find me until my shift change came in was not a good idea.

I had other things on my bucket list. Next item: returning to Vietnam.

RETURN TO VIETNAM

*A*uthor's note: I finally went back to Vietnam in April and May 2002 with three other veterans. We called ourselves 'The Peace Patrol'. The local NBC TV station interviewed me before I left and after I returned. It was a trip of a lifetime, and the best part of it was that no one was shooting at us!

The Peace Patrol with an NVA Veteran
Myself, unidentified NVA veteran, Robert Reese, Richard Webster, and Dave Gallo.

Part One:
Flight From Hell Part Ii

I'd planned to go to India in 2002 for a couple of months, but the tour company cancelled the trip after the events of 9-11. I had the time and money, but no scheduled place until I happened upon the website of a group of veterans who planned to return to Nam in the spring of 2002. A veteran, Dave Gallo of San Francisco, had put together a tour package for interested veterans.

The final group consisted of Dave Gallo, Richard Webster from Illinois, Robert Reese from Georgia, and me. We'd all served in the same basic area of operation in Vietnam during the war; the others former members of the 1st Infantry Division. Armed with our individual callings, we had in common that we wanted to see what had become of the base camps, the battlefields, and most importantly, the people.

The plan was to meet everyone at the airport for a flight that left half-an-hour after midnight. I arrived much too early, thinking I could get rid of my bags and relax, but the ticket counter didn't open until a couple of hours prior to the flight. There was nothing to do all afternoon but sit around with my baggage.

My old classmate and friend, Karen, who'd sent me off the first time I went to Nam, wanted to carry on the tradition; this time we had dinner at the airport.

Eventually I checked in, said goodbye to Karen, and went to the boarding area to meet my fellow travelers for the first time. They instantly impressed me, and I felt good about the guys with whom I'd spend the next three weeks. Although everything about my traveling buddies was positive, I did have a nagging feeling about getting on the airplane. I chalked it all up to a case of emotions since the return to that place and time in my life might open some emotional and spiritual wounds. I began to feel as if I might relive my first Pacific crossing to Nam back in 1966.

As I waited to board, the inner-feelings worsened. Something was wrong with this flight. And I knew that once the plane lifted off the runway there was nothing I could do about it.

The plane was full. There was not that much space for my legs or my butt, and I'm a little guy. I thought back to my original flight in 1966 which didn't help take my mind off that nagging feeling; it had been the 'flight from hell'.

I tried to sleep but it kept coming back to me that something was wrong with the flight. Then I looked out of the window and saw jet fuel freely flowing from the wing tanks. My mind went to town with this information. It looked as if the fuel was being pumped from the tanks to lighten the load for a landing, or to crash. We were over the Pacific Ocean, two and a half hours from the coast of California, so a landing did not figure into the scenario.

I poked my seat mate, Robert. He confirmed my concerns as the aircraft made a slow 180 degree turn. The intercom crackled and the captain announced 'minor technical difficulties' had caused us to turn back to San Francisco.

We'd flown far over the Pacific Ocean before turning around—would end up five hours of flying nowhere. I knew it had to be more than a technical problem and wondered what might happen next.

When we arrived over the coast of California, we circled the Bay Area several times. I looked down at a row of red flashing lights of emergency vehicles on the runway. Our runway.

The approach and touchdown was flawless; I was relieved to be on the ground, even if it was where we had started. I went forward to ask what had happened and overheard conversation through the open door of the flight cabin—something about a broken windshield. The 'minor technical difficulties' had been the crew's concern about having the windshield blow out, which (they felt) would have sucked them out of the cockpit.

We had to find a place to sleep for half a day before catching a late afternoon flight to Hong Kong. In the ripple effect of delays and 'minor technical difficulties' we missed our connections and had to spend a night in Hong Kong as well. By the time we got to Vietnam we were two days into our adventure.

Much like the first trip in 1966, I was tired and wearing the same clothes as I'd started with. All my bags were on the original plane.

I wondered what great adventures awaited us. I was ready for anything. Welcome back to Nam!

Part Two:
Dream Reunion Near The Iron Triangle

The weather was exactly like before. The humidity was the biggest factor; my shirt constantly glued to my skin. However, in present-day Vietnam air conditioning cooled our rooms and also refreshed the interior of the van in which we traveled around the countryside.

William "Rev. Bill" McDonald Jr.

We took in some sights in Saigon before heading out to see the country we thought we knew. Each of us wanted to see where we'd been stationed, so each day we went to see our old base camps, airfields, and battlegrounds. It was amazing how much everything had changed—and for the better. Reclamation work had turned airfields into acres of natural grasses and trees. Base camps had been removed or reoccupied by the People's Army, as was the case for Phu Loi, my old camp.

One of our trips, on April 18, 2002, exploring our old areas of operation, took us down Highway 13—Thunder Road we'd called it back then. The road travels right through the heart of the 'Iron Triangle' where I was shot down on April 16, 1967. Essentially a thirty-fifth anniversary to the month. Three-and-a-half decades give or take 48 hours.

As we bumped along the road I had a flashback of a dream I'd had ten years previous. I'd dreamed about this trip down this road and a specific house along the way. I remembered that in my dream we'd stopped to chat with an old VC (Viet Cong) veteran who invited me inside his house to meet his family. The images from the long ago dream were vivid. I began to get the feeling that I'd been here before in the dream experience.

I told Dave, who was leading the tour, that I wanted to stop up ahead at one of those houses along the road to talk to the people and possibly to go inside. He gave me a smile and then shared that he was about to have the driver stop so we could do exactly that—Dave had planned on stopping at a veteran's house, which was across the road from a destroyed ARVN (South Vietnamese Army) tank that had been left as a monument of the war.

Dave told me that he always stopped at this man's home for the tours he gave to American veterans. The man was a former VC officer and a double agent. During the daytime he had been an ARVN veterinarian doctor who took care of the guard dogs and other animals. At night, he rendered first aid and medical care to the VC in the tunnels.

Dave was a little shocked by the timing of my request to stop, as we were only a short distance from the house. He'd not informed any of us about the extra stop because he wanted to surprise us with the visit. I told Dave that I had already seen this in a dream. I'm not sure what he thought about that statement at the time.

When we stopped, the three of us played around on the old tank and took photos. Dave went across the street to see the Vietnamese veteran and secure an invitation. He cordially invited all of us into his home. The courtyard that led to his front door was decorated with fresh flowers, and a small shrine to Buddha was located near the doorstep.

When we entered the house we faced another altar with religious pictures and statues. The man's lovely wife—a woman of about seventy years old who stood less than five feet tall—brought us each a glass filled with ice cubes, then handed us each a bottle of American cola. Normally I'd avoid drinking anything with ice (in certain countries) but this was given with such loving care that I could not insult her by refusing it.

It was hard to believe that (35 years before) I had crashed no more than a few hundred yards from his home, and he had been my enemy. This was where the Japanese and then the French had lost hundreds of men well before the Americans set foot there and lost lives as well. It had been a stronghold for the VC—they'd always owned this territory. The irony of it amused me, but also made me feel good that real recovery from any war is possible. Here were all of us old warriors sitting around a former VC's dinner table talking about our grandchildren.

We had a wonderful conversation about what this gentleman did during the war years and how his 'role' affected his family. His training as an animal doctor—veterinarian—was used by the VC as he was put into service to treat casualties. He asked us about America, where we lived, and what we did.

His daughter and a grandchild also came in to see us. Spending that afternoon with him and his family was a pleasant experience, and I was happy to have had such a unique opportunity.

Furthermore, when we prepared to leave his home—and take a few photos of the area—he insisted he take photos as well, and that we appear in them with his family.

I told his wife and him that I'd dreamed about this house, his family, and this day's events ten years previous. They looked at me with loving eyes and he said, "Yes, I believe that is true." Neither one doubted my dream or thought it was strange that I'd dreamed it and told them about it. It was as if I had said the sky is blue. They fully understood what I had told them. They each gave a long hug.

I left there feeling much better about life, the aftermath of wars, and the hope that people could learn to live together in peace. This showed me that forgiveness and understanding were as much a part of nature as were the devastated forests and jungles of Vietnam that are growing back. I still can see that old man's face with his smiling wife at his side. They had lived through violent times and events and seemed none the worse for it. In fact, they seemed to enjoy life. There seemed no bitterness about the many years he had spent fighting the Japanese, the French, the Americans, his own countrymen, and the Cambodians. Those wars were long over for him; he lived in the present moment—his secret to finding peace within.

Me with former VC double agent and his family,
Tano, the guide, on far right.

Part Three:
Sacred Ceremony In An Old Graveyard

Special permission was required to visit the national historic site of the old Viet Cong headquarters. Hidden from us during the war—along the Cambodian border—the place now plays host to tourists and comes complete with guides who are watchers more than escorts. We already had our tour guide and driver, but by the time we were set to tour—as the only tourists that day—we had one Vietnamese guide for each of us. One of the young male guides held a camera and explained he'd be taking our photos for a 'local publication'.

We didn't let any of the red tape get to us; we played the games and enjoyed ourselves. After all, we were not spies or the enemy. We established a warm relationship with these three men and one woman.

On the way back to our hotel I mentioned I'd wanted to visit one of the war graveyards which were not far off the highway. The one we stopped at had huge Soviet-made statues that looked very impressive as they cast long shadows over the graves at sunset.

It took a little convincing for all to get out and visit the graves, but this is what we did. This particular cemetery was filled with soldiers from both VC and NVA units. The dates on the gravestones indicated that our own wartime units had possibly killed these men and women—each of us had direct or indirect responsibility for those buried there. It was emotionally moving to think about it in that way.

Based on those thoughts, we decided we could not ignore what had happened to their warriors as well as ours. We decided to perform a simple ceremony to honor all of those killed; both sides.

By the time we gathered a large handful of incense together, darkness had fallen on the graveyard.

Our guide, Tano, lit the bundle on fire.

A blazing bright rush of fire and smoke billowed up from the incense in his hands. He waved the sticks around until the ends were red smoking embers then handed each of us several dozen of the smoking incense sticks to carry inside the little temple.

Situated on a small rise of ground above the graves, the temple, which might have been able to hold a dozen people, had open spaces instead of doors or windows. A tile roof protected the shiny, marble floor. Buddha sat at the front of the temple; faced us as we walked in to the sacred space.

Despite the open spaces (for doors and windows) the temple became cloudy as it filled with the mysterious mist of our fragrant incense. We stood in front of the Buddha and each said a few respectful words with the greatest devotion to honor all fallen warriors—soldiers from our units, their units, and all comrades who had lost their lives in battles long forgotten.

We each placed some of our smoking incense in the sand-filled bowl in front of the Buddha statue, bowed silently, and said our prayers. We continued in silence, walking out to the gravesites and placing the remaining sticks of incense alongside several hundred grave markers. The smoke trailed skyward into total darkness.

Though we were each absorbed by our own thoughts, I noticed our guides were observing us. The ambiance within the setting made me believe that they had never seen this done before (by Americans) and I believe they were moved by our respectful gesture. I hoped our visit incited newfound respect for American veterans.

We climbed back in the van and extended the quiet and peace, feeling (not speaking) the spiritual connection with the place and with each other.

Part Four:
Chance Meeting At Black Virgin Mountain

The mountain was officially known as Nui Ba Den, but locally as 'Black Virgin Mountain' because of a legend of a woman who jumped off the mountain to avoid marrying someone she did not love. The mountain itself is said to still contain her feminine energy.

It was the location of many fierce battles during my Vietnam tour of duty. In fact, we lost a Huey and its entire crew there. They were shot down and crashed into the side of that great mound of earth and rock. We may have been on the top of it in 1967, but Charlie and his friends owned all the real estate from the bottom of that hill right up to the edges of our barbed wire fence at the top.

Nui Ba Den is visible from many locations; a sentinel watching over all the flatland. We knew we wanted to visit it, but were warned that it would not be as we remembered it.

The mountain was honeycombed with natural caverns where the VC could safely hide during the war. We could still see bullet pockmarks on the rocks.

During our trip we learned from viewing a metal plaque that one of the caverns contained a hospital during the war.

I could have been knocked over with a feather.

We pulled into a parking lot at the bottom of the mountain and saw the signage. Unbelievable!

The place had been transformed into amusement park.

It got stranger: we climbed into a children's train in order to get to the cable car. The 'Disneyland' type cable car took us up over the tops of trees and rocks on a steady climb to the summit. Each 'compartment' hung by a thin cable—Robert was not too happy about it. I watched his car in front of me rock and roll from side to side as it lurched forward on the main cable.

The view was incredible and looked like it did when I'd flown in the Huey—but no one shot at me now. I looked below me and made out people walking up thousands of stone steps almost hidden under the canopy of trees. The cover was dense, even though we were moving slowly a few feet over the treetops. It was no wonder I could never see anyone down there when we flew over at much higher altitudes and faster speeds during the war.

Next to the cable lift was the park's newest attraction, a slide for tourists to ride down in little car-type vehicles. Final testing for the 'slide-ride' took place while we were there; it was opening that afternoon and there would be a ceremony and local celebrities.

We got off the cable cars near the top and hiked up flights of rock stairs to reach the mountainside temples. Such contrast to the modern amusement park: the eastern grandeur and elegance as well as the spectacular works of art and devotion were awe inspiring. The pilgrims that we saw making their annual trek obviously thought so, too.

There was a building next to the temple for the weary to rest, but we took off our shoes on the outside steps and went right into the temple. We walked softly, trying not to disrupt the tranquil ambiance in the building.

At the back of the sanctuary a little bald headed monk stood by a large gong which hung from a wooden frame. When we bowed to the large golden Buddha, the monk rang the gong. It sent chills through my spine when it happened so unexpectedly. I offered my incense, and another monk handed me fruit to put

William "Rev. Bill" McDonald Jr.

on the altar, and passed me a folded, old paper currency note and a small amount of rice to keep.

The monk seemed intrigued by all of us, and kept his gaze focused on me while I sat on the floor and said a short prayer and meditated. When I finished and bowed to the altar, I could see and feel his watch. Our eyes connected and shared a smile. He placed his hands together as if praying and bowed slightly to me. I returned the gesture and slowly backed out.

When I sat down on the step outside and put on my shoes I was overcome with emotion. The whole place felt so peaceful, the experience so satisfying, and the mood utterly welcoming.

We climbed to more temples, negotiating steep, rocky stairs. On the way to the last temple, a young man selling birds approached us—not selling in the usual way, rather asking us to pay for their release into the wild. These birds had been captured, or bred and raised, and it was good luck and a spiritual gesture to pay for their release. We were to say a prayer for someone we loved, and then let the bird go.

I decided to release two birds, one for each of my children. I offered a prayer for each one as I released the little birds from my opened hands. They soared skyward, racing with my prayer, no doubt, to heaven. It was amazing to watch them fly away with my prayers across the same sky from which—35 years previous—I'd fired machinegun bullets into this mountain.

The symbolism of it all moved me; an earth shifting moment where I held my position, absorbed in the moment.

That day we met several NVA veterans who were on tour from Hanoi and the northern area. They were on a holiday, enjoying the peace and serenity of this sacred mountain, just as the four of us American veterans were.

We approached one of the veterans who had on his old medal-decorated uniform. We all hugged and talked and took photos together. He pulled up his shirt to show us where he had been wounded by a B-52 bombing raid on the Ho Chi Minh Trail when he was coming down from the north. There was no anger from him at all. That astonished me.

When we came down off the mountain and were walking by the concession our new, old NVA friend found us. He wanted us to meet some of his buddies and have photos taken together.

And we did. As we were all in the moment, enjoying each other's company, a man in a military uniform approached me. He invited me to meet a famous woman veteran who was in the back of a small limousine.

The car had tinted windows so I could not see inside, but before I reached the vehicle the door swung open. Inside was an elderly, heavyset woman with rows of medals draped on her jacket. She had a walking cane next to her, so I assumed she had a physical problem. Her hair was white and her teeth slightly stained, but her smile was truly genuine and warm. She extended forth her hand to shake mine. I shook her hand and stood at attention. I gave her a crisp military salute. She cupped her hands together over her mouth as an indication of her surprise, and the joy she felt. Her tear-glistened eyes said it all and she returned my salute.

A gesture of friendship and respect between old warriors, but it meant so much more to both of us at that moment.

I stepped back and happened to look at the bus that was parked alongside her car. There were several dozen veterans in their old uniforms standing near the windows saluting me. I whipped my hand to the brim of my hat and returned the gesture. Everyone smiled; we had all bonded. We looked at each other for several more seconds until I slowly turned to rejoin my friends. I heard loud cheering coming from the bus. I turned around to see that all of them were waving goodbye to me.

My return wave was filled with love for each one of them.

There was a feeling of love in the air. I do not know any other words to explain it. All my feelings about my former enemy and the war melted into an understanding that we are all just brothers and sisters on this small planet of ours. I loved these people, and it seemed they loved me—us—too. Perhaps it was respect born out of battle, but whatever it was, I was happy to have shared that moment in time with them.

The famous 'Peace Patrol'

IN THE SHADOW OF THE BLADE

A DOCUMENTARY FILM AND JOURNEY

*"I am centered in my belief that God called us to make a
film because that film has a mission of its own.
Beyond the film...the mission is not ours; it belongs to the veterans.
If we can help—and it is God's intention that we do so—we will."*
Cheryl Fries - Arrowhead Video and Films Creative Director

Our Veteran Crew
Mike Venable, Bob Baird, and me
(the missing veteran is Gary Roush, who took this photo)

William "Rev. Bill" McDonald Jr.

Author's note: I had the good karma of getting involved with a documentary project called 'In the Shadow of the Blade'. It was a film that recorded the experiences of people who were affected by the Vietnam War. This film took all of us, who were on the film crew, over 10,000 miles across America in a restored Huey helicopter that had actually been used in combat. In fact, it was from my old sister company the 173rd Assault Helicopter Company (The Robin Hoods) out of Lai Khe, Vietnam.

Part One: Heart Of The Project

It took Patrick and Cheryl Fries several years of soul-wrenching work to bring their dream to fruition. Their belief in the making of a documentary film was so strong that they never gave up—no matter the roadblocks—until one day there were no more barriers. They were in the sky.

The concept was to have a Huey helicopter buzz around America and bring the familiar *whop-whop-whop* to veterans and others affected by the Vietnam War. Patrick and Cheryl hoped that those who could run their hands along the OD (olive-drab) fuselage, climb aboard and strap in to relive the rush of warm air at takeoff would be able to have their long-locked-away stories fly as they shared them with other Americans.

The filmmakers were right; we found thousands of tales in America's heartland waiting to take off and soar.

I was involved at the earliest stages of this dream when asked for the names of veterans who might be interested in being interviewed. One thing led to another; the filmmakers took an interest in my poetry and stories, and I became one of the people interviewed for the film.

The original plan was for the Huey to fly from Texas to California, up to Washington, and across the northern states before dropping down the East Coast to Florida, but that plan fell through because of the tremendous costs involved.

At one point in the summer of 2002, the project was grounded for lack of funding but I kept e-mailing Patrick and Cheryl that it was going to happen—that in fact it had already happened in the future, and they simply needed to continue working to have it materialize. Two years of acting as their spiritual and emotional cheerleader and I wasn't giving up on them or the project.

Finally, the project plans went from idle to full RPM as funding became available and the right people added their talents. The Huey inched closer to the launch pad, even though there wasn't quite enough money to complete the cross-country trip.

As with any project, there were lots of risks and unknowns involved.

"Take a leap of faith, and go for it," I advised. *"Let the universe find the missing parts of the puzzle."*

Then one Sunday night in August 2002 Patrick called me and asked for a couple of minutes of my time. He asked if I were willing to fly to Fort Rucker, Alabama to offer a prayer for the mission's takeoff—at my own expense. It was fitting that the mission should begin at Fort Rucker, the home of Army Aviation. I told him 'yes', I was willing to give him anything he needed. I believed in their dream.

Then we talked about personal life. Two minutes turned into two hours as he opened up. Toward the end of the conversation, I explained the meaning of his recurring dreams he'd had over the years about flying. He'd long wondered what these nighttime adventures meant. I explained that the dream was about his spirit, and I went into detail about what I sensed as the meaning of these dreams; other aspects of his life too.

He mentioned that he was upset about his young daughter, and he had left his house without resolving a conflict—he was at his office in downtown Austin. I instructed him to go home, hug his daughter and kiss her right between the eyes on the forehead. Tell her, 'I love you,' I said.

We finished the conversation with my explaining that I felt something would transpire, that night, which related to his dreams of flying.

The next day he called to tell me that his daughter had crawled in bed with him and his wife early that morning. She was excited and wanted to tell them about her dream of flying. She had never talked about her dreams before, and for her to wake him up to share it was very special to him. He understood what my words meant.

Then he asked me to come along on the crew and fill a sacred role.

William "Rev. Bill" McDonald Jr.

Arrowhead Film Company took an entirely different route with this movie than most other documentary films. They added a compassionate touch to the interviewing process by appointing me as their mission chaplain. My job was to provide emotional support to those interviewed. Patrick and Cheryl didn't want anyone who had vetted their souls to be emotionally abandoned after the lights and cameras went off. They truly intended the whole documentary process be a complete healing mission for all involved.

Author's note: Several weeks after we began, I had a dream in which I saw Patrick's black SUV in a minor car crash. I sent an e-mail warning him to stay alert and be careful. He never had any accidents, so I wondered how I could be so wrong about my dream. When I talked to Cheryl, she mentioned she had been in a car accident while driving Pat's black SUV. Right car, but I had warned the wrong person. I felt really bad about it, but nobody is right all the time. I had assumed that because it was his car that he was the one having the accident.

Bill McDonald and Cheryl Fries in Austin, Texas

William "Rev. Bill" McDonald Jr.

Part Two: We Begin The Journey

Our Huey took off October 2, 2002 from Fort Rucker, Alabama, the home of Army Aviation—the perfect place to begin the journey. The night before, the Army hosted a huge party at the Aviation museum—first class, fully catered—with several hundred invited guests.

I finally got to personally meet Eric, the son of one of my unit's pilots who was killed in Vietnam in 1967. We'd met on the internet a few years before. Eric, an Army career man himself, had never gotten to know his father.

We both hugged, and he introduced me to his beautiful wife. I felt bad because I couldn't talk much with him as I had many people to visit, but it felt good to finally connect with him, and I was happy he'd been invited—I'd secured him an interview for the film.

The next day the Army had a band and color guard unit to send us off. Our crew and passengers were introduced to a gathering of several hundred people. There were a number of speeches, and then I gave a blessing for the mission.

We marched out to the aircraft while the Army band played. Film crews from CNN and four other networks shot footage of the event. It was a moving moment for me. After all the years of no recognition for my war experiences the band finally played for me and for all the veterans who'd not been welcomed home so many years before.

Half a dozen modern Army helicopters aligned to escort us on the first leg of our journey.

In our own Huey, Mike Novosel, a Medal of Honor recipient and dust off pilot, took the left pilot's seat. (Novosel Street at Fort Rucker is named after him.) An honorary crew of Vietnam veterans represented each branch of the military service. I was thrilled that the film company had my old buddy, Private Doug Ward, from the Robin Hoods (173rd Assault Helicopter Company) to represent the U.S. Army.

It was one of the greatest honors of my life to sit in the aircraft with such a fine group of soldiers. When we lifted our skids it hit home that we were truly realizing Pat and Cheryl's dream.

Our first official Landing Zone (LZ) was at the South Wall in Florida. The 'scaled down' replica of 'The Wall' in Washington, D.C. is no less emotionally powerful.

When we made a low pass over it, our blades made the popping sound that is so familiar to any GI who ever served in Nam. It is a distinct and unforgettable *whop-whop-whop*. All eyes were on our Huey as we made another low-level run over the group standing around the LZ, right next to 'The Wall'.

We gently landed in the middle of a grassy knoll, and the men and their families slowly approached the helicopter as the blades came to a stop. Our honorary crew members got off the aircraft, and our film crew interviewed them.

We repeated this process at each LZ, picking up passengers and taking them to the next LZ. Riding in our Huey was part of the healing experience that we wished to capture on film. We had two cameras mounted on the inside of the Huey to record the passengers' reactions. For some it was their first ride in a helicopter since leaving Vietnam 30 to 35 years before.

One man told me he hadn't known we were coming; he'd come to 'The Wall' as a better way to understand his father who was hospitalized and dying. He came to find some quiet time and certainly hadn't expected to find a Vietnam War helicopter landing right next to him. He was emotionally overwhelmed by the coincidence of our landing there at that exact moment. He'd been depressed and was looking for support—even answers. I put my arm around his shoulders, and we walked away from the crowd. I asked him to tell me about his dad, which he did.

I asked him if he would like me to pray for him and his father. He softly replied that he would really appreciate that, so we prayed together out of sight of the cameras and the media. He immediately broke down sobbing and I held him. I gave him some words of comfort, then I had to leave him because I could see a line of others waiting to talk to me.

Next, the wife of a Vietnam veteran approached me. She was not sure what to do about her husband who had not spoken about Nam, nor had he cried. At this moment he was a short distance from the helicopter—sobbing. She asked if I'd speak to him.

When I put my arms around her tear-choked husband and told him, "Welcome home, brother," he broke down.

"Bill, don't worry about me. These aren't sad tears, but tears of joy for bringing the Huey here and for coming to honor us veterans," he said.

We had a long conversation. But just as time flies, we knew we had to as well. There were many other people to meet—several in wheelchairs, but we had less than an hour to make it to our next LZ. I did my best to comfort all in a short period.

The blades began to rotate. We jumped in for another leg of the trip. Others would be waiting for us at every LZ in which we landed.

As I looked out from my seat in the helicopter, I saw the young man who talked to me about his dad. He saluted me as I did him. I wish I'd have spent more time there; too many broken hearts for such a short stop. I knew that in the next 10,000 miles we were going to see many more people in need of spiritual and emotional healing. I prayed I'd be up to the job.

Author's note: This documentary was an absolute labor of love for all of us, but it zapped our emotional and spiritual energy. We met thousands of veterans and their families and supporters of all kinds in every LZ. Everyone had a story. Some could not talk in front of the camera, but they unleashed their emotions and told their stories to me. Some days I felt as if the weight of the world were on my shoulders; always wondering if I could have done more or said something else to each person. The thing that kept us going was the love we received—the intensity of which helped us continue each day.

We had two helicopters on our journey, our Huey and a Bell JetRanger that we used as a camera ship for aerial photos and movies. We also had three to five vehicles on the ground with equipment and personal items. We picked up other fixed-wing aircraft and helicopters along the way. We had National Guard helicopters, sheriff department helos, TV media, and government aircraft tagging along on various legs of the flight.

Fort Worth, Texas, in front of old 091

Part Three: Angel Fire, New Mexico

Author's note: I felt great spiritual energy in New Mexico at the place that gave birth to the first Vietnam Veterans' Memorial of any kind in the world. This location had been made sacred by ancient Native Americans centuries before. It became a landmark that captured the heart and soul of our documentary film, 'In the Shadow of the Blade'.

9,000 feet up in the mountains of New Mexico—covered in powdered snow when we landed there—ice crystals caught the early morning sunlight and reflected it like diamonds on our parked Huey—a jewel on the hillside.

It was here that I met an Apache Indian Vietnam veteran who made a lasting impression on me.

I'd been looking forward to one of our last Landing Zones (LZs) because I knew that the people working in New Mexico had put their hearts and souls into making everything right. After all, the first Vietnam Veterans' Memorial (of any kind) was located there.

One veteran in particular, Earl Waters, devoted time, effort, and money into making our stay the most memorable possible; I knew when I met him that he was a good man.

I first saw Earl with a group of veterans waiting for us at the Tucamcari Airport above Albuquerque, New Mexico. We landed our Huey, refueled it, and loaded him and his buddies onboard for the ride of their lives. We rolled over the mountains and swooped down toward our next LZ where over 1,000 people waited to greet us—including a bagpipe player. He played *Amazing Grace* while standing in the shadow of our Huey. A group of teary veterans and families clung to every note.

The next morning the Huey lifted off and headed to Angel Fire, the site of the world's first Vietnam Veterans' Memorial. The helicopter climbed up and over the snow covered Sangre de Cristo Mountains before landing close to the 9,000 foot level—in the snow.

It was an inspiring sight with a Veterans' Day crowd of around 800 people all huddled on that cold, snowy hilltop next to the Memorial Chapel that was built as part of the monument.

The helicopter made several passes, playing that 'sound of freedom' as the blades popped and the engines roared. Our aircraft was escorted to the LZ by a formation of New Mexico National Guard UH-60 Black Hawk helicopters.

William "Rev. Bill" McDonald Jr.

As we flew over the snow covered hill the other helicopters broke away and our Huey came in for a landing. The blizzard caused by the rotor wash created a spectacular entrance—our own personal snowstorm.

There was a ceremony and many speeches, including one from me. So many respectful, healing, and kind words from everyone. The thrill of the morning for me, however, was witnessing the men in the front row; a dozen of the last living Navajo code talkers from WWII and Korea. These Native American Elders sat wrapped in traditional blankets—think sunsets and sunrises—turquoise and orange. Their presence was to honor the crew, but we were the ones truly blessed by their presence.

When the ceremonies were over and everyone had left the hillside the Huey remained a sentry for the night—alone in the snow.

The next morning the director of the documentary, Pat Fries, took a couple of cameramen and a soundman to the top of the hill to film the sunrise. I went along to be a part of that gloriously golden moment.

Two Native American Veterans, who were also musicians, greeted us when we arrived on the hilltop. One of them was my new friend, Ernie Dogwolf. We'd bonded the day before when I'd met him and his wife. It had been such a natural and familiar meeting, like old friends seeing each other for the first time in a long time—a kindred spirit reunion. I sensed he was spiritually sensitive to life and the world around him.

I found Ernie to be someone who commanded others' attention and respect. He did this by projecting an aura of tranquility—he was in tune with his surroundings. Though he had the look of a courageous warrior there was gentleness about him. We became instant friends as we spoke the same spiritual language.

The director asked the two men to play their musical instruments and to do and say anything they wished. Pat wanted to capture the early morning moments as the sun peeked over the mountain and turned the helicopter into the largest diamond in the world. As I watched Ernie's breath steam into the single digit temperature I anticipated the sunrise and its promise of a new day.

Then Ernie raised his arms skyward and held his Native American flute in one hand and offered some thoughts about life and God. Out of the sky flew a large black raven which circled behind my Navajo friend. He addressed a message to the bird and in turn the raven descended to a perch on the chapel steeple. The winged creature watched as Ernie changed his focus to his music.

The film captured these magic morning moments along with the sounds of drums and flutes and the image of the Huey parked in the background covered with ice and snow.

After, Ernie and his friend walked down to the aircraft. He took out a tied bundle of sage, set it on fire, and shook it until it smoked. As the drums beat, the two Navajo warriors chanted, offering prayers for our Huey and all the men who had ever flown in it.

When Ernie reached the front of the Huey and put his hands on the pilots' windshield his head dropped and he began to weep. The music and the chanting stopped, as had the cameras. I walked down the hillside and met him on his trek back up. We embraced and he softly wept and told me what had happened.

He stated that when he touched the Huey he saw the spirits of the many men who had flown in this helicopter, and they were pleased with the blessing ceremony. He saw their eyes and felt their presence. He was visibly shaken but not saddened; more spiritually awakened might be a better way to describe his feeling. We stood there looking into each other's eyes. He and I both knew what he was talking about and feeling.

Sunrise at Angel Fire, New Mexico
Ernest Dogwolf Lovato and Fidel Gonzalez

Angel Fire, New Mexico

Early morning sunrise, at Angel Fire, New Mexico.
We had just finished filming the blessing

With a couple of the last surviving code talkers

Filming morning sunrise in Angel Fire, New Mexico

Ernie Dogwolf playing his flute for Dr. Victor Westphall,
The founder of the Angel Fire Vietnam Memorial

Dr. Westphall who died before the film was released

Part Four: Baby Kathleen

Author's note:We heard a story on our journey about a baby girl who'd been rescued from Nam in 1969.This became a national story on the CBS Early Show. I gave a speech at the California State Vietnam Veterans' Memorial on Memorial Day in 2003 about this story. I also had the privilege and the honor of introducing the father who adopted the baby girl, and also the 'grown up' version—the woman herself.

The crew was at the aircraft at sunrise. It was already hot and humid—we knew it would rain that day. We loaded both helicopters with camera equipment and people, and fired up the engines. Then it happened. A red indicator light on the helicopter's cockpit dash began to flash. The tail rotor chip detector indicated trouble. We shut it down and waited while Bruce, our aircraft commander and a certified aviation mechanic, climbed up to examine the magnetic plug in the gearbox. He cut the safety wires and pulled out the magnetic plug to check it for metal shavings or chips of metal.

The visual inspection yielded nothing; it was clean. We had to make a choice; did we believe the warning light or did we put our trust in what appeared to be a clean plug? If there were metal chips in the gearbox that would have indicated a gear failure, and could freeze up in flight causing a tail rotor failure—serious trouble.

We gathered around our leader, Bruce, who would be the one to make the decision whether we went forward with or canceled our flight plans. There was much more involved than just being late or a no-show at the next Landing Zone (LZ). A large part of Kennesaw State University's student body, along with an ROTC color guard and a band, were waiting. As well, many veterans were in attendance and some waiting to tell their stories. Camera and sound crews, a director, and other media all sat outside in the rain waiting for our Huey.

It was not a small decision, but Bruce reminded us that safety was the number one priority. It didn't matter what or who was waiting for us, he would cancel the flight if he felt it was unsafe to fly the aircraft.

Bruce decided he was comfortable with the trip taking place, but said that any of us could veto that decision. He didn't want to make us go on the aircraft if anyone was uncomfortable about the warning light. One 'no' and we'd all stay on the ground. We each gave our opinions.

As a former crew chief, I told him I felt perfectly safe after looking at the plug. There was no doubt in my mind that it was a defective warning light and not the gearbox. Everyone else felt the same way and stated that we should go. We all boarded and took off with the red light still flashing on the dash.

When we got to the university, it was pouring rain and we were late, but there was still a crowd waiting for us. We had a nice ceremony followed by a luncheon in the cafeteria.

Afterward, at the helicopter, a woman approached us with a photo album tucked under her arm. Donna explained she had been a nurse with the 3rd Field Hospital in Saigon in 1969. She said that she was tired of hearing stories about American 'baby killers' and that she had a story that proved the opposite. She opened her photo album and turned to a page with a picture of an infant. The cameras rolled as Donna began her spellbinding story about a 1969 rescue of a three-week-old baby in a village in Vietnam.

The crowd around the Huey grew quiet as Donna related that a group of infantry soldiers from the Big Red One (1st Infantry Division) had come across a hamlet that had been attacked by the Viet Cong (VC). Huts had been burned. Bodies were scattered everywhere. Everyone was dead—people and animals had been slaughtered about three days prior.

The soldiers had been saddened by what they saw as they walked among the corpses of what was once a peaceful mountain community.

Then the sound of a crying infant came from nearby. The soldiers rushed to a body of a young woman lying face down. Her arms were tucked underneath, as if she was holding something.

One of the soldiers turned her over—a violation of one of the golden rules of combat because the VC sometimes attached explosive devices to dead bodies; if a soldier moved a body he could be killed or maimed. But this mattered not to the young soldier who turned her because he reacted to the sound of life. He and the others wanted nothing more than to save the helpless infant.

The three-week-old baby was tightly wrapped in the arms of her mother. The baby had several wounds but the pressure of the mother's grip had prevented massive bleeding and helped keep her alive for all that time.

The soldiers immediately called the 3rd Field Hospital. Donna, the triage nurse, broke the rules by telling them to transport the child *with* the mother's body to the hospital. American medical facilities were only for American GI casualties. Normal procedure would have been to transport this child to a Vietnamese hospital for treatment, which Donna knew meant certain death for the baby.

The soldiers brought the child and mother to the hospital, and the medical personnel went to work to save the baby. They knew that they had to act fast because once they removed the baby from the mother's arms the infant's blood pressure would fall.

Nurse Rowe went a step further; she wanted to ensure the child had a chance at a decent life. She knew a Catholic baptism might lead to a spot at the orphanage which could result in adoption.

She sent for the Catholic chaplain and gathered some of the staff. While they moved the baby girl to the operating room, the chaplain baptized her. Everyone became a godparent to the child, and Nurse Rowe named her Kathleen Fields: Kathleen, from the old Irish ballad *Take me home again Kathleen*, and Fields because she was at the 3rd Field Hospital.

There weren't many dry eyes as Donna told us this story.

She went on to explain how they made diapers for her out of women's personal hygiene products and medical rags. They created a makeshift crib. Everyone became attached to baby Kathleen. Several days later three young, muddy soldiers arrived asking to see 'their' baby. They had been the ones who'd found little Kathleen in her mother's arms. The staff permitted them to have some time alone with the baby—an emotional time for all three men.

As I listened to Donna's story I couldn't help but think of the three wise men that came to visit baby Jesus.

Donna said she wasn't sure what had happened to the baby after she had left the hospital, but she'd heard rumors that a Navy officer had adopted her and taken her to the United States.

Shortly after, the Atlanta Journal-Constitution ran a story about 'Baby Kathleen' as told by Donna Rowe. The story appeared a day or two after we had left town and were headed to another LZ.

We finished filming, but Donna's story of Baby Kathleen stayed with us. Then something wonderful happened.

'I am that baby Kathleen.' The message was posted on our film's website.

She lived in California and had a family of her own. She stated she'd like to make contact with Donna and the others who had saved her life. We were all happily surprised by the good fortune of it all. The director of the film immediately contacted Kathleen, as did I. We talked to her and found out that she lived a short drive from my house in northern California. Her dad, the naval officer who'd adopted her in 1969, lived on the edge of my town in the Elk Grove area.

Arrowhead Film Company put together a plan for a reunion in San Antonio, Texas. Although the documentary filming had wrapped up, they reassembled the entire crew.

The cost was going to exceed $35,000—more than any of us could afford—but after a request for help the funds were raised. Several people came forward and provided. Southwest Airlines donated 17 roundtrip airline tickets and cash for hotel and food for Kathleen and her family.

The spirit of giving was incredible—and none of the angels who helped asked for a single thing—not even a mention in the media.

We'd been able to get in touch with almost all the parties we could identify who aided in some way with the rescue effort. We even found the actual helicopter pilot who'd transported baby Kathleen to the hospital. When we contacted him, he was elated to find out that something he had done in the war had a positive impact on someone's life. According to his friends he'd suffered depression for many years and his life was affected by alcohol. He had never really gotten over the effects of the war. The news was a gift of sunshine for him. He was excited about coming out to meet everyone at the reunion. We arranged for an airline ticket for him, but a few days before he was to fly to Texas he caught pneumonia and died a day or so later. He never made it to the reunion, but his friends have said that he died a much happier man for having heard about baby Kathleen and the reunion.

The reunion took place April 14, 2003, at Fort Sam Houston, Texas. All of the media, including CNN, covered the event. The timing, however, was such that all the news' focus that week was on the ongoing war in Iraq and the release of our POWs (prisoners of war). In spite of that, CBS arranged for Kathleen, Donna, and one of the medics to go to New York City to do a 15-minute segment on the CBS Early Show.

Kathleen and I talked on the phone several times about how she had spent years trying to find out something about her life. She wondered who the people were who had helped her when she was an infant. Now she finally had some sense of fulfillment. She said she has often expressed her concern about why this happened to her and what it meant. I do not have all the answers, but I do know that her story has brought much inspiration to many veterans who now feel that they did something of real value during their tour of duty in Vietnam.

Author's note: During all the rush for the reunion with Kathleen and her rescuers, no one thought to include her dad, Marvin Cords. The dashing and loving naval officer had to fight through almost a year of paperwork, which included getting the president of South Vietnam to sign off on the adoption. Initially the orphanage stated there was a problem providing the birth certificate but military medical staff applied pressure, letting the orphanage know that medical supplies from the 3rd Field Hospital might be curtailed.

Marvin Cords had already adopted three children (he eventually adopted six children) when he happened to hear baby Kathleen's story from the chaplain during a church service in Saigon. It was then that he began his long quest to bring Kathleen home.

In one of my phone conversations with Kathleen, she mentioned that her father was feeling rather rejected and left out of the whole reunion process. No one had even called him or interviewed him. He wasn't even offered a ticket to fly to Texas.

I decided that Marvin deserved his day in the sunshine. When I gave my Memorial Day speech in Sacramento's State Capitol Park, I told Kathleen's story. At the end of speech, I told the audience and the media that I had a very special treat for them, and I introduced Marvin. The crowd of mostly wet-eyed veterans gave him a three-minute standing ovation after which many hugged him or shook his hand.

Finally, I introduced 'baby' Kathleen, a 33-year-old mother of three daughters. She walked up to the microphone and offered healing words to an attentive and respectful audience which included veterans and families. So much joy, love, and healing took place that day. Everyone showed visible signs of having been moved (including the media and the MC for the event, local CBS TV newscaster Dave Bender).

Kathleen's speech:

Hello, my name is Kathleen Cords-Epps and, when I was just three weeks old, my tiny life was saved by American GIs, nurses, and doctors who took great risks to save me.

I am tired of hearing in the media about American 'baby killers'. I was an orphaned baby in Vietnam. The VC killed my mother, and the entire village, and I am alive and healthy today because of veterans like you.

When you came back you were never welcomed home as the heroes that you were, and I have never had the opportunity to say what I have wanted to say for so many years.

Welcome home and thank you very much. God bless you and your families.

REFLECTIONS FROM THE ANDES

An Epilogue

After all the months involved with the making of the documentary film 'In the Shadow of the Blade', a good friend and I flew down to South America to spend most of December 2002. We spent the time exploring the Andes Mountains and Inca ruins in Peru and Bolivia. We thought of ourselves as the spiritual version of Butch Cassidy and the Sundance Kid.

Taking a break from ministering to many people afforded me the opportunity to reflect on the past year: my trip back to Vietnam, meeting former President Jimmy Carter, my daughter's wedding, and working on the documentary which entailed flying thousands of miles around the country in a Huey helicopter. It was a year in which I delivered many public speeches, was interviewed by dozens of newspapers, and more than 75 television stations—including multiple times for CNN.

I had listened to the thousands of stories from countless veterans, families of veterans, widows, and orphaned sons and daughters of veterans. I had shared their tears and their pain. I had embraced their suffering and had given all of myself in an effort to help them move past their heartaches. I was not always successful but, for many, spiritual and emotional healing could begin. The film crew witnessed many miracles of the heart and soul, but it took its toll on me. By the end of the year I had to find a way to recharge. I'd been a sponge for sorrow, but I had no regrets. I'd had a year like no other Vietnam veteran could have ever dreamed. Come to think of it, I did dream it.

While in Peru I experienced many wonderful and mystical moments, but I also almost died from a heart attack when I was hiking in Bolivia.

William "Rev. Bill" McDonald Jr.

At the time I said nothing to my fellow travelers—I didn't want to worry them because I was uncertain how serious it was. Looking back I recognize the classic signs, but when I was in the moment I passed it off as being out of shape in high altitude.

The incident, however, did make me get serious about my life.

Never in all my travels have I been to a destination where it looked better than airbrushed postcards or National Geographic spreads. Machu Picchu is such a place.

As I stood on a hillside overlooking the famous Lost City of the Incas I was beyond awestruck; dazzled and dizzied, stunned and captivated. The sacred energy cannot be captured through the camera's lens. It is a phenomenon which must be personally and soulfully experienced.

While my travel buddy attempted to capture the light within the shadows within the light within the shadows—infinite layers—I immersed myself in a review of my life; particularly the last year. I found myself at a crossroads—no longer a young man and no longer viewing the world as I had before.

Though I was much like the Lost City, shrouded in my own fog, there existed clarity within—secret chambers opened, their ancient locks released with a series of gentle clicks. Advantaged by age and experience, purpose not only revealed itself but defined itself on a scroll in an inner-library.

I realized that my childhood, even though it had a certain amount of sadness and pain, had helped to educate and shape the young man who went to Vietnam. My experiences in Nam taught me valuable lessons of life and death, and sharpened my faith. Those experiences were the groundwork for my role as husband and father. This past year of filmmaking—flying around the country and meeting people— taught me the splendor of possibility and probability: that wounds can and do heal, that people can overcome anything once they make up their minds to do so.

I recognized that I am the luckiest man alive. I would not trade any one experience or event in my life because the collective created the individual that sat on this mountaintop. And I liked this person. I enjoyed my own company. I knew I was still madly and unapologetically in love with life. And I knew there were still things I wanted to do—one of which was to record stories from my life experience for my family and friends. I wanted to share it all.

So ends what I believe is the first half of my life. Wonders wait for discovery in the second half. More importantly, what wonders and glorious things await your discovery? What gems are perched on mountains or are hidden in full view for your exclusive purpose.

I think everyone has a song in him or her that needs to be sung. I hope you enjoyed mine. I shall listen for yours in that glorious breeze that circles the globe and sings to us all.

Do not wait too long. We know not how many wondrous days remain. If my time is over tomorrow, I am fulfilled and satisfied. Please let my epitaph read:

He was a spiritual warrior who sang his own song.
He loved his children and grandchildren without measure.
He was a faithful and loyal husband, citizen, soldier, and poet.
He came. He saw. He helped. He believed!
Honor, courage and faith were his creed.
But love motivated everything he did!
And by the "amazing grace" of God, he lived his life.

ACKNOWLEDGMENTS

I am forever grateful to my wife Carol; you taught me the value of love

Josh and Daya: There are no two children who could make me more proud
To my grandchildren:
Spencer McDonald, Colton and Calle Marlow
Daylana, Gianni and Jesse Beard
You are my greatest inspiration.

My deep appreciation to life-long friends and personal advisors:
Karen Wilson, Linda Provance and Mahaila McKellar

For each being an integral part of my life journey:
Shadoe Stevens ~ Brahmachari Carl ~ Joane Schaublin ~ Dave Nye ~ Maria
Edwards
and
fellow brothers of The 128th Assault Helicopter Company

A huge debt of gratitude goes to my literary guru Gayle Lynds.
Special thanks to President Jimmy Carter and his wife.

Thanks to Pat and Cheryl Fries for the greatest helicopter 'ride' of my life.

Kudos Jan Hornung for your energetic input to my first book *A Spiritual Warrior's Journey*

In memory of my high school friends: Bob Amick, and Dondee Nettles

Deepest respect to:
Pete Conaty and Chief Sonne Reyna, my super veteran buddies
To actor Danny Glover: your interest in my books is greatly appreciated
My spiritual warrior friends Cabot Smith, and Robert Mackie:
I remain ever grateful for your support

Adrian Stanga—my high school principal
You honored me at my 50th High School Class Reunion
by telling me and others that I was your personal hero
Mr. Stanga, Sir: You are mine
Go Sunnyvale Jets!

And a smile to all those behind the lens who called out 'say cheese'

There's a moment of decision right before the end of every project when an artist waffles between *done—don't touch it* and *maybe one more look*. I'm unsure if the final draft was pried or spirited from my hands, but it was moved to its final stage by Marie and Richard Beswick-Arthur. In trade for my acknowledgement of their fine work they insist I state any errors are theirs, not mine.

ABOUT THE AUTHOR

Award-winning poet, author of several non-fiction spiritually based books, artist, consultant to film and TV documentaries, serving as an interfaith minister and chaplain to many groups and organizations, 'Rev. Bill' McDonald packs a lot of living into life.

An International Motivational Speaker and relationship workshop facilitator, meditation teacher, and non-paid veteran advocate and lobbyist, his advocacy work has popularized him in all media. He's counseled several thousand veterans over the past three decades and been recognized by the US Congress and the State of California for his tireless assistance to veterans and their families dealing with Post Traumatic Stress Disorder. Bill filled an integral position on the flight crew for the Vietnam War documentary, *In the Shadow of the Blade*, released for theaters in the fall of 2003 by *Arrowhead Films*, and later shown on *The Military Channel*. He was one of the producers, narrators, and had an on screen presence for the *PBS TV* documentary called *The Art of Healing*. He helped inspire a 'hopeful and upbeat' rewrite of the ending for the classic indie film "*Trooper*".

A Vietnam veteran with the famed '*Tomahawks*' (*128th Assault Helicopter Company)* in Phu Loi, South Vietnam—October 1966-October 1967, McDonald was a crew chief/door-gunner on a UH-1D Huey. He was shot down, survived numerous adventures, and received recognition for his courage and service, which included **The Distinguished Flying Cross, The Bronze Star Medal, The Purple Heart**, 14 **Air Medals**, and numerous ribbons and medals.

Rev. Bill is the founder of two of the largest author organizations in North America – *The American Authors Association* and *The Military Writers Society of*

America. He has helped hundreds of writers get published and media exposure. He fervently encourages veterans to tell their personal stories—as he puts it: saving history one story at a time!

On his return from Vietnam, he earned a B.A. degree at the University of San Francisco and an A.A. at San Jose City College. During 30 years in management at the US Postal Service Rev. Bill was active in his community—after hours—which continued after retirement.

Always assisting the veteran community, Rev. Bill is a member of *The American Legion, AMVETS, Vietnam Veterans of America*, and *The Military Order of The Purple Heart* and does chaplain work for other military organizations.

Bill and his high school sweetheart, Carol, married since January 1970, reside near Sacramento, California, and have two grown children and six grandchildren.

*Rev. Bill's life story continues to unfold in an upcoming book "**Alchemy of an Old Warrior's Heart**", which details a decade of his life after 2004, and documents travel to India, near-death experiences, and his spiritual quest for meaning and purpose.*

Other books by author:

A Spiritual Warrior's Journey
Purple Heart: Poetry of the Vietnam War
Sacred Eye: Poetry of in Search of the Divine
Alchemy of An Old Warrior's Heart

Contributing author:

Spinning Tales: Helicopter Stories
Angels in Vietnam: The Women Who Served
Stories of Faith and Courage from The Vietnam War
Divine Moments: Ordinary People Having Spiritually Transformative Experiences
Gottliche Momente (German Edition of Divine Moments)
Our Voices: Military Writer's Society of America – an anthology
Silent Battlefield: 2012 MWSA Anthology
God in the Foxhole: Inspiring True Stories of Miracles on the Battlefields
Baby Its You: Messages from Deceased Heroes

Partial Listing of Films Associated With:

In The Shadow of The Blade (Military Channel – Discovery Channel)
The Art Of Healing (PBS TV)
The Trooper (Indie Film)
Veterans Village (Indie Documentary)

With former President Jimmy Carter, July 2002

Made in the USA
Las Vegas, NV
16 April 2024

88766693R00184